*The East-West Conflict*

*The Organization of International Relations in the Twentieth Century*

# *The East-West Conflict*

## *The Organisation of International Relations in the Twentieth Century*

*Werner Link*

*Translated by Jackie Bennett-Ruete*

**BERG**
*Leamington Spa*
*Heidelberg*
*Dover,* NH

**Berg Publishers Ltd**
24 Binswood Avenue, Leamington Spa,
Warwickshire CV32 5SQ, UK

Panoramastr. 118,
6900 Heidelberg, West Germany

51 Washington Street, Dover,
New Hampshire 03820, USA


Originally published as *Der Ost-West-Konflikt: d. Organisation d. internat. Beziehungen im 20. Jh.*
Translated from the German by permission of the publishers
Verlag W. Kohlhammer GmbH


**British Library Cataloguing in Publication Data**

Link, Werner
The East–West conflict : the organisation of international relations in the twentieth century.
1. World politics—20th century
I. Title II. Der Ost–West–Konflikt. *English*
327'.09'04 D443

ISBN 0–907582–05–2

Printed in Great Britain by Billings of Worcester

# Contents

# *Tables*



## *Figures*

# *Acknowledgments*

This volume is based on the original German edition, published in 1980 under the title *Der Ost–West–Konflikt. Die Organisation der internationalen Beziehungen im 20. Jahrhundert*. The first two chapters, which deal with the theories of international relations, have not been included in the English version. Instead, I have revised the German Introduction, adding to it a brief discussion of those theoretical problems which seem important for an understanding of the subsequent analyses. The final chapter is new and deals with the post–1980 period; in it I have incorporated material from my recent study *Die neueren Entwicklungen des Ost–West–Konflikts* (*Veröffentlichungen der Deutschen Gesellschaft für Politikwissenschaft*, pt 1, Cologne, 1984).

I would like to thank my secretary, Frau Elfriede Schreiber, and my colleagues at Trier University — Paul Tücks, MA, Michael Meimeth, MA, and Peter Schell — for their support and, in particular, their help in tracing the original English quotations. Finally, special thanks are due to Dr Marion Berghahn and Berg Publishers, to the translator, Mrs Jackie Bennett-Ruete, and to the editor, Mrs Sonia Argyle, for the care and attention that they have given to the publication of this translation.

**Werner Link**
*Trier*
*October 1985*

# *Abbreviations*

| | |
|---|---|
| ABM | Anti-Ballistic Missile |
| *ADAP* | *Akten zur deutschen Auswärtigen Politik* |
| AFL | American Federation of Labor |
| ASEAN | Association of South East Asian Nations |
| CMEA | Council for Mutual Economic Aid |
| CPSU | Communist Party of the Soviet Union |
| CSCE | Conference on Security and Co-operation in Europe |
| DGAP | Deutsche Gesellschaft für Auswärtige Politik |
| DGFK | Deutsche Gesellschaft für Friedens- und Konfliktforschung |
| EC | European Community |
| ECOWAS | Economic Community of West African States |
| ECSC | European Coal and Steel Community |
| EEC | European Economic Community |
| EPZ | European Political Co-operation |
| ERP | European Recovery Programme |
| ESECS | European Security Study |
| *FAZ* | *Frankfurter Allgemeine Zeitung* |
| *FR* | *Foreign Relations of the United States* |
| GATT | General Agreement on Tariffs and Trade |
| ICBM | Intercontinental Ballistic Missile |
| IISS | International Institute for Strategic Studies |
| KPD | Kommunistische Partei Deutschlands |
| LAFTA | Latin American Free Trade Association |
| MBFR | Mutual and Balanced Force Reductions |
| MIRV | Multiple Independently Targeted Re-entry Vehicle |
| MLF | Multilateral Force |
| MPLA | Popular Movement for the Liberation of Angola |
| MX | Missile, Experimental |
| NATO | North Atlantic Treaty Organisation |
| OAPEC | Organisation of Arab Petroleum Exporting Countries |
| OAS | Organisation of American States |
| OAU | Organisation of African Unity |
| OECD | Organisation for Economic Co-operation and Development |
| OEEC | Organisation for European Economic Cooperation |
| OPEC | Organisation of Petroleum Exporting Countries |
| SAG | Sowjetische Aktiengesellschaft |

| | |
|---|---|
| SALT | Strategic Arms Limitation Talks |
| SEATO | South-East Asia Treaty Organisation |
| SELA | Sistema Económico Latinoamericano |
| SIPRI | Stockholm International Peace Research Institute |
| SLBM | Sea-Launched Ballistic Missile |
| SPD | Sozialdemokratische Partei Deutschlands |

# Introduction

There is strong support in political and academic discussion for the view that the East–West conflict has been the predominant feature in world politics since 1945. However, opinions as to the nature and development of the conflict and its present state vary considerably, to say nothing of the different views when it comes to assessing individual events in this global conflict. Moreover the past few years have witnessed a general lack of direction ever since the traditional interpretations of the Cold War, and then the concept of détente politics, were called into question. At the same time a new global conflict has emerged, the conflict between the industrial and the developing nations, which has complicated the discussion. Is the East–West conflict losing some of its importance compared with the North–South conflict, or is it being extended to the Third World? Is détente attainable in both arenas? 'Maintenance of détente', 'geographical indivisibility of détente', 'realistic détente', 'sliding back into the Cold War' and a range of similar terms appear as new key-words which block, rather than open up, paths to an understanding of world politics. A lack of direction, an escape into stereotyped thinking appear to be the alternatives.

This state of affairs may result from the fact that international relations — in contrast to intra-state politics — never, or very seldom, form the basis of the citizen's experience through direct participation. World politics, assisted by the mass media, is so near and yet so far. Newspaper readers, radio listeners and television viewers are provided with news from all over the world, presented to them without any visible coherence. Affirmations of goodwill and agreements on co-operation, disputes and conflicts, wars and threats of war, peace negotiations and calls for peace, state visits with wordy final communiqués or the ceremonial signing of treaties, international conferences with speeches and opposing speeches, with resolutions and counter-resolutions, appear like a badly fitting jig-saw puzzle. The media's habit of personalising political affairs adds to the confusion. With the fast-changing ebb and flow of domestic politics in individual countries, new characters appear on the stage of world politics — actors whose affairs in the context of home and abroad remain unknown or are only sketchily summarised. An impression is created that international relations lack any form of order or structure. Such an impression is understandable. That it is also inaccurate may be discerned only with some mental effort.

The overall context of international relations can be roughly characterised in that it basically concerns (1) the decentralised community of formally autonomous states which (2) has been modified by elements of a quasi-institutionalised association of states and in which (3) the activities of social groups, cutting across boundaries, have created a network of transnational relations.

Although individual states are formally equal and 'sovereign' in this decentralised international system, in reality they are extremely unequal and depend on one another to various degrees. In order to realise their security and welfare commitments they are more or less dependent on collaboration with other states (and partly dependent on foreign companies, transnational corporations, etc.). Tension between the extreme fragmentation of the international system into individual states and mutual dependence (which is, as a rule, asymmetric) gives rise to the need for a reliable order which not only complies with endeavours to 'preserve national identity' (R. Löwenthal), but also allows for international co-operation.

This structural problem is difficult to solve. Because of far-reaching differences and sharp contrasts between states and groups of states in social, economic, ideological and cultural areas it is impossible to establish a world government which could function satisfactorily; there is not enough mutual interest to allow the setting up of a world order along the lines of a state (with a monopoly of power). Under the conditions of a decentralised, quasi-anarchic association of states each state has to look after its defence alone or in collaboration with allies. States find themselves in a 'security dilemma', which John Herz (1959, p. 231) describes as follows:

> The 'security dilemma', or 'power and security dilemma', is a social constellation in which units of power (such as states or nations in international relations) find themselves whenever they exist side by side without higher authority that might impose standards of behavior upon them and thus protect them from attacking each other. In such a condition, a feeling of insecurity, deriving from mutual suspicion and mutual fear, compels these units to compete for ever more power in order to find more security, an effort which proves self-defeating because complete security remains ultimately unobtainable.

In view of this basic constellation it is understandable that power is the first regulating principle defining the groupings of states. The Great Powers assume *de facto* the task of creating such order; they are the 'managers' of the global political system (Modelski, 1972) and they organise it as an international order with zones of influence, alliances and demarcations. They evoke the building up in return of a balance of power. This applies not only in the sphere of national security, but also in the economic and trade policy sector. For example, the power of industrial nations, expressed in the existing world order, leads to the building up of a balance of power on the part of developing nations. In the final analysis power and the building up of a balance of power provide the foundation of international order.

States take pains to reduce general insecurities and uncertainties concerning the future behaviour of other states through mutual agreements on standard behaviour (through universal international law, treaties). However, at the international level there are none of the sanctions possessed by individual nations to guarantee that actions conform to these standards, i.e. there is no effective enforcement mechanism. Despite this limitation, the common interest of states or groups of states in reliable collaboration has often led to the institutionalisation of their relations. Not only have alliances continuously been formed, but many regional and global international organisations have also been founded.

States do not simply have common or parallel interests, they also have opposing interests, giving rise to regional or global tensions which can generate international conflict (such as the East–West conflict). At worst this conflict is decided by the use of force, i.e. by war. Because the term 'conflict' is used in an exaggerated and imprecise way in everyday language a short discussion of the term seems necessary.

Using Kurt Singer's theoretical studies of conflict (1949), we shall define 'conflict' as a process in the course of which incompatible (or apparently incompatible) tendencies and interests (1) are placed before the protagonists, (2) determine their actions and (3) produce critical tension which appreciably affects the organisation or structure of relationships. An incompatible tendency exists when the protagonists represent standpoints or pursue goals which — in reality or apparently — are mutually exclusive or cannot be realised simultaneously.

This definition makes it possible to differentiate between situations of competition and conflict. Competition is also characterised by differences in standpoint and by incompatible, or apparently incompatible, tendencies. If the protagonists are aware of this and if it determines their actions, then it is a matter of manifest competition. Only when critical tension arises out of the situation, appreciably affecting the organisation or structure of relationships (i.e. affecting the structure of relations and/or existing arrangements between the protagonists), can one properly speak of conflict.

This explanation of the term 'conflict' is as important for our analysis of the East–West conflict as the question of possible solutions to, or regulation of, conflict. Theoretically there are two conceivable alternatives: the solution of conflict can be sought either at the source of critical tension, i.e. in the incompatible, or apparently incompatible, tendencies, or in the effects of critical tension, i.e. in the organisation of relations.

The first procedure, viewed as an ideal type, leads either to a compromise between the opposing tendencies or to the success of one tendency.

The second procedure has four different ideal types of conflict regulation:

(1) Raising the degree of organisation, increasing relations (integration);

(2) Diminishing the degree of organisation, reducing relations (regression);

(3) Destroying the organisation with the object of a fundamental restructuring of relations (revolution, war);

(4) Withdrawing from relations (isolation).

On the basis of our definition of conflict, two structural world conflicts can be discerned which have developed during this century and are still with us today: the so-called East–West conflict and the so-called North–South conflict. Because the East–West conflict was, and still is, of major importance it seems admissible to concentrate empirical analysis on this conflict and its respective concretisations.

This analysis focuses on attempts to find solutions and to regulate conflict of the type mentioned above. That is to say that the organisation of the whole of international relations is our main interest. In order to make use of the four types of conflict resolution for an analysis of structural world conflict in our age, some hypotheses may be tentatively formulated as a rough analytical device.

(1) Withdrawal from international relations and total isolation (type 4) is feasible — if at all — only for small, insignificant states and/or for relatively short periods of time as a limited possibility.

Actual present-day international relations throughout the world make isolation improbable as a principle of global organisation, the more so because the social and political costs are too high.

(2) Military solutions to conflict, i.e. the destruction of the existing international order by antagonistic great powers (through world revolution and world war), aimed at the subsequent creation of a completely new organisation (type 3), seem unlikely in our day and age as a conscious and intentional approach to the resolution of conflict in view of the danger of nuclear self-destruction. This is not to say that it is improbable as an unintentional 'solution'. The availability of conventional and tactical nuclear weapons in regional and local conflicts (and the increasing proliferation of nuclear weapons) creates the possibility of the use of war, short of global war, as a means for structural change. The escalation and extension of local and regional wars to a global level cannot be excluded. On a global level, structural determinations are no longer conceivable through a single act — such as the victory of one state or of an alliance in war. This is why incremental (gradual) changes are becoming increasingly important. This is the global dimension of regional and local wars and war-type solutions to conflict.

(3) Regressive solutions of conflict are the most probable outcome once a multitude of incompatible, or apparently incompatible, tendencies, tangible asymmetries and few mutual interests exist between the great powers (type 2). Reduced relations, the delimitation and stabilisation of spheres of interest (regional hegemony and regional non-hegemonic integration with increased co-operation between the members) are expressions of this development. However, actual interrelations and interdependencies considerably limit the possibility of global regression, because global regression would considerably diminish the chances of fulfilling common tasks. Regression makes transnational relations, which are important for the organisation of exchanges of information, goods and capital, more difficult, or even impossible.

(4) Integration by increasing the degree of organisation of the network of relations (type 1) relies on a high level of agreement on values and common tasks. It entails an attempt to institutionalise solutions to conflict and competition by co-operative competition. Johan Galtung (1970) developed the conditions for 'peaceful co-operation' (symmetry, homology, interdependence, supra-national institution-building and dispersion). These can be used as indicators to test the appropriateness of an integrative solution to conflict, i.e.

the more these elements exist in reality the sooner an organisation based on an integrative solution to conflict will become possible. Because societies would thus be more closely linked, and material and ideological exchange would be furthered consciously, transnational relations are of greater significance in this type of conflict solution. However, as long as states remain the authoritative centres for decision-making, the organisation of political co-ordination remains the most important problem; autonomy and decentralisation narrowly restrict integration at a global level (whereas greater opportunities exist at a regional level, where there is more homogeneity).

Total integration (the extreme variant of type 1) would involve the setting up of an effective world government as a central and ultimate authority at a global level — whether in a hegemonic form or even by universal governance of a single world power. Such a 'solution' would not only abolish the existing systems of autonomous states, but also take care of the power and security dilemma and thus imply a radical structural change. In view of existing material and ideological heterogeneities and contradictions, especially between the Great Powers, this total integration was, and is, improbable at this time (nor, for that matter, would it be desirable). One should rather assume that the law or tendency discernible in the past will continue, namely that once a state or a group of states attempts to erect a world hegemony or world governance, competing states will in response build up sufficient power to prevent this — whether by increasing power internally (through armaments), or by the external extension of power (for example through alliances, hegemonic spheres of influence, the establishment of military bases, etc.) or through a combination of these measures. The following dual hypothesis can thus be formulated. Accelerated attempts at integration would probably arouse suspicions that attempts were being made to achieve universal hegemony or world domination and this would inadvertently produce counterbalancing tendencies and lead to regression. Even when there is mutual agreement on an integrative solution to conflict, the limitations of such policies must also be noted. Ambitious policies which attempt too high a degree of organisation (measured against the existing common interests) may nurture vain hopes and similarly cause a switch to regressive behaviour.

Ideal types do not exist in reality. We have to expect, and shall indeed find, mixtures of different types. In view of the common interests and contradictions, of compatible and incompatible (or apparently incompatible) tendencies in world politics in our time, a mixture of integrative and regressive elements would be a possible and obvious pattern of conflict solution (see the similar argument in G. Zellentin, 1976). The theoretical and practical difficulty is to find the right organisational mixture corresponding to the existing level of the development of world society and of the global distribution of power. Not only too great a regression, but also too intensive an integration, can become counter-productive (as I have hinted above). Integration can sharpen conflict, or even create new conflicts, and have destructive effects or suddenly lead to regression.

This problem was formulated by Harold D. Lasswell as early as 1946 at the beginning of the post war period:

> The nature and timing of world organization depend upon the global correlation of power with other elements in society. If the rate of attempted organization outruns the growth of strong sustaining elements in world society, collapse will surely follow . . . If, on the contrary, world organization lags behind the level which is capable of being attained by political skill at any particular time, humanity will remain under the shadow of atomic disaster.

Seen in the light of these problems, the development of the East–West conflict, which is analysed in the following chapters, can be understood as a course zigzagging between levels of global organisation which are either too high or too low, as a fluctuation between an intensification and a lessening of the degree of organisation in international relations.

# 1 *Interpretations of the East–West Conflict*

Assessments and interpretations of the East–West conflict and the Cold War have generated much controversy among both non-specialists and scholars. The best way to overcome the contradictory explanations and to provide a meaningful synthesis of their partial insights is to undertake a study which focuses on the organisation of international relations as a framework of analysis. Such an interpretation is made possible through the availability of comprehensive studies of diplomatic history (see in particular Martin F. Herz, 1966, W. H. McNeill, 1953, and more recently Yergin, 1977) and voluminous editions of official documents (e.g. the series 'Foreign Relations of the United States').

However, so far the debate has been characterised by a marked tendency towards reductionism. Typical reductionist interpretations explain the global East–West conflict, which expresses itself at the international level, in terms of the peculiar attributes of individual states and societies, i.e. they analyse an international phenomenon at a national level. There are two main schools of thought which, though diametrically opposed in all other respects, share this approach.

(1) The liberal and moderate conservative approach resulting in an 'orthodox' explanation holds that the very nature of the Soviet regime is responsible for the failure of various attempts at co-operation, and hence for the Cold War. Although the theory of the Soviet Union's exclusive 'guilt' (originally argued by Western governments) has often been modified, the socio-political structure of the Communist regime and its ideology are considered to be the real determinants of the Cold War. Thus, for example, Arthur Schlesinger, a pillar of the Liberal Establishment in the United States, argues that even the most rational American policy could not have prevented the Cold War: 'The Cold War could have been avoided only if the Soviet Union had not been possessed by convictions both of the infallibility of the Communist world and of the inevitability of a Communist world' (Schlesinger, 1967; repr. in Gardner *et al.*, 1970, p. 76). In short, Communist ideology made the Cold War a tragic necessity.

According to Hans J. Morgenthau (in Gardner *et al.*, 1970) who can be regarded as the leading representative of the 'realist' school, the conflict arose primarily out of a clash between two incompatible concepts of order — between the Soviet principle of carving out spheres of influence and American universalism; to this extent it resembled earlier conflicts. The new dimension which distinguished this from past conflicts and which transformed it into the Cold War was 'the Communist character of the Soviet state and of its foreign policy', the combination of the principles of Communism and traditional Tsarist expansionism.

(2) In contrast, the revisionist approach (originally put forward by radical liberals and later represented primarily by neo-Marxists) identifies the causes of the Cold War with the inherently expansionist policy of the capitalist United States of America. Following the penetration of the North American continent, the dynamic American economy required new fields of action. This domestic need was expressed in the 'open door' policy which, by opposing the creation of zones of influence and preference, was bound to collide with Soviet policy (W. A. Williams, $^{2}$1962 and his 'Wisconsin' school; see also Link, 1971; H. J. Schröder, 1976, and the fundamental criticism of R. J. Maddox, 1973).

According to the neo-Marxist version of this theory, the capitalist mode of production and distribution is 'irreconcilable with the existence of other autonomous centres of production and distribution by reason of the development of its own inherent laws' and therefore 'naturally directed towards expansionism' (Krippendorff, 1970, pp. 461 ff.). For neo-Marxists the East–West conflict is an aspect of the 'international class struggle'; that is to say, it can be attributed to the 'struggles and collaboration between social classes, class factions, social strata and groups within socially antagonistic societies' (Arons and Jahn, 1973, p. 90).

On occasion both schools of thought (see in more detail Gaddis, 1972) qualify their arguments by referring to individual, personal factors, using Stalin's character or Truman's mentality as additional explanatory models. Nevertheless, the most crucial factor is seen to be the inherent need for expansion on the part of the respective societies or states. At their most extreme these versions of the two schools present mirror images of anti-capitalist or anti-Communist interpretations of modern history. They are at one and the same time reductionist and determinist.

Furthermore both main schools of thought have been given a

theoretical or philosophical foundation which reinforces their determinism. For neo-Marxist authors the antagonism between capitalism and socialism is an inevitable manifestation of the process of historical development which leads to the triumph of socialism on a world scale. The irreconcilable struggle between the two social orders and their embodiment in the nation-state system is a necessary period of historical transition. Just as feudalism was replaced by the bourgeois capitalist stage following a transitional period of international conflict, socialism is regarded as a historical necessity — the only difference being that in this event the global victory of socialism really would emancipate the people from international domination and tyranny. From the perspective of this theory of history, the East–West conflict is a manifestation of the 'age-old' North–South conflict from which it is derived in the sense that 'the founding of the Soviet Union in 1917 produced the first counter-strategy of liberation from the tyranny of capitalist industrial society at a national level' (Gantzel 1972, p. 105). Despite the inclusion of states as actors, it is the class struggle that remains the decisive level of interaction. Moreover, since the international class struggle is seen as an antagonistic and irreconcilable conflict, compromises over central questions cannot be justified. Temporary agreements are merely stages in a historically necessary process of conflict which will achieve its final objective only with the victory of the proletariat organised by the Communist parties, a victory which will also eliminate international exploitation. This concept is expressed in the theory of peaceful coexistence as a principle of the transitional phase in official socialist doctrine, both in its political propaganda and in socialist international law (see Jegorow, 1972; Uibopuu, 1971; Royen, 1979).

Although the liberal-conservative philosophy of history is less certain as to historical purpose, it is nevertheless no less determinist than the Marxist view when dealing with the classification of the East–West conflict within historical development. Of the general interpretations of the Cold War advanced within the framework of the liberal-conservative philosophy of history the most impressive is that undertaken by Ernst Nolte.

In the course of a wide-ranging examination, Nolte (1974) has analysed the most important ideological and intellectual movements and counter-movements and their historical roots and identified the 'European liberal system' as the most significant development in recent history. By this he means 'the multifaceted character of a society which can allow what is new, unexpected and unplanned to spring into existence since it is able to develop in the shelter of its diversity, free from any rigid control of a too powerful centre' (p. 86). It is a flexible, competitive, pluralist, open society which is reflected at an international level in competition between secularised, but still closely connected, states (p. 102). It is a society which 'is characterised by an expansiveness which eliminates the 'yes, yes – no, no' and indulges both the unimpeded development of the extreme left as well as the countermove from left to right in certain circumstances' (p. 103). The Soviet Union has withdrawn from this system by institutionalising the leftward tendency and, as the state of the extreme left, has destroyed openness and variety in its organisation. The United States was also originally conceived as a state of the left, but she remained 'sufficiently rich and diverse' for her pluralism to be identified as an offshoot and constituent of the European system (p. 130). It is the very pluralism of this system that accounts for the fact that, whilst developing specific answers to historical challenges at home and abroad, it can never itself be that answer; nor could it be the answer to the 'state of the extreme left'. On the contrary, Fascism was the requisite answer to the Bolshevik revolution and this specific answer 'had to be[!] more antagonistic than and at the same time similar to it than the European system could ever be . . . and if it had not occurred (which is out of the question) it could have been constructed theoretically.'

The choice between the two revolutions had to be made by the system 'which was older than both and which contained the basis for both' (p. 138). That is to say, the United States was predestined for the role it actually played in the defeat of Fascism. National Socialist expansion indeed produced a relationship between both systems with the anti-Fascist war coalition — which, according to Nolte, was neither a simple emergency coalition nor an explicit ideological alliance, but rather represented a relationship in which traditional ideological, neo-ideological and power-political aspects were inextricably linked. But this uneasy alliance was short-lived. Nolte explains the failure of co-operation after the defeat of the common enemy with the axiom that 'internal political stability . . . is the precondition of any significant co-operation between states' (p. 179). Since this condition existed in neither state and since 'all attempts at domestic self-assertion' necessarily 'contain negative implications for foreign policy', co-operation was bound to fail:

> How could the United States and the Soviet Union — culturally alien, ideologically hostile despite certain affinities, incapable of exploiting common economic interests for political reasons — have remained allies once the reason for their co-operation, Hitler and National Socialism, ceased to exist? (p. 181)

This rhetorical question emphasizes the ideological, rather than the economic, difference between the systems as the decisive factor in an explanation of the origins of the Cold War. Policies of both the Soviet Union and the United States are explained by the irreconcilable contradiction between the principle of the Communist system, which precludes the possibility of a new dissenting majority from developing, and the nature of the European liberal system, characterised by pluralism. Thus conflict between the Communists and the United States was 'inevitable'. The reason that it erupted only after a transitional period lay in the Soviet Union's interest in maintaining its 'anti-Fascist appearance' and in the existence of various schools of political thought in the United States, some of which also pursued anti-Fascist policies.

East–West conflict and the Cold War are thus portrayed as predetermined both ideologically and by the nature of the systems. Historical opportunity and inevitability result from the nature of an ideological 'system': the analytical device is in effect reified; the European liberal system is said to have characteristics; it negotiates, develops solutions, etc. Thus neo-Marxist socio-economic determinism is replaced by a kind of ideological determinism which, despite its greater empirical content, is equally problematic.

All determinism removes from the individual and the collective actors the opportunity for choice and decision-making. It corresponds to a mechanical philosophy which is as out of place and outdated in the humanities and social sciences as it is in the natural sciences. Relations, on the one hand between political and social systems which as such are created and changed by man, and, on the other hand between individual negotiators or collectives, cannot be characterised by blunt determinism, but have to be understood by looking at mutual and reciprocal limitations and forms of 'plastic' or soft control (see Popper, 1966). With regard to the East–West conflict it was at the height of the Cold War that R. H. S. Crossman warned against deterministic analyses:

> There is no scientific validity in the phrases 'inherent contradiction' and

> 'inevitable conflict'. In so far they are not just untrue, they merely express a pessimistic conviction that human beings will always fail to find a sensible method of resolving a dangerous situation. (Crossman, 1951, p. 10)

Arguments of historical philosophy that point to the inevitability of international confrontation are all the more threatening to current attempts to relax tensions and manage conflict. Daniel Yergin (1977) has criticised past interpretations of the Cold War from a similar standpoint and has opted instead for an analysis based on individual and group psychology. He emphasizes the perception and the axiomatic outlook of respective actors and groups of actors, the diplomats and leading politicians:

> There has been too much of a tendency to assume that all that happened was of a single piece, foreordained and determined. But how world leaders perceived their interests and acted on those perceptions counted for a very great deal. . . . The understanding American leaders had of events and possibilities controlled their own actions and reactions in the dialectic of confrontation. (1977, p. 8)

Using this theoretical concept, Yergin has painted a highly informative picture of diplomatic history. It is, however, debatable whether the classification of two alternative groups of thought (the Riga group versus the Yalta group) is either conclusive or convincing. The main objection is that Yergin's basic approach involves a fallacy of psychological reductionism. The analysis of perceptions clarifies American actions and reactions, but not the result of the policy — the failure of the projected establishment of an international system of peace. So this analysis pays insufficient heed to the structural limitations of the 'operational environment' (Sprout and Sprout, 1965) which are independent of those perceptions and affect the realisation of specific policies and contribute to the outcome.

In order to avoid both reductionism and determinism in an analysis of the East–West conflict it is necessary to consider the following. Since so-called East–West conflict is generally agreed to be an international phenomenon, an explanation must be sought at the level of global international relations — their structure and organisation. The fact that such an explanation will not attempt to reduce matters to the domestic socio-political level nor to the individual or group-psychology level does not, of course, mean that these factors will be ignored. And it certainly does not mean that, instead of seeing international conflict as being determined by domestic socio-political or individual psychological factors, it will simply employ another kind of determinism which explains actions of societies or states only by international factors. On the contrary, this analysis also accepts the significance of a reciprocal, 'plastic' control and a reciprocal effect between international and national or social structures and actors, in this way incorporating the fragmented results of past research.

Since the East–West conflict is understood as a structural conflict, we must ask which constraints on political actors result from the general structure of world politics. And according to the theory of conflict (see the Introduction), it is important to differentiate between competition and conflict. We must also ask which incompatible tendencies and interests have actually been pursued (= competition) and have generated a critical tension which threatenes the organisation of international relations (= conflict); and which solutions or sorts of conflict management have been tried.

# 2 *The Genesis of the East–West Conflict*

Many scholars hold that the East–West conflict, when seen as ideological and partially organised clash — as the expression of antagonistic interests or conflicting ideas of domestic, social and international order — is older than the Cold War. This is undoubtedly correct. Moreover, the antagonistic tendencies are also older than the East–West conflict, older than the conflict between the Soviet Union and the democratic countries of the West. These incompatible tendencies, which at first produced tensions only within societies rather than internationally (although they were relevant to international organisation from the very beginning), did not arise as geographically located clashes within the state system. Their character was, on the contrary, transnational. The concept of a co-operative order, i.e. of the organisation of international relations co-operatively (*genossenschaftlich*) as a 'social world community' (see H. C. Schröder, 1968, p. 77) opposed the traditional organisation of international relations based on the formal autonomy of each state and the actual domination of the Great Powers.

The ideological and theoretical reasons for this counter-tendency were given by Marx and Engels at a time when Britain dominated the world through the *pax Britannica*. Historically, the counter-tendency became important when mass socialist parties adopted the co-operative concept for their transnational relations. This development was accelerated during the phase of global politics in which Britain's power gradually declined and oligopolistic imperialist competition increased between the Great Powers. The fundamental principles of this counter-concept thus manifested themselves in the transnational relations of socialist parties at a time when attempts were being made — stimulated in particular by Germany's 'grasping for World Power' (*Griff nach der Weltmacht*) (Fritz Fischer, 1967) — to bring about a rearrangement within the global state system which ended in the First World War. The concept of a co-operative new world order was thus contrasted in a militant way by parties united in the Socialist International with the traditional system of competition between states characterised by these parties as imperialism and colonialism on the part of the Great Powers: 'Once the proletariat has gained political power, traditional divisions between states will fall with a number of other traditions' (Kautsky, 1908, p. 36).

However, it would be difficult to maintain that in the prewar period the global thrust of this counter-tendency (in contrast with its internal social importance) determined the actions either of the socialist parties or of international politics in general, unless one attributed more significance to International Congresses and resolutions than is justified in view of their internal disunity, particularly in international matters such as colonialism and imperialism (see the dispute at the Stuttgart International Socialist Congress of 1907 and the vehement argument between Lenin, 1917, and Kautsky, 1914, on the question of imperialism; cf. recently Kraus, 1978). At the very latest, on the outbreak of war, when transnational relations broke down and orientation in the direction of the nation state prevailed it became clear that internationalism did not determine the everyday policies of the social-democratic parties. It was only after the Bolsheviks had gained state power in Russia that a specific configuration of conflict emerged — and this is the nub of the theory quoted above — which was thenceforth superimposed on the traditional oligopolistic competition of the Great Powers, eventually to become an aspect of competition between them. Only after socialist ideas (in their Bolshevik form) were combined with the power of the Russian state and when the transnational relations of the Communist parties were bound to Soviet Russia through the Comintern did the controversy over the reorganisation of world politics (which was inextricably bound up with the controversy over domestic structures) become an important factor in international relations. This generated (at first only in part and for relatively short periods) the critical tensions that threatened the very organisation of international relations; that is to say, only then did competition develop into conflict. It may be defined as an East–West conflict since the antagonists were, and are, geographically located in that way. Conflict in the international arena, however, remained relatively muted for as long as one of the antagonists, the Soviet Union, was a relatively weak state. For now and in the future the relative power of the antagonistic states, rather than transnational movements, was to determine the process of conflict.

This state of affairs was the expression and result of the fact that, contrary to Marxist-Leninist predictions, the world revolution —

the militant destruction of the existing world order and its replacement by a socialist-Communist organisation — did not take place and of the fact that conflict had become permanent because of the failure of a revolutionary reorganisation of world order. This had two implications:

(1) Conflict was reformulated, in practice and in theory, as conflict between states, governed by the rules of the state system;

(2) Solutions to conflict had to be found which began with, and took into account, the split in the international system.

In order to understand the fundamental restructuring of the shape of conflict it is necessary to present a short account of the theoretical and ideological development.

In their original theories Marx and Engels applied the thesis of simultaneous and direct development towards a world market under the conditions of capitalist means of production and distribution seeing in this the prerequisite of a world Communist revolution. Thus the assumption was that bourgeois industry and bourgeois trade would create a world market and develop modern productive forces which would then be 'harnessed' by the simultaneous proletarian revolution and subjected to the 'collective control of the most advanced peoples'. So in the original Marxist concept the irreconcilable tendencies contained differing concepts of the organisation of international relations which were understood as a unity (a 'world market'). How this organisation 'collective control' would look remained open at first and would later be only sketchily described as a free association. The one thing that was clear was that the nation-state principle in world politics and national restrictions and barriers would no longer constitute a problem even before (and even less after) the world revolution. Marx saw the economic, and with it the historical, development as a widening of the gulf between capital and labour — the bourgeoisie and the proletariat — and as an extension of this relationship (spanning and devaluing nations) into a global problem, as the struggle between the unified international proletariat and the unified international exploiting class. For Marx world revolution meant the simultaneous transformation of the capitalist world market into a world-socialist system; lengthy global divisions were not envisaged (Marx, *Frühschriften*, 1845–8, pp. 361 ff.). The possibility that the antagonism between states could consolidate interests seen as irreconcilable between world proletariat and world bourgeoisie contradicted the thesis that the organisation of national states had already become meaningless precisely because of the capitalist world market and that the revolution would occur simultaneously in advanced parts of the world. However, since in fact 'initially' a revolution occurred in only one country (and in a country that could in no way be described as highly developed) the problem of global economic organisation was inextricably bound up with the problem of universal political organisation.

Marx had already failed to develop the links between the central categories of 'world market', 'revolution', 'class' and the categories of global political organisation in the state system (see Soell, 1972). Lenin was only partly successful in describing the links in the theory of uneven development, shortened to the vulgarised formula of the struggle between classes and nations. It was decisive that states (i.e. states having opposing internal orders) should be taken seriously as organisational units structuring world politics and that the thesis of two antagonistic world systems should replace the concept of the unity of the international system. The two systems were seen as confronting each other as both social and state systems: a 'conglomerate made up of classes, states, parts of the population, revolutionary movements' (Schmiederer, 1973) which is, and was, difficult to define more precisely.

Following the withdrawal (after the separate peace treaty of Brest-Litowsk) of revolutionary Russia from the network of relations established during the World War, practical politics were first shaped by an internationalist world revolutionary concept of the Soviet leadership. However, they had already been adapted to the actual circumstances of power politics under Lenin (in the context of the New Economic Policy). Stalin's decision to construct 'socialism in one country' (as opposed to the Trotskyist course of 'permanent revolution') meant that in foreign policy priorities were set in favour of Russian power politics according to the rules of the traditional state system which, however, would be supported by the transnational activities of the Comintern. This meant that Soviet foreign policy developed an 'opaque duplicity' (Stökl). In Stalinist ideology the 'chief interests of Communism . . . were fused with assertions and increases of the power of the Soviet regime in Russia' (Ruffmann, 1977,[7] p. 212). This meant that revolutionary internationalism was equated with, or subordinated to, the unconditional partisanship of the Soviet Union 'because the USSR is the basis of the world revolutionary movement' (Stalin, 1927). This view provided an ideological justification of the restoration and the eventual expansion of the Russian Empire as revolutionary imperialism. However,

Stalin's policy of coexistence was at the same time an acknowledgement that the structure of the international system imposed limits on Soviet policy which would, for a long time, prevent a revolutionary reorganisation of the international order. The Soviet state was too weak to revolutionize the international system alone and was faced with the same dilemma as that of all other states — the securing of power and defence. This was seen as a particular threat precisely because the extreme divergencies of politics and economics could not be reduced in the short term. Thus the traditional concept of the balance of power was employed as the standard for Soviet foreign policy (see Stalin's statements of 1925, quoted by Ruffmann, [7]1977, p. 186). Stalin's pursuit of a balance of power was certainly unrealistic when one considers the striking difference between the power of the Soviet Union and that of the democratic capitalist countries. However, if the transnational relations of the Comintern are included, the picture becomes more realistic. The Comintern's activities were in fact only formally separated from the Soviet Union's official foreign policy. In reality the totalitarian unity of state and party left no room for even relative autonomy in foreign activities. Whilst Communist parties in democratic countries had a certain freedom of action within their social and political systems, the guiding principles were determined by the Comintern, who acted more for Soviet Russia than transnationally. The CPSU's domination of the Comintern and the subordination of their paratransnational policy to the interests of Soviet power politics made it possible for the Soviet leadership to give voice to a strategy of conflict resolution through world revolution whilst actually pursuing an integrative policy between states on the basis of the dualistic world structure. The components of world revolution were only occasionally interwoven with practical foreign policy. In practical politics Machiavelli usually triumphed over Marx; considerations of power and security politics decided the issue (B. Moore, 1951).

The Soviet Union's militant approach to conflict during the revolutionary phase (with the explicit justification of global intervention in favour of the revolution) mirrored the policy of military intervention practised by Great Britain, France, Japan and the USA which aimed at maintaining the international structure. This policy, which commenced in the summer of 1918, — as historical research has clearly shown — was adopted primarily because of 'old' conflicts, i.e. the conflicts that determined the World War. It aimed at preventing a joint German-Russian front and at blocking unilateral

Japanese influence. Again, *Machtpolitik*, aimed at state expansion, was primarily the impulse behind Poland's war of intervention in 1920. However, these military interventions also had an anti-Bolshevik character; the Great Powers strengthened counter-revolutionary forces in the Civil War without being able to prevent their defeat. Inasmuch as this intervention strove to overcome Bolshevik rule, or to prevent its consolidation, it was an attempt to maintain the existing state system and the capitalist world market by the re-integration of a non-Bolshevik Russia. The economic counterpart was Herbert Hoover's Food Relief Programme, envisaged first for Russia and then implemented as a 'proto-Marshall Plan' (Levin, 1968) in East European states in order to contain the Bolshevik revolution.

These attempts to bring about a military solution — following Germany's defeat — were never consolidated by consistent military action on the part of the Allies. French plans for a great anti-Bolshevik crusade were wrecked by British, and more by American, resistance just as the attempts of a defeated Germany to bring about an understanding with the victorious powers by constructing a united anti-Bolshevik front failed. However, there is evidence that even at the Versailles Peace Conference the question played an important (albeit not an exclusively dominant) role as to the re-organisation of the international system in view of the Bolshevik revolution in Russia and the means of containing Communism (see Arno Mayer, 1967, and John M. Thompson, 1967). Thus at this stage the prototype was forged that would hence forward characterise international relations. Bolshevik Russia and the liberal-capitalist democracy of the United States became the main forces representing opposing ideological and regulatory policies at state level. These policies were: Lenin's world revolutionary concept and Wilson's reformist concept and the conflicting ideas of a socialist and a liberal-democratic internationalism. However, Wilson's politics were directed not only against Lenin's revolutionary 'anti-imperialism', but also against the 'traditional imperialism' of the West European Great Powers and Germany. It was the 'vision of a global order beyond power politics' that was to characterise free world trade and co-operation between nations on the basis of international law, democratic power structures and life-styles and international capitalist trade relations (Levin, 1968, p. 3; Arno J. Mayer, 1959, Epilogue: 'Wilson vs. Lenin'). The 'Western democratic counter-movement' represented by Wilson in America had 'tried to overcome classic state power politics both from within and at the same time on an ideological level' (Bracher, 1963, p. 122). However, the close link of democratic ideals with the nation state meant that the orientation on the state as a structural principle of international politics could be overcome only in a very limited way. The replacement of the nation state as the main structural principle by the principle of class politics propagated by Marxism met its contrary equivalent for the first time in the biological racial principle of National Socialism.

# 3 *The Regulation of Conflict in the 1920s*

## *The Connection Between Partial Isolation and Integration*

The reintegration of a non-Bolshevik Russia into the existing state system, or rather into a new world order projected by Woodrow Wilson, was achieved neither by military means (through interventionist wars) nor through the economic-humanitarian measures of the Hoover Programme. The new world order was realised only in a rudimentary form, distorted by power politics. Following this failure, at first a policy of isolating Soviet Russia was adopted by West European nations and by the United States. The establishment of a *cordon sanitaire* of Eastern and Central European states aimed both at preventing the spread of the Bolshevik revolution to Western Europe and at impeding the formation of a united front between Soviet Russia and defeated Germany.

This policy of containment was part of the general concept of world politics expressed in the Versailles Treaty, but it was never fully implemented. The concept of collective security, on which the League of Nations was based, could be realised only in so far as French security requirements — which increased further when American and British promises of guarantee did not materialise — and Britain's balance-of-power policy were pursued by the traditional means of power politics. The reality of power politics did not correspond with the legal rules of the League of Nations which discriminated against the potentially strongest continental European state, i.e. Germany, and which at the same time lacked universal validity because of the exclusion of Soviet Russia and the absence of the United States of America (Walters, 1952; D. C. Watt, 1975). In the eyes of the United States, the up-and-coming world power, this made it necessary to pursue the positive aim of the stabilisation and reintegration of a democratic, liberal-capitalist Germany into a Western 'community of ideals, interests and purposes' (Secretary of State Hughes). If this task were not accomplished, world stability seemed to be unrealisable. Germany was to function as a 'bulwark' against Communism. The policy of diplomatic non-recognition of the Bolshevik regime was to keep the way open for the future reintegration of a democratic Russia and was at the same time intended to make such a path attractive to dissident forces in Russia. Thus the policy of geographical, political and diplomatic isolation was seen as a factor in American policy. The Soviet Union in no way chose isolation, it came about through decisions taken overseas (a point which cannot be stressed too strongly in view of the different interpretation of modern theorists of disassociation). However, isolation was never total, and was increasingly combined with integrative methods. A number of European states — with Great Britain, Germany, Norway and Austria in the lead — departed from the strict policy of isolation, at first in the area of trade. In 1922 Germany also officially broke away politically from the united Western front and henceforward the Soviet Union was gradually recognised *de facto* and *de jure* by other countries. The year 1924 was the 'year of recognition'. Great Britain, Italy, Norway, Austria, Greece, Sweeden, Denmark, China and France recognised the Soviet Union, although the United States officially maintained a policy of isolation until 1933. Great Britain and France were still independent Great Powers in the power game and operated accordingly in their policies towards the Soviet Union.

Immediately after the October Revolution and in the following years, the Soviet leadership began to speculate on America's economic interest in the Russian market and tried to normalise political relations through direct and indirect offers of negotiation (including the settlement of debts incurred under the Tsar). But all this was of no use. References to the bright prospects for American capital and industrial investment in the Soviet Union understandably met with a certain positive response in American business circles orientated towards exports. But this did not improve the US Administration's willingness to recognise the Soviet Union, first because other economic groups, in particular the American unions (AFL), energetically advocated an uncompromising policy, and secondly because, in view of the clash of American and Russian interests in Asia, a restructuring of the Pacific area was considered more worthwhile for America as long as Russia was excluded from that region (Washington Conference of 1921–2). Nevertheless, there were forces within the US Administration that were the more inclined to consider economic co-operation (albeit below the level of official recognition), as the imminent breakdown of the Bolshevik regime appeared less likely and competition amongst Western European states for advantages in trading with the Soviet Union became stronger. They justified this policy with an argument which henceforth appeared in many variations at all phases of détente as follows: 'In all probability it will be easier to hasten its [i.e. the Soviet Government's] transformation into a more or less normal representative government, having a more or less normal economic policy, by beginning to do business with it than by holding off' (Memorandum from the Chief of the Russian Division [Office], US Department of Commerce, E. D. Durand, 2 Feb. 1922).

Similar arguments were employed by Germany in her efforts to harmonize her East and West policies, culminating in the Berlin Treaty of 1926. Germany maintained that Soviet Russia had to be included in peace policies 'in order to moderate her and make her conform, at least to a certain extent, with civilised countries' (Conversation of Under-Secretary of State von Schubert with the American Ambassador, 7 Apr. 1926, ADAP, Series B, Vol. II. 1, p. 283). Upgrading relations and increased organisational links (the integrative solution of conflict) seemed appropriate for an international peace policy, as pursued in the era of the Locarno Treaty and the Kellogg Pact.

In the US State Department developments took a different turn in the first half of the 1920s under the aegis of the Secretary of State Hughes. Hughes, too, advocated the use of economic methods to effect a change in the Soviet regime. He did not, however, regard a policy of economic involvement as suitable, but preferred economic isolation. He wanted to draw an economic *cordon sanitaire* round Russia and bring about the collapse of the Bolshevik system by refusing both co-operation and badly needed credits. Hughes felt it necessary for Western governments to co-operate 'to teach the Soviet government by keeping away'. This policy prevailed even after the change of personnel in the US State Department in 1925. The influential Governor of the Bank of England, Montague Norman, could rightly assume that official politics in America would sympathise with his policy of 'financial starvation' in order to force the Soviet Union by admittedly 'very drastic and brutal means', 'to listen to reason and create the possibility of reopening the doors of the Great Russian Empire and to return to healthy economic — if not political — conditions' (Conversation with the German Ambassador Dufour, 6 Apr. 1926, ADAP, Series B. Vol. II. 2, pp. 318 f.).

A long-term international perspective was essential. The antagonism between the United States and the Soviet Union did not arise primarily from the fact that individual problems, such as the repayment of American loans, were unsolved. The Soviet government had already declared its readiness to negotiate on this issue. The heart of the matter was rather the more fundamental problem of containing the world-revolutionary influences emanating from the Soviet experiment and the Comintern which, in the eyes of the American power élite, threatened the capitalist system on a global scale. Orientation towards world revolution, as voiced in the Comintern, reduced the value of the Soviet Union's diplomacy aimed at economic co-operation:

> It is the conviction of the Government of the United States that relations on a basis usual between friendly nations cannot be established with a governmental entity which is the agency of a group who hold it as their mission to bring about the overthrow of the existing political, economic and social order throughout the world and who regulate their conduct towards other nations accordingly. (*FR* 1928, III. 822)

America's strict policy of isolation was to help to prevent this global success for the Soviet Union, even if it meant that partial and short-term economic advantages could not be realised. The United States had become the financial centre of the world and the State Department hoped that an American block on loans would deprive the 'so-called Soviet Government', 'the present rulers of Russia' (*FR* 1928, III. 824) of the support of an increasingly impoverished population. However, no united Western front was established. The economic *cordon sanitaire* had long been violated even by American industry. The transnational relations of the business world could not be completely controlled under the conditions of a liberal-democratic regime. Moreover the peremptory interest in expanding exports was increasingly inconsistent with the policy of non-recognition and isolation. This contradiction was insoluble and could at best be eased by allowing American industry to enter into private trade and economic relations (but leaving individual firms to take all the risks). Whilst business concerns interested in exports to the Soviet Union fought to change the official hard line of Washington's policy by employing arguments similar to those of official Soviet policy in order to create the conditions for a further increase in American–Russian trade, the State Department referred to the fact that, despite the absence of diplomatic relations, the total of American exports between 1924 and 1927 exceeded those of Germany or Great Britain. In the interest of its own policy on exports, the US Administration accepted that, despite the official embargo on loans, American firms had strengthened relations with the Soviet Union and thereby contributed indirectly to the failure of the official policy of isolation.

From all this it emerges that the Soviet Union's main antagonist was acting politically rather than economically. The fear that 'a union of purpose' could develop between a defeated Germany and an isolated Soviet Union was one of the factors responsible for the United States' seizing leadership in the critical area of tension in international politics, namely the matter of reparations, despite the fact that she was not a member of the League of Nations since she wished to retain her freedom in international trade and did not want to take responsibility for an international order based on the Versailles Treaty (see Link, 1970). The United States thus temporarily stabilised the international system and integrated Germany economically, as well as politically, into this system.

The Dawes Plan brought economic peace in the shape of a *pax Americana* by revising the Versailles Treaty and stabilising international relations. The Locarno Treaty and Germany's entry to the League of Nations (1925–6) were the most visible expressions of the new international order which, with the accession of the Soviet Union to the Kellogg Pact (1928), developed a universal character. Even in economic matters a global perspective — beyond partial economic interests — determined America's policy towards Russia.

Those leading Americans who, like Parker Gilbert, the 'King of the Dawes Plan', worked on a definitive settlement for German reparations and the repayment of debts by the Allies in the second half of the 1920s in the interest of a functioning world economy, identified the main problem as 'how to bring Russia back into the global economy of the community of Europe and the world'. The alternatives were either the speedy reconstruction of Russia or the cancellation of debts. Plans to found a Bank of International Co-operation also aimed at an international solution to the Russian question: reparations and the payment of debts were to be linked to the development of the Russian market with the offer of credits to Russia. One reason for the failure of all these plans was that Soviet Russia favoured bilateral or trilateral co-operation and wanted to prevent any establishment of a united Western front. As far as bilateral co-operation was concerned, the economic aspects of the policy of coexistence already practised by Germany made the re-orientating of American policies towards Russia an attractive proposition worth aiming at both for export industries interested in business with Russia and for the new Democratic Administration.

However, new developments and considerations in world politics were more important. Japan's overtly imperialist policy and Germany's switch to an aggressive nationalism, which threatened international order at the beginning of the 1930s, seemed to recommend a reorientation of American attitudes towards the Soviet Union and at the same time fostered the hope that, under pressure of this dual threat, the Soviet Union would be ready to agree to a conciliatory settlement of questions bound up with recognition. In earlier attempts to establish contacts the Soviet government itself had continually introduced the Japanese factor into discussions, either by referring to the Japanese threat or by conjuring up the spectre of a Russian–Japanese understanding.

Following Japan's attack on Manchuria and Secretary of State Stimson's fiery response (the Stimson–Hoover Doctrine, 1931) this argument had become reality. The Soviet Union hoped that American recognition would restrain Japanese aggression and sought a safeguard in Europe by approaching France, the strongest continental power, who, in the face of nationalistic tendencies in Germany, was ready to reduce her political distance from the Soviet Union. Thus the Soviet Union was able to pursue a reorientation of her European foreign policy which, in 1931–2, led to a system of bilateral non-aggression pacts with Finland, Latvia, Estonia, Poland and France. The catchword 'collective security' opened up the way for the Soviet Union's membership of the League of Nations in 1934 and for the Soviet Pact of Mutual Assistance with France and Czechoslovakia in 1935. In spite of socio-economic and ideological differences, there was a rapprochement of world political interests on the part of the formerly revisionist Soviet Union and the main representatives of the Versailles Treaty. France (and her allies in Central and Eastern Europe), fearing a nationalist or National Socialist Germany, was prepared to integrate the Soviet Union into the existing international system without changes in the regime and, for the same reason, the Soviet Union was convinced that 'the security of the Soviet state had become dependent on the stability of the international system' (Alexander Fischer, 1977). The Soviet policy of co-operation with Western democracies within the framework of the existing international order also led to a corresponding alignment of the transnational activities of the Comintern. At the Seventh World Congress in 1935 the Communist parties in democratic countries pledged themselves to a popular-front policy which was to serve as an effective safeguard of international co-operation at national level — a strategy which produced a notable, albeit short-lived, success with the Popular Front government in France between 1936 and 1938 (see Braunthal, [3]1978).

In the United States it was the Democratic Administration of the New Deal that undertook a change of course in the direction of an integrative policy towards the Soviet Union. It responded to the altered international situation and accomplished what the Republican Administration had begun. The American policy of peaceful change was pushed to its limits with Japan's attack on Manchuria, the failure of the Geneva Conference on disarmament and Germany's unilateral rearmament. The Stimson–Hoover Doctrine, which pronounced the non-recognition of violent revisions as a basic principle of American politics, had already switched direction, thus 'binding the USA to anti-revisionist philosophy' (Moffat, Department of State). Global political trends of the otherwise highly divergent states in the West and the Soviet Union met in the common interest of containing military aggression — in the interest of 'the preservation of the world's peace machinery'. This was to indicate the pattern of the later anti-Fascist war coalition, although at the same time links continued to be maintained, on the one hand, for an understanding between Western democracies and National Socialist Germany and, on the other, for the pursuit of co-operation motivated by 'state politics' between Germany and Russia and re-invigorated in 1939 in the Hitler–Stalin Pact (Niclauss, 1966). In 1933 changes in international relations, occasioned by Germany and Japan, and the corresponding reaction of the Soviet Union (her policy of collective security) were decisive for America's eventual switch to a policy of including Russia in global politics without requiring a change in the Soviet Union's political and economic system: 'The idea was forming in both Roosevelt's and Hull's minds that Japan and Germany might be sobered if the breach between the United States and the Soviet Union were healed' (Feis, 1966, p. 311).

Once Japan had broken away from the 'community of ideals, interests and purposes' and Germany, after a temporary reintegration into the existing world order, had set off along the same path, it was felt that efforts should at least be made — despite her internal structure — to bring in Russia, as she was ready to co-operate. The policy of isolation was partly replaced by a policy of co-operation which did not exclude reciprocal attempts to interfere, but regulated matters in such a way that continuing opposing tendencies would not escalate to a critical level of tension (see the Roosevelt–Litvinov Agreement, Bishop, 1965).

# 4 *The Revolution of International Order*

## *Antagonistic Cooperation Between East and West During the Second World War*

The assumption of diplomatic relations between the United States and the Soviet Union in 1933, the Soviet Union's membership of the League of Nations in 1934 and the Soviet Union's pacts of mutual assistance with France and Czechoslovakia in 1935 were the most visible signs of the global political decision taken by the main parties in the East–West conflict to pursue a strategy of integrative conflict regulation within the framework of the existing state system. Conversely, this policy corresponded with the withdrawal of Japan and Germany from the League of Nations in 1933 (and eventually of Italy in 1937) and the grouping of these countries into the so-called Anti-Comintern Pact (1936–7), which, despite its anti-Communist tone, had a strong anti-British character. When the revolutionary threat to international order arose from what were to become the Axis Powers, Japan, Germany and Italy, i.e. with the development of a new pattern of international conflict, the strategy of integration based on intensifying the degree of organisation became structurally relevant to global politics in the relationship between the antagonists in the East–West conflict (though, as has yet to be shown, it was not first structurally determining).

The essence of the new conflict originating from the Axis Powers likewise concerned the structure and organisation of international relations. A new structural global conflict was superimposed upon, and eventually supplanted the East–West conflict. Japan strove for a 'Greater East Asian Co-prosperity Sphere' and Fascist Italy for a Mediterranean Empire. In both cases old, traditional imperialist concepts were revived in new guises. National Socialist imperialism also drew together, and reinforced, traditional German expansionist and hegemonic goals (Hillgruber, 1969). It was a 'modern imperialism' interspersed with 'pre-capitalist' elements (Joseph A. Schumpeter, 1953). However, not only was the 'systematic addition' of all previously more or less diffuse proposals for expansionist aims new:

the decisive element of its qualitative newness was the arrangement of such proposals in a racist programme which aimed at forcing the historical process into a 'biologically determined final order' (K. Hildebrand), into a *pax Germanica* (H. A. Jacobsen). Just as the state had been replaced as an international unit of organisation by class in Communist ideology, race was the central structuring principle of the global historical philosophy of National Socialism. This racist claim was the actual revolutionary impulse of National Socialist politics for state and society not only at home, but also internationally. The destruction and radical recreation of a domestic social order 'were the prerequisites of all military expansion, preparing the way for, and accompanying, its realisation, which was to lead . . . to the goal of racially determined conquest and domination on a global scale' (Hildebrand, 1974, p. 650). Rauschning formulated this racist revolution in the National Socialist structure of the international system by summarising Hitler's ideas as follows:

> Nations are the manifestations of our history. Thus I have to recast these nations into a higher order, if I want to strip off the waste of an absurd historical past. And for this my concept of race is useful. It dissolves the old and creates the possibility of new relations. France, with the nation concept, brought her revolution across her borders. National Socialism, with the concept of race, will conduct its revolution until it has brought about a new world order. Just as the idea of the nation was somewhat revolutionary compared with the historically dynastic, feudal countries in the way it introduced the biological idea of the people, so our revolution is a further step or rather the ultimate step towards conquering historism and recognising pure biological values. (quoted in Faul, 1954, p. 362)

However, the transnational content of the racist programme of National Socialism was only fictitious. Whilst the international class struggle of the Communists corresponded to actual social groups within states and societies whose co-operation across frontiers was organised by the Comintern, only specific Germans abroad and groups of ethnic Germans outside the 'Greater German Reich' offered possible links of transnational relations for the National Socialists. It was such links that the National Socialist *Aussenamt* (Foreign Department) tried to activate in support of the Third Reich's foreign policy (see Jacobsen, 1968; Freye, 1967). The racist programme was inextricably bound up with the greater German *Machtstaat*, the 'German Reich of the German Nation'. Conversely, the real opponents of the development of National Socialist domination were not social groups, but states.

Like the beginning of the East–West conflict, when the United States became the main antagonist of the Soviet Union very early on, the programme (and eventually the reality) of the National Socialist world revolution also culminated in confrontation with the United States. As Andreas Hillgruber (1965) and Klaus Hildebrand (1971) have shown, despite all pragmatic adaptations and variations, Hitler was orientated towards a 'plan of expansion by stages' developed first in the 'key documents' of the 1920s — *Mein Kampf* and Hitler's *Second Book* (1928):

> Regaining the position of a great power in Central Europe would create the conditions for the domination of a continental empire stretching from the Atlantic to the Urals, which would in turn facilitate the establishment of a 'world power' position rounded off with naval bases and overseas colonies, and then allow for the struggle against the United States from continent to continent, in order finally to rise from a leading power in the world to world domination. (Hildebrand, 1976, p. 183).

Whereas the first steps were to be taken within the framework, and with the methods, of power politics in the traditional state system, the consummation of Hitler's vision was to be the 'last battle' of National Socialism, i.e. the final struggle for world hegemony between Europe (dominated by one Germanic race 'with its African extensions') and North America. The world domination of National Socialism would transcend every frontier of the nation-states and would have its 'steely hard core' in an international élite of the German race. Thereafter the dynamics of power politics would come to an end and, although there would still be a conquered world, there would no longer be anything to conquer. The racial domination of the German people was to guarantee the continuation of this state: the new man, like a God, would guarantee the world domination of German blood and safeguard it against all changes. Thus world history would reach its projected, racially determined goal. The dynamic of the historical process would lead to a biologically fixed static state of 'Utopia' (Hildebrand, 1971, pp. 27 f.). Hitler's 'super-Machiavellianism' founded on racist biology (Faul, 1954), was the inner force of the National Socialist revolution of the international system.

The principle of racist organisation was as incompatible with the traditional principle of state organisation as the Communist principle of class organisation. Like the principle of the class struggle, it never determined actual foreign policy in its purest form or without contradiction (the contradiction in German demands for domination and the alliance with Asian Japan was obvious). However, it was precisely this combination of racist and traditional elements in the power politics of National Socialism that constituted its disruptive force in the international system, although at the beginning the competing states were unaware of this.

As long as the first step, i.e. retrieving for Germany a position as Great Power, determined Hitler's foreign policy; and as long as the concept of racist ideology (if one disregards foreign policy propaganda) showed its real consequences 'only' in domestic politics, it was still possible, in the view of the competing Great Powers, to regard an orderly revision of the international order as a sensible policy — considering different factors in isolation and employing the conventional standards of power politics. In particular, such an evaluation provided the basis for British policy, which strove for a conflict resolution which would integrate National Socialist Germany. This policy developed in contrast to the French policy of isolation, which aimed at establishing a bloc against National Socialist Germany, seen by Paris as a power upsetting the status quo. France tried to win Britain over to her policy of alliance with the Soviet Union, although it must be added that the Franco-Russian Pact — founded on the idea of mutual assistance by military convention — was also disputed within France. Instead of a policy of isolating Germany, Britain strove for a 'general agreement' with Germany, employing methods of peaceful change of the status quo in order to reintegrate her into the European power system and to avoid an escalation into war. This policy of peaceful change and appeasement, which acquired negative connotations only because of its failure, was pursued with great flexibility and persistence (though without adequate resources of power), through bilateral agreements (which achieved their most spectacular result in the Anglo-German Naval Agreement of 1935) and through multilateral attempts at conference diplomacy (culminating in the Munich Agreement of 1938). It was pursued partly by reference to the potential for revision contained in Article 19 of the Charter of the League of Nations, at the same time drawing in the Soviet Union. (The British even considered the use of Article 19 for a general agreement with Germany.) It was also pursued outside the League of Nations and excluding the Soviet Union. However, in all instances, this policy linked resistance to the use of force with efforts for conciliation. It was to help Britain maintain her traditional room for manoeuvre, her policy of non-commitment, and to avoid any war that would threaten the Empire. This dual policy — guided by the concept of the balance of power — aimed at the containment of aggressive policies and at promoting a readiness to compromise on the basis of new agreements. It was a policy adopted towards both Germany and Japan: the attempt of an old world power, Great Britain, 'to ensure that the traditional state system remained efficient and powerful in view of both the revolutionary ideology of Bolshevik Russia and the superior potential of bourgeois-capitalist America' (Niedhart, 1972, p. 277).

However, Britain was a declining world power. In the light of her true potential strength it would have been sensible for the United States to take over a leading role in the construction of a unified policy towards the Axis Powers. But the concept of the preservation of freedom of action and of the avoidance of fixed political or alliance-type obligations was even more deeply rooted in the United States than in Britain. Since America's territorial security was not at first directly threatened by the Axis Powers, German expansionism was primarily experienced as an economic and ideological threat: 'the penetration of the informal American Empire in Latin America' (Schröder, 1970), the setting up by the Third Reich of a *Grossraum* economy in south-eastern Europe and the ideological attack of the National Socialist regime in North and South America necessitated, from the American point of view, not a military, but an economic policy of containment linked to efforts to find a political *modus vivendi* with National Socialist Germany. Similarly Japan's *Grossraum* policy in Asia clashed with American globalism, particularly with the concept of the 'indivisible world market' (Junker, 1975).

The World Depression had intensified the economic and political fragmentation of the international system. American Secretary of State Hull therefore concentrated on re-establishing a self-regulating economic and trade system. Proceeding from a maxim typical of a competitive society, i.e. 'that the economic approach should be the spear-point of the approach to peace' (Hull, *Memoirs*, I. 525), multilateral trade relations, based on unconditional, mutual, most-favoured-nation treatment and non-discrimination, were explicitly seen as the best means to restrain the unilateral nationalistic expansion of the Third Reich. Accordingly the US President suggested (in 1933) that the maximum possible institutionalisation of international co-operation was the transformation of the League of Nations into an 'Economic Council', and later (1937–8) he proposed a conference of neutral states, including America, aimed at establishing a fundamental normative consensus as to how to oppose aggressive nations. In his 'Quarantine Speech' of 5 October 1937 Roosevelt openly expressed the idea of isolation and regression with regard to the Axis powers and from 1936 onwards internal American debates increasingly considered the USSR as a possible partner in the event of a crisis or war (Knipping, 1974). However, only in the western hemisphere, where the economic and ideological offensive of the Third Reich hurt American interests most, did German aggression gradually lead the Roosevelt Administration from 1935–6 onwards to change the Monroe Doctrine into a defensive alliance (Offner, 1969, pp. 167 ff.). The US President had no substantial European peace programme, nor would he have been able to pursue one, considering the political opposition at home. The conclusion of the Anglo-American Trade Agreement of November 1938 prepared the way for future co-operation with Britain, but it did not alter Britain's attempt to find a settlement with National Socialist Germany which would exclude the United States — a settlement based on the idea of a European economic bloc directed against the United States. Britain's rejection of any effective co-operation with the United States and instead her attempt to reintegrate Germany into a revised international order continued until 1939:

> One essential factor in British efforts to find an economic basis for the congruent interests of the 'Big Four', which seemed to have become apparent in Munich, was doubtless that, despite the Anglo-American Economic Treaty of November 1938, Britain strove to maintain a certain distance from Washington and not be drawn away from the European Continent in America's wake. (Wendt, 1971, p. 529)

The British strategy of restoring the concept of a Europe independent of the United States failed because Britain had long since lost her former position of power. Despite all domestic difficulties, the economic potential of the United States was considerably greater. However, the Roosevelt Administration could not, and would not, transform its economic power into political action. Only after Britain's policy of integration had finally failed because of Hitler's wars did the conditions exist in Great Britain and the United States for a reorientation, and for co-operation between the Western democracies.

The East–West conflict played a varied role in attempts to find an integrative solution to the conflict with the Axis Powers and later in the decision to opt for a military solution. It was only after

Hitler's attack on the Soviet Union that the East–West conflict was, temporarily, replaced by antagonistic co-operation between the western democracies and socialist Russia. Historical research has given a thorough analysis of this contradictory process (see especially Niedhart). The normalisation of diplomatic relations and the Soviet policy of collective security could not conceal the fact that deep differences continued to exist between the systems of the Bolshevik Soviet Union and those of the bourgeois-democratic countries. The intensification of domestic political terror (e.g. the Moscow show trials) and non-compliance with obligations under the Roosevelt–Litvinov Agreement (repayment of debts, cessation of Comintern interference, etc.) intensified suspicions of the actual aims of the Soviet Union. The role of the Soviet Union and of the Comintern in the Spanish Civil War also created considerable tension, predominantly in Anglo-Russian relations.

Closer co-operation was impeded by the lack of ideological preconditions and the incentives of power politics. From a military standpoint the strength of the Soviet Union was thought to be limited. After 1937, when more than half the Soviet military leadership had fallen victim to Stalin's purges, doubts increased as to the strength of the Red Army. But for the neighbouring Western countries, Poland and Rumania, even a weakened Red Army posed a real danger. They were not, therefore, prepared to guarantee the Soviet Union the right of passage. Thus the basic anti-Communist views of the leadership (particularly in Great Britain), the presumed inefficiency of the Soviet Union's military potential and the veto of Central and East European countries all had the same effect, i.e. the prevention of the conclusion of a military alliance with the Soviet Union, advocated by France for some time, but which became possible only in 1939. Until then Britain, increasingly taking France along with her, pursued a policy of integration towards Germany, whilst the Soviet Union adopted a policy of isolating Germany. Even after Germany's invasion of what was left of Czechoslovakia and the ensuing British guarantee to Poland, Rumania and Greece, the British Government still clung to its concept of integration. Negotiations with the Soviet Union to establish a 'peace front' which now took place were envisaged as a means of bringing political pressure on Germany to force her into a comprehensive settlement. War, seen as a threat to the very heart of the British Empire, was to be avoided at all costs. British policy towards Russia was also defined by this main aim. It was nothing but a 'function of the success and failure of

British efforts for a settlement' (Niedhart, 1971, p. 55).

> The anti-Bolshevik disposition, which formed the Government's picture of Russia, never became a central point of reference or a structural component of British foreign policy. Peace in Europe was never to be achieved by building Germany up as a bulwark, but rather by integrating her into a European settlement. (Niedhart, 1972, p. 431)

Thus, in the end, it was not the contradictions of the East–West conflict, but the diverse strategies of solving the conflict with revisionist Germany that prevented co-operation between Great Britain and the Soviet Union. And when Britain eventually shifted towards a policy of alliance with the Soviet Union, it was the Soviet Union that prevented the forming of a united front to oppose National Socialist Germany and facilitated Hitler's unleashing of the Second World War with the help of the Hitler–Stalin Pact of 23 August 1939, including the additional secret protocol on the division of Poland. Such an understanding had always been a possibility from the Soviet viewpoint. It was based on a concept of 'state politics' which aimed at excluding ideological conflict from considerations of power politics (B. Moore, 1951, pp. 362 ff.; Niclauss, 1966 p. 199). In spite of all these deep-seated differences, both British and Soviet efforts to reach a settlement with National Socialist Germany and the Axis Powers were rooted in the fundamental concern of both states to maintain, or even improve, their own security. The Hitler –Stalin Pact was the Soviet version of Appeasement.

Stalin stuck unwaveringly to this policy during the European War (1939–41); he supported Hitler's *Blitzkrieg* on the one hand by providing important economic goods and on the other through the Comintern, by attempting to weaken the Western nations' resistance to German aggression; and in agreement with the Third Reich he pursued his own expansionist policy in Poland, the Baltic States and Rumania through to the attack on Finland on 30 November 1939. Up to Germany's attack on the Soviet Union, Stalin hoped that National Socialist Germany and the democratic 'capitalist' states would tear each other apart.

Despite all protests against Stalin's expansionist policy and against Soviet support for German war strategies, the policy of the Western democracies was a determination to avoid driving the USSR into a firm military alliance with the Third Reich. Only after Russia's attack on Finland did the United States extend her 'moral embargo', previously imposed against Germany and Japan, to the

USSR. The American arms industry was immediately urged to renounce voluntarily all exports to the Soviet Union and to ban Soviet aeronauts from visits to American companies; American oil technicians were recalled from Russia; an embargo was proclaimed on the charter of ships, and so on. However, this policy was revised as early as the summer of 1940 and the 'moral embargo' was eventually lifted officially on 21 April 1941, though it could be proved that some American exports to the USSR were re-exported to Germany and that some of those exports were used to replace Soviet goods supplied to Germany. The possibility of a future alliance was to be kept alive by a policy of compromise and consideration towards Russia. The alliance of the three powers, Germany, Japan and Italy (27 September 1940), and secret information received concerning Hitler's instructions for the preparation of an attack on the Soviet Union (18 December 1940) strengthened the belief of the US Administration that the USSR would soon become a powerful opponent of the expansionist policies of Germany and Japan. When, instead of this, Stalin intensified his appeasement towards the Third Reich and Japan in the spring of 1941 (by the Soviet–Japanese Neutrality Treaty of 13 April 1941) American–Soviet relations deteriorated once more — as exemplified, for instance, in the denial of licences for exports to Russia. However, in principle the aim of the Roosevelt Administration was still not to spoil the chances of co-operation with the Soviet Union at a later stage. The Lend-Lease Bill of 11 March 1941 was deliberately framed so as to facilitate the inclusion of the Soviet Union in the event of a change in coalitions. Like the British approach, American policy was also determined by 'strategic defence policy motives' rather than by the ideological contradictions in the opposing systems of the East–West conflict. Official American policies towards Russia had, since 1932–3 (even during the Hitler–Stalin Pact), depended essentially on American policies towards Germany and Japan (Knipping, 1974, p. 235). The greater the threat to American security, the more consistently American policy was determined by the imperative of creating a force to maintain the balance of power — despite the anti-Communist response with which the American public greeted Stalin's policy of appeasement and expansion.

Once the Soviet version of appeasement policy had also failed, following the attack of the Third Reich upon on the Soviet Union (22 June 1941), the mood of anti-Communism was by no means immediately reversed. For example, Senator Harry Truman gave the following advice: 'If we see that Germany is winning we ought to help Russia and if Russia is winning we ought to help Germany and that way let them kill as many as possible, although I don't want to see Hitler victorious under any circumstances. Neither of them think anything of their pledged word' (New York Times, 24 June 1941 p. 7).

However, the US Administration acted on the clear maxim of increasing security and creating retaliatory forces. The USSR immediately received massive support in the shape of deliveries of military goods, and was included in the Lend-Lease programme in November 1941, as had been planned from the very beginning (Dawson, 1959). Germany's aggressive striving for world domination was irreconciliable with American interests and with any kind of peaceful order which half-deserved the name. The two opposing powers, the United States and the USSR, were gradually forced into an 'antagonistic coalition' by the war policy of Germany and Japan. With the attack on Pearl Harbor (7 December 1941) and the German and Italian declaration of war on the United States (11 December 1941) the decisive struggle began on a global scale.

This development corresponded with the principles of Hitler's programme of expansion, but not with his timetable. The decisive struggle between a National Socialist Europe and the United States had originally been only a long-term aim, the realisation of which was reserved for a future generation. However, as the American defence potential (which was seen in very realistic terms) would benefit Britain's resistance through the Lend-Lease Programme of 11 March 1941, Hitler feared for his 'short-term goals' even without American participation in the war. At the end of 1940 Hitler expressed the view 'that we must solve all continental European problems by 1941, since from 1942 [the] USA will be in a position to intervene' (quoted in Hillgruber, 1966, p. 15). He was, therefore at pains — against the wishes of the German Admiralty — to give the United States no occasion for premature intervention. The German-Japanese Pact also served primarily to intimidate the United States. Only when, despite this alliance, Hitler feared an American-Japanese understanding and when the campaign in the East came to a standstill, did he see himself forced to accept a Japanese attack on the American position in the Pacific in preference to the possibility that Japan would disassociate herself from Germany in the increasingly probable event of American participation in the war on Britain's side. Thus his Japanese policy eventually accelerated

America's intervention in the Atlantic which it had originally aimed at preventing, or at least postponing. Hitler's strategy of a decisive struggle with the United States only after the defeat of continental Europe was revised decisively.

The anti-Fascist war coalition (the antagonistic co-operation between the main protagonists of the East–West conflict) was established in 1941 after the failure of the tactics of power politics on the part of both the Western democracies and the Soviet Union, and when National Socialist Germany sought a military solution in pursuit of a racist world hegemony. In other words, neither the planned antagonistic co-operation between the Western democracies and National Socialist Germany nor the antagonistic co-operation actually practised between National Socialist Germany and the Soviet Union could create an enduring international order since Germany strove, not for a revision of the international order, but for a radical overthrow, for an elimination, of an order based on the structural principle of autonomous states. The revolutionary-military strategy of the Axis Powers generated an antagonistic co-operation between the Western democracies and Communist Russia which aimed at creating a counterweight to prevent the racist world hegemony of the Third Reich and to defeat the aggressors. The solution to Hitler's alternative of world power or ruin was predetermined in 1941–2. What was not known was whether an integrated world order could be created on the basis of antagonistic co-operation after a victory over the Axis Powers, an order in which the continuing contradictions between Bolshevik Russia and the democratic countries, which had become so obvious in power politics in the years between 1939 and 1941, would remain below the level of critical tension and within the framework of peaceful competition.

# 5 *The Concept of an Integrated World Order of Peace at the End of the Second World War*

The Second World War destroyed the old international order which had been partly institutionalised in the League of Nations. The failure of the League of Nations and the common struggle of the United Nations against the aggressor states provided the background of experience for the development of ideas on a new order in the international system even during the War (see Claude,[3] 1964). The dominant feeling was that a new world order of peace had to be better than that provided by the League of Nations and that it had to be based on the continuation in peacetime of the war coalition. This latter aspect implied at the same time that the front line of conflict with the Axis Powers rather than the divisions of the old East–West conflict primarily determined plans for a post-war order. The New Order was to guarantee that the United Nations could jointly suppress aggressor states (which meant the Axis Powers). Therefore, in the formulation of the Atlantic Charter (14 August 1941), President Roosevelt insisted that initially any institutionalisation of the New Order should be dispensed with, that is to say no new League of Nations should be created, 'at least not before some time has elapsed during which an international police force set up by the USA and Britain has had time to operate' (S. Welles, 'Where are we heading?', pp. 14 f., quoted in Hagemann, 1964, p. 107). Accordingly, paragraph 8 of the Atlantic Charter stated that 'pending the establishment of a wider and permanent system of general security' it was essential to disarm the aggressor nations. The political conditions for a peaceful order were thus to be created in advance by the two 'world policemen', the United States and Great Britain.

Neither this timetable nor the exclusive policing role of the Anglo-Saxon powers could be maintained. By signing the Atlantic Charter on 24 September 1941 the Soviet Union entered the process of joint peace planning — albeit with reservations (see M. F. Herz, 1967). The US Secretary of State, Cordell Hull, in particular had already vigorously championed the idea of an 'effective international organisation' expressed by Churchill in his proposal for an Atlantic Charter. Hull subsequently took a specific liberal variant of this as the centre-piece of international post-war planning. The agreement reached at the Moscow Conference of Foreign Ministers (1943) to 'recognize the necessity of establishing at the earliest practicable date a general international organisation . . . for the maintenance of international peace and security' (FR 4943, I. 756), opened up the way to negotiations at Dumbarton Oaks (for the establishment of the United Nations Organization) and at Bretton Woods (for the International Monetary Fund and the International Bank for Reconstruction and Development). Official steps to found a world trade organisation were first taken in December 1945, with the USSR no longer participating in these negotiations. Once the Charter of the International Trade Organisation had failed because of domestic resistance in the United States, the General Agreement on Tariffs and Trade, GATT, took its place — its aim the liberalisation of world trade (see, e.g., Wilcox, 1949; Heiduk, 1973). Multilateral international co-operation was (1) to be institutionalised at a universal, not a regional, level; it was (2) to cover all areas of politics and economics; and (3) to be flexible through the effective consideration of the mechanisms of peaceful change.

According to Hull, by orientating the post-war development towards this concept of a global integrative order, not only the United States, but every nation could look forward to a happier future. The institutionalisation of multilateral co-operation between the Great Powers would render the establishment of specific zones of interest unnecessary. The removal of trade barriers and discriminating trade practices would stimulate the expansion of trade and raise the standard of living in all countries. Along with economic friction, which had in the past led to moves towards autarky and bilateral trade agreements, the true causes for the global use of force and war would disappear. Finally, international multilateralism would favour, or even secure, the universal establishment of peaceful political democracies like that of the United States (Kuklick, 1970, p. 276). Whilst economic co-operation was of central importance to this concept, it was not developed in a 'political vacuum' and accusations that it was 'economistic' (Richard Gardner, $^{2}$1969) cannot be sustained since the political organisation of the United Nations was to provide the solid institutional structure of international co-operation for all countries on the basis of equality.

The discrepancy in this 'idealistic' concept between the institutional establishment of the formal equality of all nations and their effective inequality in terms of power was conspicuous and could have had — broadly speaking — two divergent effects.

On the one hand, American political, military and economic superiority could have resulted in the planned global liberal system of security and trade being *de facto* a 'co-operative supremacy' (R. F. Smith, 1968) founded by the United States and subordinating the formally equal, but in reality weaker, states. Smaller and medium-sized nations could be expected to accept this subordination, but not the main allies, Great Britain and the USSR.

On the other hand, the institutional guarantee of equal treatment for all nations could have given the majority of small and medium-sized states the opportunity of restraining the American freedom of action and use of actual might on the part of the Great Powers (including the United States) by the formation of coalitions and by majority decisions. Such a possibility was unacceptable to *all* the Great Powers.

Political 'realists' such as President Roosevelt, Secretary of War Stimson, Prime Minister Churchill, Secretary General Stalin and Foreign Minister Molotov ensured a change in these idealistic principles by:

(1) modifying the principle of universalism through its combination with the regional principle, and

(2) institutionalising the political supremacy of the four or five Great Powers and at the same time limiting the possibility of peaceful change.

(1) The principle of regionalism was most forcefully represented by Churchill. In his opinion (expressed in May 1943), although close co-operation between the United States, Great Britain and the USSR should be institutionalised by means of a supreme world council, this should be firmly grounded in European, American and Far Eastern regional organisations. Like a three-legged stool, the world council would rest on the three regional councils and its stability and effectiveness would depend on them. 'It was only the countries whose interests were directly affected by a dispute who could be expected to apply themselves with sufficient vigour to secure a settlement' (Churchill, 1951, vol. 4, pp. 718 f.). This concept was based on the idea that the Commonwealth and the

United States would participate in all three regional councils and that a close Anglo-American alliance would to a certain extent provide the political link between these groupings. This would of course secure Britain's global interests and at the same time take the necessary precautions to restrain Soviet politics without abandoning co-operative understanding. Significantly, because of his realistic political approach, Stalin did not at first oppose the regional principle. Moreover, in Tehran Stalin reacted to Roosevelt's plans for a world organisation by suggesting as a possible alternative the creation of a European or a Far Eastern Committee and a European or a worldwide organisation (Conversation with Roosevelt on 29 November 1943; FR. *The Conferences at Cairo and Tehran*, 1943, p. 531). Although Stalin soon began to favour a universal organisation rather than regional organisations, not least because he strongly rejected Churchill's plans for a federalised Europe, at a later stage he was again inclined towards a model combining the two principles. Within the framework of the concept of a global order both Stalin and Churchill thought in terms of spheres of interest. Indeed a year later — in October 1944 — they were in a position to agree secretly on the respective demarcation of Central Europe (Churchill, 1954, Vol. 6, p. 198).

At the same time the Soviet leadership made its concept of a combined organisation publicly known (N. Malinin, 'On the question of creating an internationl security organisation', in: *The War and the Working Class*, 1 Oct. 1944). Malinin argued for a decentralised United Nations structure in order to relieve the general organisation of local problems. Four sections were to be established for Europe, America, Africa and the Asian-Pacific Area under the umbrella of the General Assembly. Countries that had important interests in several continents would be represented in several sections. The regulation of local conflicts would be left to the region concerned — provided that the Security Council could, if it wished, decide to deal with the problem itself. Soviet interests were taken into account not only because, according to this organisational proposal, they would be represented in at least two sections. In addition, individual countries (and therefore the Soviet Union) were to be allowed to agree on so-called security zones which need not be either identical with the continental sections or directly linked with them. This was the actual power-political core of the Soviet Union's concept of organisation. Although Malinin publicly repudiated the policy of bloc-building and spheres of influence, he in fact propagated nothing less than the creation of a Soviet sphere of influence by using the unfettered term 'security zone.'

However, thinking in terms of spheres of interest met with strong resistance from the American leadership. President Roosevelt undoubtedly took account of the power structures that might emerge in Central and Eastern Europe under the influence of the Red Army (Yergin, 1977, p. 58). But with regard to the structure of security policies in post-war relations, he was decidedly against regionalism, because he envisaged a global role for his country and, in view of the political climate at home, had to assume that the American public would only accept global military commitments on the part of the United States if they were mediated by a general international order. The State Department, and Hull in particular, opposed regionalism even more strongly, for reasons of both power politics and economics. In Hull's opinion, regional organisations tended towards the construction of closed areas of trade and systems of preference. They accordingly threatened the central concept of liberal multilateralism and the 'open door' policy which had already been agreed in the Atlantic Charter and which, above all, was to break up the British system of preferences. Regionalism was seen to prejudice not only the multilateral regulation of international economic and trade relations, but also the organisation of political relations. In Hull's opinion, the construction of economic blocs led, without fail, to antagonistic groupings and eventually to military conflicts which an international organisation could no longer control.

Politicians, such as Secretary of War Stimson and his deputy McCloy, who favoured *Realpolitik* also feared that the establishment of large regional organisations involved the danger of war between whole regions and that such developments would take 'the meat out of the world organisation' (quoted in Kolko, 1968, p. 472).

The American leadership, however, wished to retain its own regional organisation in the Western hemisphere (which at the same time was being vigorously expanded); and this was the flaw in the American argument. On the one hand, the United States wanted to ensure that she could operate in her own sphere of influence without the impediment of a possible Soviet veto. Accordingly only a loose tie between the regional organisations and the Security Council was desirable. On the other hand, she wanted to keep open the option of 'being able to intervene promptly in Europe'. The pursuit of this goal inclined the United States against a European regional organisation and — if that was unavoidable — in favour of its strict subjection to the Security Council in order to prevent the Soviet Union from adopting a privileged position in Europe similar to that occupied by America in the Western hemisphere. Thus the United States adopted a position aptly described by Under Secretary of War McCloy, when he said: 'We ought to have our cake and to eat it too.'

Even before the problem was solved through the Charter, it became increasingly obvious that the USSR had *de facto* established a sphere of influence in Eastern Europe and that Britain was beginning to organise co-operation with Western European countries, in order to build up a Western zone to counter the Soviet sphere in close collaboration with the Commonwealth. In the event of failure in co-operation between the Great Powers, traditional British policy, which relied on creating a balance of power, would subsequently have something to fall back on and an alternative security policy. However, neither Great Britain nor the Western European countries were sufficiently powerful to create an effective counterweight to the Soviet Union, a fact clearly recognised by the Americans:

> Since there is no longer power to balance in Europe, Britain would logically turn to the United States as the greatest potential source of support in developing an adequate counterpoise to Russia. Without the assured support of the United States, any combination of powers which Britain might be able to assemble would still leave Russia preponderantly strong. (FR, *Conference of Berlin*, I. 259).

In this situation the US Administration sought to do all in its power to delay the consolidation of Eastern and Western spheres of influence in Europe and to subordinate regional organisations to the Security Council. This appeared to be the only way to avoid the threat to peace which such arrangements would produce.

This subordination was prescribed — though not without notable contradictions — by the United Nations' Charter: '. . . no enforcement action shall be taken under regional arrangements or by regional agencies without the authorization of the Security Council' (Article 53). However, enforcement actions against former enemy states were exempt, particularly in the event that such actions were also undertaken on the basis of regional arrangements. Thus regional agreements in Europe (which already existed in part) were legitimised. The exemption clause was not, however, extended to American regional agreements. The insertion of Article 51 into the

Charter was a precaution against the Security Council being brought to a standstill by the veto of a Great Power. In that event the regional organisation concerned, and the attacked states, could take military action by invoking the right of collective self defence. In this way regionalism appeared to have been made partly compatible with universalism. At the time of the signing of the United Nations Charter and during preparations for the Potsdam Conference, official American policy still gave priority to maintaining co-operation between the Great Powers:

> The need of the moment is to promote understanding between Great Britain and Russia on all matters in dispute. We should do all we can in this connection and direct our best efforts towards smoothing out the points of friction between the two, thereby fostering the tripartite collaboration so necessary to lasting peace. However, American policy must be attuned to events in Europe *as a whole* and to the consequences of general European conditions on the stability of Great Britain. Specifically, it is not in our interest to deny to the United Kingdom protection against possible dangers from the Soviet Union, especially since the Soviets have established domination of Eastern Europe and since the International Security Organization would not be effective in case of a clash between the Soviet Union and Great Britain. Until it is determined which course events in Europe will take — i.e. whether Russia will colloborate or not — we should not take a positive stand one way or the other on this proposal to draw the nations of Western Europe into closer association. (Briefing Book Paper, British Plan for a Western European Bloc, Washington, 28 June 1945, in FR, *Conference of Berlin*, I. 264).

If the integrative solution of conflict embodied in the universalistic concept of the United Nations were to fail, both Europe and Latin America had recourse to the right of collective defence which was constituted outside the chapter on regional arrangements in the United Nations Charter (see below).

(2) The second change in the 'idealistic' concept was more decisive and gave universalism its oligarchic character by allocating jurisdiction on peace issues to the Security Council and by granting the right of veto to its permanent members. For the Big Four (or Big Five), the institutionalisation of co-operation was adapted to the actual relations between the powers — without, however, reflecting them exactly (see below). Roosevelt's idea of establishing a police committee of the four Great Powers as a true organ of power was integrated into the Security Council by the regulation of the right of veto. Co-operation according equal rights to the Great Powers (including the Soviet Union) was the essence of the projected order

of peace (see Range, 1959, pp. 162–89). Whereas the principle of voluntary co-operation was envisaged for relations between the Great Powers, international order could — when other states were involved — if necessary be compulsorily enforced, provided that the Great Powers reached a voluntary agreement on the issue. And this meant (as Roosevelt clearly saw, and as his successor Truman confirmed in June 1945) that a co-operative understanding was of fundamental importance (see Hagemann, 1964, p. 110) and 'that without continued unity of the Big Three there would be no reasonable prospect of peace.'

The concept of a new international order envisaged close relations between the Great Powers which had not previously existed, despite the contradictions in their respective systems. However, because of the rule of unanimity, the degree of integrative relations between the Great Powers was made dependent on the degree to which their actual interests concurred and could be accommodated.

Once more it was the *Realpolitik* politicians, Stimson and Churchill, who drew particular attention to the need to deal immediately with this accommodation of interests, whilst in contrast Roosevelt tended to pursue a policy of postponement. His starting-point was that American supremacy would be even greater once the War ended. In the 'directorate of the four world policemen', i.e. in the 'police committee', the United States would not limit herself to a regional role, but rather follow a global policy of creating bases through which she could bring her power to bear. Roosevelt relied on the fact that he would be able to integrate the Soviets into an assembly which would limit their ambitions and where the United States would be able to gather her supporters (see de Gaulle, 1956, p. 238, and Range, 1959, pp. 183 ff.). Close relations with Great Britain, as the United States' junior partner in Europe, were envisaged as a back-up measure. In general, however, the main precept was that American independence and freedom in decision-making had to be secured. This maxim also determined Roosevelt's reluctance for nuclear co-operation with Britain and his firm resolve not to share the nuclear secret with Russia or France. Not until September 1944 was he prepared to conclude a formal agreement with Britain on 'full co-operation . . . on atomic energy for military and commercial use' which could only be terminated by common agreement. He maintained his refusal to co-operate with the Soviet Union in nuclear matters to the very end (Bernstein, 1976).

Whilst the oligarchisation of international organisation certainly narrowed the gap between the formal structure and the real distribution of power, it did not close it completely. The formally equal four or five Great Powers possessed very different power potentials. The functioning of the international organisation relied on their voluntary co-operation, but this had to be realised under unequal conditions of power.

Such an international organisation was desirable from the Soviet viewpoint only in so far as it offered the Soviet Union effective protection from aggressors, but did not give the co-guarantors of her security an opportunity to influence her zone of power either through arbitration or through mediation. She did not want to exclude the possibility of taking unilateral military action in Eastern Europe (see the Soviet correction to the wording of point 6 of the Four Powers' Declaration of 30 October 1943). At the same time, however, she gave assurances that she did not want to divide Europe into spheres of influence (Hull, Memoirs, p. 1298). This approach expressed the desire — as Hagemann (1964, pp. 157 f.) has recognised — 'to limit the task of the organisation to be established to securing peace in the narrowest technical sense and to entrust it neither with jurisdiction over peaceful change nor with economic and social tasks.' Moreover, the mechanisms of peaceful change would have facilitated the formation of new international groupings, particularly in the light of future peace treaties with enemy states, thereby threatening the continuation of the wartime coalition. Thus co-operation between the Great Powers and the exclusion of domestic affairs from United Nations jurisdiction also constituted the basis of international order in the eyes of the Soviet Union. As Stalin stated at Yalta on 6 February 1945:

> The most important condition for the maintenance of a long lasting peace is the unity of the three Great Powers. If this unity is maintained there is nothing to fear from the German threat. Therefore one must think about how one can best guarantee a united front of the three Great Powers, to which one must add both France and China. This makes the question of the future charter of the international security organization so significant. One has to create as many checks on any future divergences amongst the three leading powers. One must draft the charter in such a way as to make the development of conflicts between them extremely difficult. That is the chief task. (transl. from A. Fischer's German edn., 1968, p. 129).

Stalin's demand for guarantees that in the event of conflict the new international order would not be mobilised or used against the

Soviet Union was answered by reference to the Great Powers' right of veto. Whilst the obligation to unanimity among the Great Powers could certainly not prevent conflicts from arising, it did elevate the integrative regulation of conflict to an essential element in the new international system.

Despite other differences of opinion, all the Great Powers therefore agreed that 'the rule of unanimous decisions was a compulsory and resolute condition for the new international order' (as expressed by the Prime Minister of New Zealand at the San Francisco Conference, 1945, quoted in Hagemann, 1964, p. 169). In the event of the failure of an integrative regulation of conflict (which at the time of the signing of the UN Charter had already become a probability) Article 51 was added at the last moment. This allowed regressive regulation of conflict as an alternative to the UN system: 'the inherent right of individual or collective self- defence' in the event of an armed attack formed the basis of a reserve security system. Should the integrative resolution of conflict, to be achieved through understanding and co-operation between the Great Powers, fail because of diverging interests and dissent and a military solution be imminent, a distancing of opponents and a regrouping of powers would be the only escape route and alternative. Such a development would also resolve the 'ambiguous compromise' (Inis Claude, [3]1964) between universalism and regionalism contained in the UN Charter in favour of policies based on spheres of influence. Seen in general terms, an alternative mechanism for the solution of conflict was contained in a kind of reserve charter which had been prepared in case the co-operation between the Great Powers broke down. Preference was given, however, to an order based on integration, to be laid down in the UN Charter as the principle of co-operative understanding between the Great Powers.

Furthermore, the institutionalisation of multilateral economic co-operation (which Hull had consistently pursued) was to supplement co-operation in the area of security. This also meant strengthening economic relations, particularly between the United States and the USSR. The basis for such co-operation had already been created during the Second World War when the United States had begun to provide aid. Immediately after Germany's attack on the Soviet Union the USSR was included in the Roosevelt Administration's Lend-Lease Programme. She received arms and industrial goods (including entire production plants) totalling more than 9 billion dollars from the United States. After the war these economic links were to be intensified. This aspect was of considerable importance from the time of the Tehran Conference until the Russian request on 3 January 1945 for a large post-war credit in excess of $6 billion. 'Russia will provide an important market for the United States after the war '(Stalin) and the Americans would 'need a great amount of raw materials', thus providing a basis of common interest which guaranteed, as Roosevelt put it, that in future 'close trade relations will predominate' between both nations (Conversations on 29 Nov. 1943, quoted in Fischer, 1968, p. 18).

The policy of integration which was to overcome conflict between East and West by strengthening relations and promoting co-operative understanding was thus a comprehensive concept, although security matters were unquestionably the main focus.

The control which the three or four powers were to exert over a defeated Germany was the concrete and, at the same time, the most ambitious, attempt to realise the idea of joint security and co-operative understanding. Furthermore, the declaration on liberated Europe of 11 February 1945 expressed the same concept of co-operation. All the participants were highly conscious of the fact that it was enormously difficult to implement, especially since there had already been many problems (diffirences of opinion and mutual suspicion) during the efforts to pursue the pre-eminent goal of defeating the Axis Powers.

# 6 *The Failure of the Concept of Integration*

## *The Beginning of the Regressive Regulation of Conflict*

The concept of a co-operative peaceful order was planned largely along the lines of power politics. Ideological and political differences between the systems apparently played no more than a subordinate role. The projected system of the United Nations was to provide the organisational framework for co-operative competition or competitive co-operation between the Great Powers. It seemed feasible that conflict between the systems could be regulated by integrative methods, just as during the wartime coalition. The agreement between the democratic countries and the socialist Soviet Union to maintain a 'conservative' order in the international state system and to protect the national state interests of the Great Powers (see Senator Vandenberg, quoted in Hagemann, 1964, p. 130) appeared to prove that the structural conflict between the principles of class and world revolution and of the nation-state had been overcome in favour of the latter. The Soviet Union, who had more or less liquidated her world-revolutionary support organisation, the Comintern, in 1943, was not only integrated into the traditional global political structure, but had also received international recognition as a Great Power. The central problem of the peaceful ordering of One World was seen in competition not between socialism and capitalism, but rather between the Great Powers and their political interests. These were to be mediated through the institutionalisation of co-operation and the strengthening of relations between the systems in a way that would ensure that no critical tensions would develop to affect the system of international relations as a whole.

A sharp difference between American and Soviet (and to some extent British) ideas on the structure was already discernible in the planning phase. It was a difference between the contradictory tendencies of multilateral universalism and the policy of spheres of interest which inevitably arose from the imbalance of power between the United States and the Soviet Union (and to some extent between the United States and Britain). Even without its nuclear monopoly (see below) American supremacy could, at least in the short and medium term, be used to full effect under the conditions of co-operation, if international relations developed without zones of interest. The American potential was particularly imposing in the economic sphere, and it was also in this sphere that political competition was linked inextricably with competition between the systems — even though this was not immediately visible. Non-discriminatory free trade and economic transactions would have created a global structure of trade and market economies dominated by the United States — thus stabilising the 'capitalist system' on a global scale. However, since both the American and the Soviet leadership were convinced that there was an indivisibility in the economic and the political systems, economic superiority would at the same time have meant political predominance. The Soviet Union would have been under dangerous pressure to conform. Resistance to this danger gave rise to the Soviet tendency to resort to demarcation. The Soviet policy — in contrast with that of Britain — of favouring spheres of interest was to that extent not only part of an international competition between states, but also the expression of a competition in the matter of political and ideological dominance. The objective contradictions between multilateral universalism and the policy of spheres of influence threatened the projected order of peace. Put in another way, it was by no means a false perception that produced critical tension, but rather the correct perception of actual conflicting tendencies. Just as the United States followed the principle of 'having her cake and eating it' with regard to her Western hemisphere, the Soviet Union wanted to protect her own spheres of interest from the control of the other Great Powers and at the same time use the international organisation to exercise global influence as an equal Great Power. Put in a nutshell, there was a dual dilemma.

The Soviet Union expected the United States and the Western powers in general to allow her, as a Great Power with equal status, to exert global influence within the framework of the directorate of the Great Powers. She also expected them to conform to agreed mutual co-operation, not only by tolerating Soviet unilateral policy in its sphere of interest in Eastern Europe, but also by helping her to arrange, protect or even extend her sphere of interest. On the other hand, the United States expected the Soviet Union to respect the American sphere of influence in Latin America and to accept the setting up of American bases on a global scale. She expected the USSR to conform with multilateral co-operation without effective protection against American dominance, which in effect meant that she would assist in strengthening the capitalist order on a world scale.

This dilemma became clear to the participants only gradually. Basically, it concerned the problem of whether an accommodation could be found between the two tendencies — between universal co-operation and the policy of spheres of interest. Theoretically this would have been possible by the linking of integrative and regressive methods of conflict regulation, i.e. on the one hand equal by a certain degree of co-operation, and on the other hand through partial demarcation and regression (e.g. a selective and moderated policy of spheres of interest). However, this problem of accommodation had to be solved not in theory, but in everyday political approaches to specific cases, the significance of which often became clear only after the event. Moreover, the policy of the Great Powers was also subject to the more general effect of human actions that individual decisions often produce undesired, or even unforeseen, effects and generate a negative cumulative effect (in the sense of a positive feedback or a reactive development of conflict).

It became clear in 1944 and 1945, and even clearer in 1946, that, in respect of decisions on concrete individual problems relevant to future political alignments, the Great Powers did little to balance the effects of material inequality, or to establish uniformity as regards participation in decisions and in the distribution of advantages. Nor did they do much to mitigate the policy of spheres of interest by the introduction of elements of global co-operation. Rather than practising balanced co-operation based on equal rights and gradually implementing this from case to case, they used existing inequalities to consolidate individual interests. Thus the following negative pattern was created. The three Great Powers co-operated mutually and with equal status at the large conferences and in the European Advisory Committee while preparing the principles of a common policy on liberated countries and the Axis Powers. This enabled them to achieve balanced compromises. However, inequalities emerged when the time came for the practical application of jointly agreed policies.

The first test case was Italy. The Soviet Union was only formally involved in the policies of occupation by being represented on an unimportant consultative committee; it had no influence at all on decisions (Herz, 1967). The Soviet Union then ensured that the decision-making process on South-eastern Europe was biased against the Western Powers, whose influence in the Allied Control Committee for Rumania, Hungary and Bulgaria was minimal. Available documents (see especially Fischer, 1968, and FR) demonstrate that the Soviet Union found the cost of co-operation with the Western powers in this region too high and too detrimental to her interests. She assumed that free elections would produce a defeat for the Communists — which the Hungarian elections of November 1945 proved to be correct. In general, she believed that a liberal-democratic system in these countries would bring anti-Communist and anti-Russian forces to power, thereby posing a threat to the Soviet Union's security. These considerations played an even more important role in the policy towards Poland, which in turn had become a test case on co-operation in American eyes (in the opinion of Cordell Hull) once the United States had agreed to the Russian annexation of East Poland. The Soviet Union used her powers as an occupying force to implement her interpretation of the imprecise compromise formula of Yalta.

The Americans reacted — referring explicitly to Russian practices in South-eastern Europe — by excluding the Soviet Union from the policy process in occupied Japan (Blakeslee, 1951). In Germany, Russia's unilateral transfer of East German territories to Polish administration and the political dispute over reparations constituted the first steps along the road of questioning the common decision-making process (see below).

Eastern Europe played a particularly important role in the sequence of unilateral decisions as the Soviet Union's unilateral policy in this region coincided with Germany's defeat, which brought about a reduction in the mutual west—east military dependence. The following groupings were created:

The presence of the Red Army meant that the Soviet Union did not depend on co-operation with the Western Powers to secure her sphere of influence in Eastern and Central Europe. However, the United States could only pursue her interests and policies there (in the sense of an 'open door' policy) on the basis of co-operation with the Soviet Union. In this area the unequal dependence involved in co-operation worked against the United States (see Davis, 1974).

From the American point of view this was contrasted with a stronger Soviet dependence on co-operation with the United States in the sector of economic and credit policy. Economic means (in particular the policy of loans) had traditionally played an important role in American foreign policy in the implementation of political goals, and in 1945 it was an obvious policy to use economic superiority as an instrument against a weakened Russia.

When deliveries were stopped on 13 May and 17 August (although these decisions were legally prescribed and later amended) it must have become clear to the Soviet Union that she could expect further aid from the United States, only if she continued to co-operate (Herring, 1969).

The American tactic was even more obvious in connection with the Russian request for a commercial loan of $6 billion submitted in a memorandum of 3 January 1945. When presenting this request, Molotov made it clear that the development of friendly relations depended on the granting of the credit. Ambassador Harriman explicitly recommended assistance by credits, but in his telegraphed report of 6 January 1945 (FR, 1945, V. p. 946) he added (and repeated the view both in telexes and verbally):

> It is of course my very strong and earnest opinion that the question of the credit should be tied into our overall diplomatic relations with the Soviet Union and at the appropriate time the Russians should be given to understand that our willingness to co-operate wholeheartedly with them in their vast reconstruction problems will depend upon their behaviour in international matters.

American documents reveal in detail the way this link was seen (see Paterson, 1969). The Americans desired Soviet co-operation in the various international economic bodies which were to realise liberal trade and world-economic relations as well as

> the establishment of a proper role for the United States in the Allied Control Commissions in Rumania, Bulgaria, Hungary, and eventually Germany; establishing a proper role for the United States in general economic relations with and the reconstruction and development of Poland, Czechoslovakia, and the Balkan nations; and establishing a proper basis in Iran. (FR, 1945, V. 960)

Authoritative circles in the US Administration believed that withholding the credits needed by the Soviet Union gave them the decisive leverage to force co-operation in these areas, in particular in Eastern Europe. When Truman took office he was convinced of an unequal dependence in American-Russian co-operation which was in America's favour ('The Soviet Union needed us more than we needed them'). He therefore believed that, whilst the United States might not be able to implement the most important demands 100 per cent, she should be able to get 85 per cent (FR, 1945, V. 232 f.). Whilst Secretary of the Treasury Henry Morgenthau in particular argued from the very beginning in favour of granting the Russian request for credit and with such a gesture of 'reassuring the Soviet Government of our determination to cooperate' (ibid., p. 963), the approach recommended by Harriman was adopted, which was to give the Russians to understand 'how lack of co-operation with our legitimate demands will adversely affect their interests' (ibid., p. 822).

The supposed leverage of credit policy had, of course, a weak point: from the Soviet viewpoint the American economy must, in view of the extended production apparatus, seek to stimulate an active export policy financed by commercial loans, in order to maintain full employment after the War — an argument presented in official contacts between 1943 and 1944 by the Americans themselves. The significance of these factors was played down by some of the President's advisers, but openly conceded by the Economic Division of the State Department: 'Purchase of 10 billions in capital goods during the transition period would provide a healthy stimulus to capital goods industries in the United States and would facilitate the maintenance of a high level of employment' (ibid., p. 973). Influential groups in American politics and business generally regarded an expansion of exports overseas as necessary to the system. However, the possible loss of the Soviet market appeared to be replaceable with other markets (Eakins, 1969).

An American loan could therefore exert little pressure and do little to compensate for the unequal dependence on co-operation in Eastern and South-eastern Europe. The Soviet Union could with some justification suppose that the granting of the requested commercial loan by the United States, linked with corresponding exports to Russia on the part of American industry, would form a balance in the relationship of co-operation.

The traditional policy of achieving international co-operation in the American sense through granting or denying loans failed. A policy of loans was shown to be effective when used against countries with the same (i.e. capitalist) structure, but not with Communist countries (Richard N. Gardner, 1969; Lloyd Gardner, 1970).

One interesting question is whether co-operation in the nuclear sector (in the sense of joint control of atomic energy which might include the Soviet Union sharing in United States' nuclear secrets) could have been used to persuade the USSR to moderate her unilateral policy based on spheres of interest in Eastern Europe by the inclusion of elements of co-operation. Conversely, the question from the Soviet viewpoint could have been whether the disadvantages that co-operation with the United States in Eastern and South-eastern Europe would probably have brought for the Soviet Union would have been balanced by the general advantage of Russo-American co-operation in the nuclear sector.

After the successful testing of the atomic bomb, the political leadership in the United States believed that they finally held the master card. In this phase the question was not whether to threaten the Soviet Union with the use of the atomic bomb. Rather, sharing the nuclear secret with Russia was to be considered only if she was prepared to co-operate with the United States in other areas and was ready to make important equivalent concessions. In view of the alternative facing the Soviet Union — risking an apparently almost hopeless nuclear arms race with the United States — some members of the US administration believed that this conditional offer of co-operation would be attractive to Russia.

It is impossible to say whether the Soviet Union would really have been prepared to compromise, since in the end the offer of nuclear co-operation was not made. According to his colleague Stimson, Secretary of State Byrnes was 'very much against any attempt to co-operate with Russia' and carried the bomb along in his pocket to both conferences of Foreign Ministers in London and Moscow in September and December 1945 'as a great weapon to get through the things he has' without actually making the atomic question an issue in the negotiations (Bernstein and Matusow, 1966; Bernstein, 1976). At the same time Stimson, Acheson and Wallace, who were against a 'policy of exclusion' towards the Soviet Union and advocated co-operation with mutual respect for each other's interests, were overruled in Washington (FR, 1945, II. 49). When Byrnes eventually tried seriously to influence an agreement at the Foreign Ministers' Conference in Moscow in the late autumn, unilateral measures had already advanced too far. The Baruch Plan, with which the United States nominally proposed international control of atomic energy whilst at the same time conducting the Bikini Tests, was in fact not a genuine offer of participation (Hewlett and Anderson, 1962; Sherwin, 1975). It allowed the United States to retain her nuclear monopoly and only to relinquish it in the final phase of gradual internationalisation. No firm or binding timetable was envisaged for the individual stages: all members of the international organisation would unanimously have to agree that the stage in question had been reached. As Lloyd Gardner (1970) has pointed out, the United States thus received an additional degree of security and veto power in respect of the realisation of the plan, whilst the veto for use in decisions on misdemeanors, enforcement actions and sanctions normally attributed to the Security Council was abolished. Thus the Baruch Plan was not an offer of co-operation, but, as Senator Vandenberg described it in 1946 'the showdown with Moscow'. The nuclear monopoly of the United States, i.e. of the Anglo-Saxon Powers, made the whole concept of a co-operative order of peace and the integrative regulation of conflict an anachronism. Since nuclear parity was unattainable through co-operation, the Soviet Union had to strive for this goal on her own (see Wolfers, 1946). This meant a critical increase in competition between the Great Powers and between the antagonistic systems they represented.

Inequality in the area analysed so far was increased all the more by the lack of readiness on both sides to accept a somewhat similar amount of rapprochement and alignment in internal matters as a consequence of eventual co-operation. On the contrary, each side intended exclusively to convert the other's system to its own ways. The Soviet Union wanted to undermine and promote the breakdown of capitalism whilst the United States wanted to encourage a breakthrough of liberal-democratic principles in the Soviet Union.

Secretary of War Stimson, for example, presupposed in his memorandum of 19 July 1945 that in the long term no reliable international relations could be established between two such fundamentally diverse systems. He also thought that in view of the reign of terror in the Soviet Union no free exchange of ideas was possible and that Russian mistrust could not be overcome. Consideration should therefore be given to the question of whether, before setting up international controls on nuclear energy and Russian participation in them, they should insist on internal changes in the Soviet regime which would actually realise the freedoms embodied in the 1936 Constitution of the USSR (FR, *Conference of Berlin*, 1945, II. 1157).

In September Stimson revised his opinion fairly radically in that he now believed 'that any demand by us for an internal change in Russia as a condition of sharing in the atomic weapon would be so resented that it would make the objective we have in view less probable' (FR, 1945,II. 41). However, he added that conversely a gradual liberalisation might be expected in Russia as a result of atomic co-operation and the atmosphere of trust this would create.

The concept of co-operation, which most consistently advanced a balanced development, in the sense of mutual rapprochement, was advocated by Secretary of Commerce Wallace in his famous speech on 12 September 1946: 'Under friendly peaceful competition the Russian world and the American world will gradually become more alike. The Russians will be forced to grant more and more of the personal freedoms; and we shall become more and more absorbed with problems of social-economic justice.'

Similarly in the transitional phase advisers in other Departments put forward a concept mediating between universal multilateral co-operation and the policies of spheres of interest, which might perhaps have had a chance. They proposed mutual respect for Soviet political spheres of influence in Eastern Europe and American ones in Latin America and at the same time close economic relations based on 'open door' policies. In view of the close link between politics and economics a concept of this sort would have required a large measure of political and diplomatic skill, a willingness to differentiate and a subtlety in forming coalitions within both countries. None of these preconditions existed. In the Soviet Union it was a prescribed maxim that socialism and capitalism were irreconcilable (at any rate since Stalin's election speech of 9 February 1946). In America Stimson, who was vacating his office, was already in the minority by September 1945 and a year later Wallace was dismissed by Truman because of the speech quoted above. With the Baruch Plan the Truman Administration then adopted a policy which, if it had been accepted by the Soviet Union, would — according to Oppenheimer — have completely changed the Soviet system. In the key areas of national security there was a switch towards a regressive policy with the decision against American-Russian co-operation on nuclear matters. The close relations of the wartime coalition deteriorated. However, in the winter of 1946–7 a certain degree of duality could still be observed. The fact that the United States was still prepared to negotiate co-operatively with the Soviet Union in the spring of 1947 on peace treaties with Italy, Rumania, Bulgaria, Hungary and Finland, thereby conceding considerable territorial and financial gains to the Soviet Union, showed that in important problem areas which directly concerned the military alliance of the Second World War she retained elements of the concept of co-operation for a relatively long period.

The Soviet Union had substantially increased her territory as a result of annexations — at first through the alliance with National Socialist Germany and then in alliance with the Western Powers: the gain was a total of 1,143,230 square kilometres. The area gained in Europe (476,900 square kilometres) included the following countries or parts of countries: Estonia, Latvia, Lithuania, areas of northern and eastern Finland, territories around Memel, north-east Prussia, east Poland, Carpathian Ukraine and areas in northern and eastern Rumania. The peace treaties legalised these annexations (contrary to the pledge of the Soviet Union of a policy of non-annexation in the Atlantic Charter).

In addition the USSR established a sphere of interest in Eastern Europe which signified not only a determining influence, but a direct domination and Sovietisation. The US Administration and the public regarded this as a violation of the Yalta Agreement although at home the view was expressed that these agreements were in no way unequivocal — they could be interpreted in various ways. Co-operation with the Soviet Union reached its limits, however, according to the unanimous opinion of the American ruling élites, where the Soviet Union openly pursued expansionist policy and aimed beyond those territories already controlled by the Red Army.

The United States' switch to a policy of spheres of influence of her own in Europe ran parallel to these expansionist attempts on the part of the Soviet Union. Within the US Administration diplomats such as George Kennan had been advocating a policy of this sort some time (since 1945), but had been unable to implement it. The time was not ripe for his concept of containment until 1947; the year 1945–6 was a transitional phase. A State Department memorandum of 1 April 1946 and the Clifford Report of September 1946 still refuted the theory of irreconcilable emnity between the socialist and capitalist worlds (in the meantime again propagated by the Soviet leadership) and emphasized the concept of co-operation, though at the same time formulating a resolute resistance to Soviet expansion:

> The U.S. together with other countries of the non-Soviet world believes that there is no objective reason, why the so-called capitalist system and Communist system cannot peacefully exist provided neither attempts to

> extend the area of its system by aggressive and ultimately forcible means at the expense of the other. However, in order to provide any basis for such peaceful coexistence of the two systems, the U.S. at the present time must demonstrate to the Soviet Government in the first instance by diplomatic means and in the last analysis by military force if necessary that the present course of its foreign policy can only lead to disaster for the Soviet Union. With respect to the extension of Soviet territorial control the U.S. should use the best methods at its disposal to check the actual physical extension of Soviet power beyond its present limits. Diplomatic and other non-military action represent the only means at the disposal of the U.S. to check this extension of Soviet power until such extension involves the seizure of regions in which the power of the Soviet armies can be countered defensively by the Naval, amphibious and air power of the U.S. and its potential allies. The Charter of the United Nations affords the best and most unassailable means through which the U.S. can implement its opposition to Soviet physical expansion. It not only offers the basis upon which the greatest degrees of popular support can be obtained in the U.S. but it also will insure the support and even assistance of other members of the United Nations. If, as may occur, the United Nations breaks down under the test of opposition to Soviet aggression it will have served the purpose of clarifying the issues before American and world public opinion and thus make easier whatever future steps may be required by the U.S. and other like minded nations in the face of a new threat of world aggression. (FR, 1946, I.1169)

The Truman Administration consistently employed this strategy and resisted any expansion of the Soviet spheres of influence either in Iran or in the Mediterranean or Aegean. The very complex connections have been competently elucidated and thoroughly described in recent historical research (Hess, 1974; Knight, 1975). The Truman Administration gradually came to the conclusion that the Soviet Union was determined to shatter the order which Great Britain had created in the Mediterranean and the Middle East, 'so that Russian power and influence can sweep unimpeded across Turkey and through the Dardenelles into the Mediterannean, and across Iran and through the Persian Gulf into the Indian Ocean' (FR, 1946, VII.2). In Iran the United States forced the withdrawal of Russian troops from the northern province of Azerbaijan through the intervention of the UN Security Council(!) with the result that the pro-Soviet separatist regime there was defeated by troops loyal to the Iranian Central Government, and the oil concession originally agreed with the Soviet Union was not eventually granted (see 6 below). The United States further prevented the Soviet Union from becoming trustee for the administration of Tripolitania, sending the US Navy to the Mediterranean as a demonstration (but avoiding escalation) to deter the Soviet Union from using force to implement territorial demands against Turkey and to secure the establishment of a base in the Dardanelles. This policy eventually culminated in the Truman Doctrine (12 March 1947) which pledged American assistance not only to Greece and Turkey, but to all free nations in the event of a military Soviet or Communist threat. In the eyes of the American ruling élites efforts already made by Tsarist Russia were being repeated in these regions under a Communist banner. And just as Karl Marx had developed a domino theory on the traditional expansionist policies of Tsarist Russia in 1853 (to which former Secretary of State Byrnes significantly referred (1947, p. 295), Deputy Secretary of State Acheson explained the Truman Doctrine to the American senators in Congress as follows:

> The corruption of Greece would infect Iran and all to the east. It would also carry infection to Africa through Asia Minor and Egypt, and to Europe through Italy and France, already threatened by the strongest domestic communist parties in Western Europe. The Soviet Union was playing one of the greatest gambles in history at minimal cost. It did not need to win all the possibilities. Even one or two offered immense gains. We and we alone were in a position to break up the play. These were the stakes that British withdrawal from the eastern Mediterannean offered to an eager and ruthless opponent. (Acheson, 1970, p. 293)

The United States took up the imperial reins which had slipped from Britain's hands (Jones, 1955). The USSR's attempts to extend her sphere of influence caused the US Administration to take over the tasks which Great Britain had been propagating as urgent since the Second World War — the creation of a counterbalance to the Soviet Union in Europe and the Middle East. In the summer of 1947 the Truman Administration came to the conclusion after internal consultation 'that we have to accept the fact that the original concept of one world, on which the United Nations was based, is no longer valid and that we are in political fact facing a division in two worlds' (Forrestal's Diary entry, 31 Aug. 1947, in Millis, ed., 1951, p. 307). It was the transition 'from the universalist dream to the reality of spheres of influence' (R. Aron). And this meant that in place of an integrative solution to conflict the shape of relations between the systems was to be determined by principles of distancing, reduced relations and regression.

For the other main protagonist in global politics, the Soviet

Union, such an approach to conflict dominated (as has been shown above) from the very beginning, and eventually found its expression in the Two Camps Doctrine. In A. A. Zhdanov's authoritative formulation, it read:

> The fundamental changes in the international situation and in the situation of individual countries brought about by the War have rearranged the whole political map of the world. A new grouping of political forces has been created. The longer the period that separates us from the end of the War, the more sharply do two main lines emerge in international postwar politics corresponding to the division of the political forces active in the global arena into two main camps: the imperialist and anti-democratic camp on the one hand, and the anti-imperialist and democratic camp on the other. (*Tägliche Rundschau*, 24 Oct. 1947; see Weingartner, 1973, pp. 69 ff.)

At the same time the doctrine served to link the aims of traditional Russian power politics with the world-revolutionary goals of the Soviet leadership. With the founding of the Cominform in September 1947 the second component also finally reappeared in an organised form. The Cominform institutionalised transnational co-operation between the Communist parties in Italy and France and the governing Communist parties of the Eastern Bloc countries under the leadership of the CPSU. Western European parties were thus officially turned into outposts and bases of the Soviet Union inside the opponent's 'camp'. According to Zhdanov, 'the USSR and the countries of the new democracies' provided the basis of the 'anti-imperialist and democratic position': 'the anti-imperialist position depends on the working-class and democratic movements in all countries, on comradely Communist parties in all countries, on the liberation movements in the colonies and in dependent nations as well as on the help of all advanced democratic forces present in every country.'

In place of the concept of symmetrical co-operation this introduced the concept of a policy of symmetrical spheres of influence, regressive demarcation and simultaneous influence in the opposing spheres of influence with the help of Cominform.

This general pattern of relations asserted itself in all areas. It showed that both sides (not least for reasons of psychological agitation) believed it impossible to have a variety of approaches in their relations.

This link between retrogression in relations with Western nations and the intensification of internal bloc relations was most clearly visible in the sphere of trade policy. By 1945 American exports to the

Soviet Union were declining considerably, whilst Russian exports to the United States had increased up to 1946. From 1947–8 American trade relations with Eastern European states and the USSR deteriorated substantially and did not begin to improve until 1954 (see Table 6.1).

Table 6.1 *US Trade with Eastern Europe and the USSR* (*in US $ m.*)

| | 1947 | 1948 | 1949 | 1950 | 1951 | 1952 | 1953 | 1954 | 1955 |
|---|---|---|---|---|---|---|---|---|---|
| American exports | 335.3 | 122.7 | 61.7 | 26.4 | 2.7 | 0.5 | 0.6 | 5.9 | 7.2 |
| American imports | 108.2 | 113.0 | 67.5 | 80.5 | 63.8 | 32.3 | 29.9 | 42.4 | 55.5 |

*Source*: US Department of Commerce, Washington, DC; quoted in Spulber, 1957, p. 463.

In contrast, trade within the bloc of Eastern European states and between them and the USSR was already considerably greater by 1948 than it had been before the war. By 1952 it constituted between 67 and 89 per cent of the total trade of the countries concerned (Spulber, 1957, p. 410). Between 1948 and 1967 trade within the West rose from 64.4 to 75.7 per cent (Wilczynski, 1969, p. 46). Reciprocal policies of embargoes were the main reason for this retrograde trend (Spulber, 1957; Wilczynski 1969).

The United States had already introduced the first controls on exports in 1948 and the USSR subsequently retaliated with restrictions in strategically important areas; for example, she began to reduce exports of manganese ore, vital to American industry, and finally discontinued them so that the United States had to turn to India for supplies (Venkataramani, 1958).

In 1949 the United States and her allies adopted a systematic policy of embargoes: they established a Coordinating Committee for East–West Trade (Cocom) which — more or less successfully — prevented the export of strategically important goods to the USSR and its allies (see Adler–Karlsson, 1968). The first embargo list was drawn up in November 1949 and vastly extended during the Korean War, to include about half of all goods traded internationally. Furthermore, in 1951–2 the trade agreements between the United States and Eastern Bloc countries were cancelled (Galtung, 1966).

From 1954 onwards the embargo list was gradually reduced (Wilczynski, 1969, pp. 272ff.).

Whilst regression in trade relations had been initiated predominantly by the United States, resistance to the exchange of students and scientists in the cultural sphere came from the Soviet Union. Cultural institutions and information offices in the East and in the West were closed down in the years between 1950 and 1953.

Thus what has been labelled the 'Cold War' was not an attempt to achieve a new organisation of international relations through a military or war-type solution of conflict (or critical tension), but rather an attempt to avoid a military explosion in the international system — a 'Hot War' — through extensive regression. Nevertheless, an element of force in the settlement of conflict was retained in the pattern of relations, as was shown unequivocally by the term 'Cold *War*'. Accordingly both elements were combined in the key American foreign-policy document on the Cold War, NSC-68 (1950) in which reference was made to the prevention of war and the use of 'means short of war' as well as the realisation of war-type or contentious relationships: 'The cold war is in fact a real war in which the survival of the free world is at stake' (quoted in Etzold and Gaddis, 1978, p. 442).

At home and within the spheres of influence, regression signalled a policy of the stabilisation of the existing political order by means of a corresponding economic order. In this the United States certainly allowed a wider variety in line with her liberal values to the extent of accepting democratic socialism in Great Britain as legitimate, whilst the Soviet Union insisted on the violent imposition of its type of socialism. The maxim 'cuius regio, eius oeconomia' (Rölling, 1970, p. 178) was thus validated, albeit with the variations detailed above. With regard to the structure of domestic politics, in 1947–8 integration in the blocs was expressed on the one hand by the introduction of governments of 'peoples' democracy' in Eastern Europe, and on the other hand in the exclusion of Communist parties from the governing coalitions in Western Europe (Wallensteen, 1973).

Last, but not least, both sides found it necessary to exaggerate ideological differences in order to justify demarcation abroad, to increase national efforts and integration at home and to further a fighting spirit. An enormous ideological mobilisation (see Freeland, 1972) was possible because the Cold War, although a direct result of political competition for power between the Great Powers, exceeded this competition. Ideological conflict was not simply added to the conflict of power politics, did not represent a 'superimposed conflict.' Rather, the main competition in power politics between the Super Powers was at the time in reality (and not only in propaganda) an ideological and political conflict whose significance had been underestimated in proposals for a new world order in 1944–5.

## Excursus 1: The Iranian Conflict

The Iranian conflict is of particular importance in the developments described above and therefore deserves to be studied in some greater detail. It concerns a territorial dispute which for the first time brought confrontation to the Security Council — the organ to which a central function in the concept of co-operative world order had been allotted.

In August 1941 Iran had been occupied by the first joint action of Anglo-Russian troops and somewhat later by American troops in order to protect the overland supply route to Russia. It was agreed in a treaty with Iran of 29 January 1942 (and later confirmed at the Yalta Conference) that foreign military units would withdraw six months after the end of the War and that Iran's full territorial integrity would be secured. However, whilst the treaty established no formal regime of occupation, both the Soviet Union and the United States used the presence of their troops to establish their influence in the Northern Province and in the central region respectively, which included attempts to secure oil concessions. Once the War ended the Soviet Union (and Britain, too, at first) refused to withdraw her troops immediately. The Soviet Union insisted on a wide interpretation of the six months' limit and even sought to extend her military presence. In the meantime she supported movements seeking autonomy for Azerbaijan, coming from reformist liberal and Communist forces and directed against the conservative central government. In December the autonomous Republic of Azerbaijan and the Kurdish People's Republic were founded with Soviet support. The Soviet aim was to win a firm base of influence in this way and, in return for the partial or total withdrawal of troops, to receive oil concessions based on 51 per cent participation in the northern provinces, internal air-transport rights and a privileged position in the port of Pahlavi (on the Caspian Sea). In addition, on the basis of the Russo-Iranian Treaty of 1921, she would obtain the right of military intervention in the event of internal unrest in Iran.

The United States used this dispute to test the Soviet Union's willingness to allow the United Nations Security Council to be used to enforce Iran's territorial integrity — even against her own interests. Consequently the United States turned down Great Britain's suggestion of a commission of the Three Powers and encouraged the Iranian government to bring the matter before the Security Council in the face of Soviet resistance. The fact that the Soviet Union had not withdrawn her troops by the target date of 2 March, and had even draughted fresh troops three days later and started marching towards Tehran, led to an increasingly grave situation, which moved the US Administration to insist even more forcefully on the use of the Security Council — despite the fact that by the end of March 1946 bilateral Iranian-Russian negotiations were underway, ending in a compromise agreement on 5 April. The United States kept the Iranian problem on the agenda of the Security Council even after the Iranian government had withdrawn its case (15 April) and Soviet troops had retired from Iranian territory (May 1946).

The withdrawal of Soviet troops was seen as a victory for the United Nations. Soviet oil interests were in no way assured since the agreement concerned would be effective only after it had been ratified by parliament. The USSR complied with the directions of the UN Security Council (see Hiscocks, 1973, pp. 116 ff.). Doubtless the Soviet Union was legally obliged to withdraw her troops without having won oil concessions. But it had been established that the Security Council could be employed in a partisan way to demonstrate the power of the United States as long as a formal veto did not neutralise the Council. During the Iranian conflict the United States had opted for a policy of containment which eventually resulted in a policy of her own spheres of interest while at the same time making use of the UN. In December the United States strengthened the resolve of the central Iranian government to send troops to Azerbaijan and to overthrow the pro-Soviet provincial government (December 1946) and finally, in July 1947, encouraged the Iranian government to refuse to ratify the Soviet-Iranian oil agreements which had been concluded on the withdrawal of Soviet troops. Instead, the oil concessions were granted to British and American firms (see Geyer, 1955). So this conflict was solved unilaterally in favour of the West in 1946–7. However, the Soviet Union was able to continue to use the Communist Tudeh movement and to pursue conciliatory policies in order to influence Iranian policy. Iran thus remained a point of tension between East and West.

## Excursus 2: The German Conflict

Developments in Germany are particularly important since it was there that the most intense attempts to achieve an integrative policy on the part of the Great Powers were made and because this policy had, to a certain degree, been institutionalised.

At the Potsdam Conference (17 July to 2 August 1945) an Allied Control Council was established as a joint quasi-governmental organ. The 'principles of a coordinated policy of the Allies' envisaged that the 'supreme authority in Germany' would be exercised by the Commanders-in-Chief of the four victorious powers 'on instructions from their respective Governments', 'each in his own zone of occupation, and also jointly, in matters affecting Germany as a whole, in their capacity as members of the Control Council'. There was notable unity between the Great Powers on the maxim: 'So far as practicable, there shall be uniformity of treatment of the German population throughout Germany.' The administration of Germany had to be 'directed towards the decentralization of the political structure'; 'for the time being, no central German government' should be established. 'Notwithstanding this, however, certain essential central German administrative departments, headed by State Secretaries, shall be established' which 'will act under the direction of the Control Council.' Accordingly, it was agreed in economic matters that: 'During the period of occupation Germany shall be treated as a single economic unit.' To this end 'common policies' were to be set down. Allied control over the German economy was to ensure the implementation of the programme of industrial disarmament and demilitarisation, reparations and foreign trade, but at the same time to serve to 'ensure . . . the equitable distribution of essential commodities between the several zones so as to produce a balanced economy throughout Germany and reduce the need for imports.' Russia's demands for reparation were to be satisfied primarily through her zone of occupation, and those of the Western Powers from the Western occupation zones. In addition the USSR was to obtain 10 per cent of the industrial plants scheduled to be dismantled in the Western zones without payment or exchange, and 15 per cent in exchange for an equal amount of food, coal, potash, zinc, timber, clay products, petroleum products and other commodities. It was generally agreed that the 'proceeds of exports from current production and stocks' should 'in the first place' be used to pay for those imports necessary for the maintenance of an average standard of living in Germany.

Contrary to plans for a division, which had been advocated by all the Great Powers at Yalta, and despite the previous unilateral decision of the Soviet Union to transfer German territories east of the Oder–Neisse line to Polish administration (in so far as this had not already been ceded to the Soviet Union), the idea of German unity was laid down at Potsdam. Unity and conformity were to be realised comprehensively and in detail by institutionalised co-operation between the four victorious powers. Even the compromise on reparations, with its compensatory clause, was within the keeping of this policy of co-operation, which still had to be specified in substance by the elaboration of joint programmes in all the relevant areas.

These aims were enormously exacting and presupposed a degree of unity which, apart from the antagonism between the systems, was hard to imagine. For example, in one of the most important questions — the setting up of central administrative departments — it was not an American-Soviet clash that caused all efforts to fail, but France's policy of obstruction. Whereas France demanded the separation of the Saar, the Rhineland and the Ruhr area, and consequently blocked their inclusion into a central German administration, the USSR hoped to extend her influence upon the Western zones through a central administration, particularly in the Ruhr, whose economic value in itself was highly prized — quite apart from the expected political consequences. This explains the fact that in the Control Council the Soviet Union — despite hard bargaining — remained open to compromise for a long time. Even in 1946 the US Administration still believed it possible to arrive at a common policy if French resistance could be broken (see Gimbel, 1976). However, in the same year there were several signs that the Soviet Union — in line with her unilateral policy of spheres of influence in Eastern Europe — was also giving up the concept of co-operation in her German zone of occupation through the compulsory fusion of the Social Democrats (SPD) with the Communist Party (KPD) and the general toeing of the political line, reparations from current production, the founding of the SAG trust, non-compliance with the provision that food-stuffs or raw materials should be sent to the Western zones. This clearly violated the maxims of the Potsdam Agreement mentioned above. Russia evidently tried to make the necessary preparations to influence the whole of Germany from a sound position in her own zones, or, in the event that co-operative means of influence should fail in the Western zones, to bring her own zone within her sphere of interest, both economically (by directing East German production towards Russian needs) and politically (by constructing a 'people's democracy'). Russia even expected the United States ultimately to pay the German reparations (financed by the American taxpayer) with supplies of American food-stuffs and credits to enable the Soviet Union to use current German products primarily as reparations (contrary to the Potsdam Agreement) and thereby economically to bind the Soviet Occupied Zone tightly to the Soviet Union.

The American State Department had already warned of the consequences of such a policy in an official statement in December 1945:

> In planning the peacetime German economy, the interests of the United States are confined to the industrial disarmament of Germany and to the provision of a balanced economic position at the standard of living indicated. The United States does not seek to eliminate or weaken German industries of a peaceful character, in which Germany has produced effectively for world markets, for the purpose of protecting American markets from German goods, aiding American exports, or for any other selfish advantage. Similarly the United States is opposed to the attempt of any other country to use the industrial-disarmament plan of the Berlin Declaration to its own commercial ends at the expense of a peacetime German economy. It is our desire to see Germany's economy geared to a world system and not an autarchical system. (Policy Statement of 12 Dec. 1945, quoted in Ratchford and Ross, 1947, p. 217)

Despite this, the US Administration retained the concept of co-operation even after the decision for the establishment of the Bi-Zone, which was primarily motivated by economic factors, namely to make the American Zone viable and to relieve the burden on the American tax-payer. At the same time this prepared the way for the creation of an own sphere of influence as an alternative if co-operation should fail. The American offer to conclude a Four Power Treaty guaranteeing German disarmament for 25 or 40 years was meant to smooth the way towards joint political co-operation in Germany by strengthening co-operation on defence policy for both the Soviet Union and France. Russia's rejection of this proposal in the summer of 1946 (contrary to earlier positive declarations) coincided with her attempts to extend her existing spheres of influence and interest in the Mediterranean and Middle East. This rejection was further connected with the Soviet attempt to play the card of

German unity unilaterally (see Molotov's speech of 10 July 1946). This was seen as further evidence of the Soviet Union's negative attitude towards co-operation. The Soviet policy on Germany was seen by the Americans as yet another example of the USSR's determination to pursue a policy of extending her interests in all directions (see Link, 1984).

The concept of a co-operative peace system was wrecked by the unilateralism of both Great Powers in strategic and military matters and as a consequence of the Soviet Union's unilateral attempts to expand into the Mediterranean and Iran. This failure had very dire consequences for policy on Germany. Leading American civil servants have clearly perceived the 'tragic inevitability' (Kindleberger) of this development. In view of the deep fundamental differences of interest as to the internal order in Germany and the integration of a new Germany into the nations of the world, the conclusion was that a decline in the level of relations (regression) was more conducive to the regulation of conflict than a joint political approach. Conflicting tendencies were highlighted by the American military Command's insistence on its responsibility for the whole of Germany and by the emphasis on the Control Council's task of implementing the 'principles of a co-ordinated policy' jointly agreed at Potsdam (see Yergin, 1977, p. 230). The huge discrepancy between the low degree of agreement as to interests and the high degree of co-operation which had been created by the organisational structure and the tasks involved in the joint administration of Germany made an organisational change, in the sense of distancing and reducing relations between the Soviet Union and the Western nations, necessary, but at the same time extraordinarily difficult. Benjamin Cohen's comparison with a divorce elucidates this state of affairs: the separation of two people can, in the main, be enforced less dramatically, or even with more understanding, than the legal dissolution of an institutionalised marriage. The liaison between the victorious powers, created by the Control Council, led increasingly to 'conflicts about co-operation'. It no longer seemed possible to save the relationship, but at the same time a separation by mutual consent was unattainable.

The aggravating circumstances themselves are not, of course, covered by this analogy. The regressive policy of incorporating the Soviet Occupation Zone into the zone of Soviet dominance and of incorporating the Bi/Tri-Zones into the Western spheres of interest did not mean demarcation along national boundaries, but rather the division of the German nation and its capital and the consolidation of this division with the founding of two states — the German Democratic Republic and the Federal Republic of Germany. This created a 'dual conflict' (Richard Löwenthal) which shaped the Cold War in Europe in the same way as the division of Korea and Vietnam did in Asia:

> On the one hand the Federal Republic of German together with the Western Powers was party to a general conflict of systems in which the West sought to prevent the expansion of the sphere dominated by the Soviet communists into central and western Europe or even to ensure the maintenance or re-establishment of a liberal democracy and the capitalist system; on the other hand, the Federal Republic of Germany was faced with a specific conflict in its interest in re-unification and with its non-recognition of the German Democratic Republic and the frontier with the East. (Knapp, 1975, p. 29)

In other words, conflicting tendencies between the Soviet Union and the United States became enshrined in the European system of relations and also in Germany, within the framework of national relations. And during the phase of the Cold War the method of demarcation — regressive regulation of conflict — was chosen for both conflicts (see End, 1973).

Because of Berlin's geographical position, the policy of regression could not be implemented consistently unless the West accepted an expansion of the Soviet sphere of power. The Soviet Union's unilateral and violent attempt to settle the conflict over geographical frontiers with the Blockade in 1948–9 was countered not only by the people of West Berlin, but also by the Western Powers with the help of the Berlin Air Lift. Berlin thus became the place where the dual international and national conflict most visibly merged into one and where, at the same time, despite the dominance of the regressive regulation of conflict, rudiments of an integrative control on the part of the Four Powers (most noticeably in the Allied Air Control) were retained. In this sense, too, Berlin was an 'island' in the Cold War system of relations. It was appropriate to this particular logic that this bone of contention also provided the link between the Super Powers' détente and relaxation in Europe with the Four–Power Agreement on Berlin of 3 September 1971 (see below).

# 7 *Structures and Procedural Patterns in the Cold War and Détente*

The basic design of the Cold War is colloquially termed 'bloc building' or 'polarisation'. This pertinently expresses that the cooling of East–West relations (regression) was accompanied by an intensification of relations between the Allies (integration), with the respective leading power providing the focal point and exercising a determining influence (hegemony) or even forthright domination (for an explanation of the difference see Triepel, 1943). In both Western and Eastern spheres of interest, blocs were established based on alliances which strove for a relatively high degree of co-operation and strong links between the respective members. That is to say, on the one hand bloc-building and regression in relations between the blocs and on the other hand, integration within the blocs led by the United States and the USSR, characterise the mutually related elements of the structure and processes of the Cold War. Conversely, in the phase of détente, relations between the systems were strengthened anew. Efforts were made to establish links, exchanges and even agreements between the blocs in order to reduce the risk of confrontation and war.

In order to trace this pattern of structures and processes, we have to identify the power potential (which changed with the passage of time) of the main powers which shaped these structures, i.e. the polarity, as well as their gravitational pull on medium-sized and smaller countries, i.e. the polarisation.

## The Structural Patterns of Polarity

The 'polarity' of the system of states is determined by the number of leading powers and how one allocates their power potentials (see Link, German edn., Ch. 1). To determine how much power individual states actually have is indeed very difficult. Power is based on material and intellectual resources and on the ability to mobilise these resources (see above). In principle, intellectual resources elude quantification, but even material resources cannot be determined precisely, since the choice of indicators and their significance is disputed and the available data and statistics are often incomplete or rely on measurements which cannot be compared (e.g. the UN statistics provide the net *social* product of market economies, but the net *material* product of socialist countries). Because of these and other difficulties (which will not be examined here ; see Vogel, in DGFK Jahrbuch, 1979–80) individual statistics and a general index of material power potential can provide only an approximate guide. Consequently, the current polarity can only be roughly determined. This rough pattern is, however, sufficient for our purposes, namely to clarify the structural changes of polarity over a period of time.

A first impression may be gained by a juxtaposition of statistics (see Tables 7.1 and 2; see also Larson, 1978). The comparison shows a clear American superiority.

Amongst the many attempts to construct a complete index of material power potentials, that of Wilhelm Fucks (1965) has found the widest recognition. Fucks argues convincingly that steel and energy production, as well as population, are the most important indicators for determining the power potential of a country. His considerations on the importance of these factors — which will not be referred to individually here — led to the formula 'power (potential) equals the average steel and energy production figures multiplied by the cubed-root of the population figure.'

By means of this formula the ten largest potentials of state power have been calculated for four different years and ranked in order of precedence (see Table 7.2).

The quotients of the power potentials of the list of states in this Table show the differences between the states. The greatest quotient value shows where the dividing line runs between Great and Middle Powers (measured by their power potentials and without regard to the degree of mobilisation). Further, the US values were set at 100 and the values of the other states related to that, in order to view the differences in power as well.

These tables show that as regards material power potentials the state system in 1948 cannot be described as one of bipolarity. On the contrary, there was a unipolarity because of the United States' universal superiority. At this time the USSR is not yet a world power of equal standing, and the former Great Powers, France and

Table 7.1 *Survey of state power potential*

| | GNP (in billion dollars) | Population (in millions) | Military manpower (thousands) | Strategic nuclear systems | % of world exports[1] |
|---|---|---|---|---|---|
| **1952** | | | | | |
| USA | 350 | 157.5 | 3550 | 800 | 20.6 |
| USSR | 113[2] | 184.8 | 4600 | — | — |
| China | 59[3] | 586.9 | — | — | — |
| GB | 44 | 50.7 | 890 | — | 10.4 |
| France | 29 | 42.4 | 645 | — | 5.2 |
| FR Germany | 32 | 48.7 | — | — | 5.4 |
| Japan | 16 | 85.5 | 114 | — | 1.7 |
| **1962** | | | | | |
| USA | 560 | 186.7 | 2827 | 1835 | 17.4 |
| USSR | 229[2] | 221.7 | 3600 | 865 | 5.6 |
| China | 79[3] | 689.0 (1960) | 3000 | — | 1.2 |
| GB | 81 | 53.3 | 445 | 90 | 9.1 |
| France | 74 | 47.0 | 742 | — | 5.9 |
| FR Germany | 89 | 54.8 | 389 | — | 10.6 |
| Japan | 59 | 94.9 | 216 | — | 3.9 |
| **1972** | | | | | |
| USA | 1152 | 208.8 | 2253 | 2165 | 12.4 |
| USSR | 439[2] | 250.5 | 3425 | 2830 | 3.5 |
| China (1971) | 128[3] | 800.0 | 2880 | 150 | 0.6 (1971) |
| GB | 151 | 55.8 | 352 | 144 | 6.1 |
| France | 202 | 51.7 | 503 | 92 | 6.6 |
| FR Germany | 259 | 61.7 | 475 | — | 11.6 |
| Japan | 317 | 106.0 | 266 | — | 7.1 |

1. For 1952 non-market economies are not included.
2. Net Material Product (0.72 Rubel = 1 dollar).
3. Constant $ (1970).

*Source*: Buchan, 1974, pp. 322 ff.

Britain, are no longer in the top group (and also unable to re-establish their colonial power). It was not until the 1950s that an American-Soviet bipolarity developed even if it continued to be very biased in the United States' favour. Within this bipolarity, relations between power potentials increasingly changed in the sense that the distance between the United States and the USSR narrowed. At the

Table 7.2 *World ranking according to power potential (Fucks' formula)**

| | Index | Standardised weighting (USA = 100) | n / n + 1 |
|---|---|---|---|
| **1948** | | | |
| 1. USA | 3620 | 100 | |
| 2. USSR | 984 | 27 | 3.68 |
| 3. GB | 419 | 12 | 2.35 |
| 4. Western Occupied Germany | 216 | 6 | 1.94 |
| 5. China | 120 | 3 | 1.79 |
| 6. India | 118 | 3 | 1.02 |
| 7. Poland | 110 | 3 | 1.07 |
| 8. France | 94 | 3 | 1.18 |
| 9. Japan | 89 | 2 | 1.06 |
| 10. Soviet Occupied Germany | 55 | 2 | 1.60 |
| **1955** | | | |
| 1. USA | 4434 | 100 | |
| 2. USSR | 1916 | 43 | 2.31 |
| 3. GB | 458 | 10 | 4.19 |
| 4. West Germany | 358 | 8 | 1.28 |
| 5. China | 314 | 7 | 1.14 |
| 6. Poland | 156 | 4 | 2.02 |
| 7. India | 150 | 3 | 1.04 |
| 8. Japan | 133 | 3 | 1.13 |
| 9. France | 130 | 3 | 1.02 |
| 10. Canada | 73 | 2 | 1.77 |
| **1963** | | | |
| 1. USA | 4639 | 100 | |
| 2. USSR | 2698 | 58 | 1.72 |
| 3. China | 1364 | 29 | 1.98 |
| (EEC) | (678) | (14) | (2.01) |
| 4. GB | 421 | 9 | 3.24 (1.61) |
| 5. West Germany | 421 | 9 | 1.00 |
| 6. India | 296 | 6 | 1.42 |
| 7. Japan | 219 | 5 | 1.35 |
| 8. Poland | 200 | 4 | 1.10 |
| 9. Canada | 159 | 3 | 1.26 |
| 10. France | 149 | 3 | 1.06 |
| **1976** | | | |
| 1. USA | 6506 | 100 | |
| 2. USSR | 5797 | 89 | 1.12 |
| 3. China | 3058 | 47 | 1.89 |

Table 7.2 *Continued*

| | Index | Standardized weighting (USA = 100) | n / (n + 1) |
|---|---|---|---|
| (EEC) | (1236) | (19) | (2.47) |
| 4. India | 558 | 9 | 5.48 (2.22) |
| 5. Japan | 536 | 8 | 1.04 |
| 6. GB | 421 | 6 | 1.27 |
| 7. West Germany | 411 | 6 | 1.02 |
| 8. Canada | 388 | 6 | 1.06 |
| 9. Poland | 352 | 5 | 1.10 |
| 10. Australia | 154 | 2 | 2.28 |

* Calculated by Anton Viehbeck from data in the *UN Statistical Yearbook 1948–78.*

same time, the Chinese People's Republic increased her power potential. Measured in terms of her resources, China became one in the top group of world powers in the 1960s, thereby creating the foundation of the pattern of tripolarity in the division of power potentials (below the level of nuclear strategy). If one takes the new power potential of the nine member states of the EEC as one unit, Western Europe ranks directly below the main powers. Neither does Japan belong to the group of Great Powers (because of its small population and low energy production), but, like India, she belongs to the medium-sized powers.

The essential features of our calculation are confirmed by the indices of power developed by Singer and his colleagues (1972) and by Hopkins and Mansbach (1973), using indices of population, urbanisation, use of energy, iron and steel production, military expenditure and military strength. These also show unipolarity in the first post-war phase, a reduction in the difference between the United States and the USSR in the periods following, and China's elevation to the group of Great Powers. However, the Hopkins –Hansbach index appears to be less realistic than that of Fucks. For example, for 1938 it puts the Soviet Union in first place above the United States, Germany, Great Britain, Japan, France and Italy and, furthermore, it identifies a tripolarity as early as 1955.

Cline (1977) arrives at a different result by employing a formula to estimate the *perceived* power of states or politico-geographical zones. In this formula the 'objective' data on population, acreage, production and military strength are subjectively evaluated and adjusted, added together and then multiplied by a factor 'calculated' from a subjective evaluation of strategic intentions and the decision to pursue a national strategy. Thus there emerges, not an index of actual power resources, but one of perceived power. Since perceptions elude quantification this method is dubious and its results are of limited value. For example, Cline arrives at the grotesque conclusion for 1977 that the total of territorial, population and economic factors puts the EEC (362 points) way ahead of the United States (274) and the USSR (205). The total of perceived power potentials, which includes all the factors mentioned above, apportions 618 points to the group of countries led by the USSR, thus ranking above the group of Western and North European countries — calculated at 558 points — followed by the North and Central American group with 523 power points. These perceptions of power are hardly generally accepted. Nevertheless Cline's study is useful in that it contains extensive statistics and lists of actual objective data on the economic and military spheres of individual countries. However, Fucks' formula is more useful for the construction of an index of the division of power resources, as it is limited to 'hard' quantifiable data, though nowadays performance in the field of microelectronics seems to be more important than steel production. A revision of the formula should be considered accordingly.

The rough guide derived from Fucks' formula can be clarified further when one looks at important individual elements of these potentials. As the nation-state system has remained essentially an anarchic self-help system, the allocation of military power potential was, and is, of the greatest importance. Military expenditure is usually chosen an indicator; however, it is precisely in this area that data are particularly inexact and inadequate. Even the otherwise reliable SIPRI (Stockholm International Peace Research Institute) Yearbooks often present different figures for individual countries and years — with many reservations because of the difficulties in evaluating currency and prices. The policy of concealment employed by governments often necessitates making guesses. Taking these lists of data as the basis, the hierarchies and quotients (calculated as described above, but not reported here in detail) present a somewhat modified picture of the development of polarity. A bipolar structure has existed in military expenditure from since the end of the Second World War — a bipolarity which was at first slightly tipped in the Soviet Union's favour, but which during the 1950s swung in favour of the United States. The Chinese People's Republic has also joined the group of Great Powers in this sphere, though not until the 1970s.

Whilst information on military expenditure is useful, that relating to the entry of countries to the club of nuclear powers is more reliable. After the United States (1945) and the USSR (1949), Great Britain (who had been America's junior partner ever since the war) undertook her first atomic test in 1952 followed by France in 1960, the People's Republic of China in 1964 (SIPRI Yearbook, 1972, p. 462) and India in 1974. Although the number of nuclear powers has increased to six and the danger of further growth exists, despite the Non-Proliferation Treaty of 1968 (see SIPRI Yearbook and Harald Müller, 1977), up to now there has been a change in the distribution of power only at the level of nuclear strategy (especially with the development of nuclear delivery systems) from unipolarity to bipolarity. The United States and the USSR, the two main parties in the East–West conflict, determine the global structure of power.

In order to identify changes in the imbalance during the dynamic development of this polarity it is necessary to concentrate not so much on a numerical comparison, but rather on the (anticipated) effectiveness of nuclear weapons and delivery systems. The decisive factor is the strategic capability to inflict unacceptable damage on an opponent. K. Goldmann has come to the following conclusion relating to the development of polarity based on this criterion of '(nuclear) strategic capabilities':

In the beginning the United States had a clear nuclear monopoly, but not a strategic capability (phase1); only in 1950–1 did the United States have a large stock of nuclear weapons at her disposal. By then Russia had successfully tested atomic weapons, but her nuclear potential was still insignificant, i.e. there was a period of American strategic monopoly in the mid 1950s (phase 2). The period that followed — up until the middle or end of the 1960s — was a transitional phase (phase 3) in which the Soviet Union increasingly gained the capability to attack America on her own territory and to inflict serious damage there. But during this period only the United States had sufficient second-strike capability, whilst the USSR was gradually working towards such a capability. It is hard to establish precisely when a balance of arms was achieved — when the transitional phase ended and symmetrical polarity was achieved at the strategic level. According to Goldmann (1974, p. 199) the conflicting opinions can be summarised as follows:

> . . . the number of operational Soviet ICBMs appears to have increased from less than 100 in 1962 to about 300 in 1966 (*The Military Balance 1972–1973*, p. 67). Until 1965 or 1966, however, only some of the Soviet ICBMs were put in hardened silos (Wolfe 1970, p. 433), whereas all the new SS-9 and SS-11 ICBMs that entered service in the latter half of the 1960s were protected in this way (Slocombe 1971, p. 5). Moreover, the Soviet Union lagged far behind the United States with respect to SLBMs as well. Apparently it was not until 1968 that Soviet submarines came so close to the United States that their missiles could reach targets there [ . . . ] ; the 'Y-class' ballistic missile submarines, the first Soviet ones roughly comparable to the Polaris system, did not begin to enter service until 1968–1969 (Slocombe, 1971, p. 5; *SIPRI Yearbook 1969/70*, pp. 368–75). One observer concludes from the available evidence that a sufficient second strike Soviet capability came into being some time between 1962 and 1966 (Slocombe, 1971, p. 1). Another observer maintains that the change did not occur before 1965, and that even this limit may be too early. [Secretary of Defense] Schlesinger said in early 1974 that the period 'in which the United States did retain close to a disarming capability against the Soviet Union and recognized it' prevailed 'into the latter 1960s'. (see also Gantzel, HSFK-Mitteilung No. 4)

These contradictory estimates are characteristic of the general uncertainty and instability of the transitional period. The SIPRI calculations (Yearbook, 1972, pp. 6 and 20) point to a later, rather than an earlier, date for the achievement of a strategic balance. Whatever the case may be, by the end of the 1960s at the latest, both sides possessed a second-strike capability (phase 4), and this situation of a bipolar strategic balance or strategic stability can be used to describe the international system up to the present day.

All other nuclear powers (China, Great Britain and France) have no, or only a very limited, strategic strike capability and certainly no second-strike capability. To this extent at the strategic level there is, as before, a bipolarity (see Fig. 7.1).

The discussion so far has concentrated on the global distribution of power within the international system. This has to be supplemented by a look at a different type of distribution of power potentials (polarity) in Europe, since in the power struggle between the Soviet Union and the United States, Europe was, and still is, of great importance.

The conspicuous characteristic of Europe at the end of the Second World War was the Soviet Union's predominance in terms of potential power — a superiority which has been essentially strengthened since that time. This conclusion is arrived at by the use of Fucks' formula to determine the index of power (Table 7.3).

Figure 7.1 *The five strategic nuclear powers, 1977*

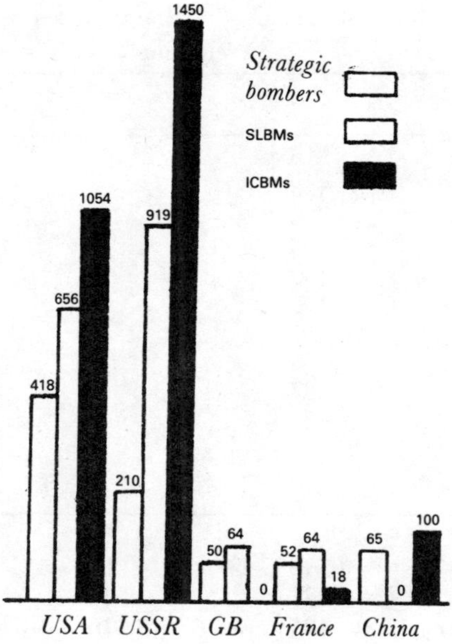


Source: Cline, 1977, p. 96.

Table 7.3 *European ranking according to power potential (Fucks' formula)**

| **1948** | Index | Standardised Weighting (USSR = 100) | $\frac{n}{n+1}$ |
|---|---|---|---|
| 1. USSR | 984 | 100 | |
| 2. GB | 419 | 43 | 2.35 |
| 3. West Germany | 216 | 22 | 1.94 |
| 4. Poland | 110 | 11 | 1.96 |
| 5. France | 94 | 10 | 1.18 |
| 6. Soviet Occupied Germany | 55 | 6 | 1.70 |
| 7. CSSR | 40 | 4 | 1.39 |
| 8. Belgium | 31 | 3 | 1.28 |
| 9. Spain | 19 | 2 | 1.67 |
| 10. Hungary | 15 | 2 | 1.26 |

Table 7.3 *Continued*

| | Index | Standardised Weighting (USSR = 100) | n / n + 1 |
|---|---|---|---|
| **1955** | | | |
| 1. USSR | 1916 | 100 | |
| 2. GB | 458 | 24 | 4.19 |
| 3. West Germany | 358 | 19 | 1.53 |
| 4. Poland | 156 | 8 | 2.30 |
| 5. France | 130 | 7 | 1.20 |
| 6. East Germany | 100 | 5 | 1.30 |
| 7. CSSR | 61 | 3 | 1.64 |
| 8. Rumania | 38 | 2 | 1.62 |
| 9. Belgium | 37 | 2 | 1.01 |
| 10. Italy | 31 | 2 | 1.22 |
| **1963** | | | |
| 1. USSR | 2698 | 100 | |
| (EEC) | (678) | (25) | (3.98) |
| 2. GB | 421 | 16 | 6.40 (1.61) |
| 3. West Germany | 421 | 16 | 1.00 |
| 4. Poland | 200 | 7 | 2.11 |
| 5. France | 149 | 6 | 1.34 |
| 6. East Germany | 105 | 4 | 1.43 |
| 7. CSSR | 98 | 4 | 1.07 |
| 8. Rumania | 58 | 2 | 1.71 |
| 9. Italy | 55 | 2 | 1.05 |
| 10. Spain | 31 | 1 | 1.77 |
| **1976** | | | |
| 1. USSR | 4797 | 100 | |
| (EEC) | (1236) | (21) | (4.69) |
| 2. GB | 421 | 7 | 13.76 (2.93) |
| 3. West Germany | 410 | 7 | 1.02 |
| 4. Poland | 352 | 6 | 1.17 |
| 5. Holland | 148 | 3 | 2.37 |
| 6. Rumania | 132 | 2 | 1.12 |
| 7. France | 128 | 2 | 1.03 |
| 8. CSSR | 122 | 2 | 1.05 |
| 9. East Germany | 110 | 2 | 1.10 |
| 10. Italy | 99 | 2 | 1.10 |

Calculated by Anton Viehbeck from data in *UN Statistical Yearbooks 1948–78.*

As Table 7.3 shows, the distribution of the power potential in Europe (even when the EEC is counted as one unit) is polarised at one extreme (unipolarity). The centre of power is the Euro-Asian USSR. Only American commitments in Europe helped, and help, to redress this imbalance. West European countries and the United States have employed, and employ, a policy of building up a balance of power in Europe which in the global framework is employed by the USSR to counteract American superiority.

The strategic balance, particularly in Europe, was and remains, dependent on an American policy of involvement. Whereas at first 'only' conventional Soviet military superiority in Europe was balanced by American commitments, the situation changed in the mid 1950s. At that time Russia had built up her nuclear potential to a point where, though still not having a second-strike capability, she was nevertheless in a position (according to estimates contained in the Gaither Report of 1957) to inflict tremendous damage on American territory — damage which was unacceptable to American despite her second-strike capability. This situation made it possible for the Soviet Union to hold Western Europe hostage:

> The Soviet Union could obviously inflict damage on Western Europe that would be considered to be unacceptable by Europeans, and it could obviously do so even after it had suffered a first strike from the United States. But would damage deemed unacceptable by West Europeans be deemed unacceptable by Americans? This question was the core of the great debate about the credibility of the United States commitment to the defense of Europe. (Goldmann, 1974, p. 197)

Once the international strategic situation had been stabilised by mutual second-strike capability, it became increasingly necessary to establish an American nuclear defence in Europe as a counterbalance to the Soviet Union's potential, since the British and French nuclear potential have no second-strike capability. This objective distribution of power explains the vital interest of the countries of Western Europe in a military and political alliance with the United States, not only during the Cold War, but also in the era of détente, which is characterised by a depolarisation in non-military spheres.

## Patterns of the Polarisation Process

Under the conditions of the unipolar distribution of power potentials, global East–West bipolarisation of countries occurred as a result of the unipolar division of power potentials during 1947–8 in the relations (interactions) between states, in the course of which this unipolarity was transformed into a bipolarity of power potentials. The bipolarisation of relations is the true characteristic of the Cold War, just as conversely the de-bipolarisation (subsequently referred to as simply 'depolarisation') in different spheres of action and relations — running parallel to continued bipolarity of strategic power potentials — characterises the phase of détente.

This process of polarisation in the international system and in Europe has best been described by Roger Wall (1975) and documented graphically and statistically for the three areas of policy in the formation of alliances trade and diplomatic relations.

Wall calculated the data on the degree of bipolarisation in the arena of policy in alliance-making with these indices: 0 = no alliances, 1 = neutrality or non-aggression pacts, 2 = mutual defence alliances not institutionalised by military collaboration and 3 = bilateral alliances or alliances for collective defence institutionalised by military collaboration. Trade relations were calculated — in simplified terms — by identifying the value of trade between individual countries and the two Super Powers and comparing the two. In addition to the degree to which the flow of trade is orientated towards one Super Power (uni-orientation), the degree of polar dependency of the individual countries (i.e. the relation between one country's trade with the Super Powers and its total trade) and the relative importance of the country (i.e. the percentage of its trade compared with world trade) were taken into account. (See Fig. 7.2.) By establishing the lowest value of the degree of polarisation at 0 and the highest at 100, Wall was able to draw polarisation curves for all three areas and to compare them (see also Väyrynen, 1977, p. 65). He thus provided a picture of polarisation tendencies, making it possible to see increases and decreases in polarisation. From an examination of the different phases and dimensions of polarisation in Europe significant variations become visible:

(1) The bipolarisation in the sphere of alliances is the central variable in the dynamic process of bipolarisation in Europe. However, this occurred later than in the global system — not until 1948.

(2) From 1948 onwards, bipolarisation in Europe in the sphere of trade increased, reaching its peak in 1950. However, by 1952 the depolarisation process had already begun in this sphere, and continued with occasional interruptions (1955–7, 1959, 1963–6).

Figure 7.2 *The international system*

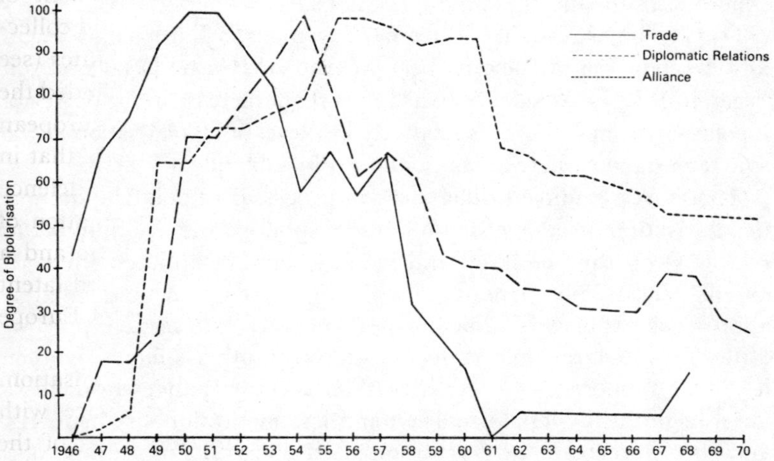


Figure 7.3 *European bipolarisation*

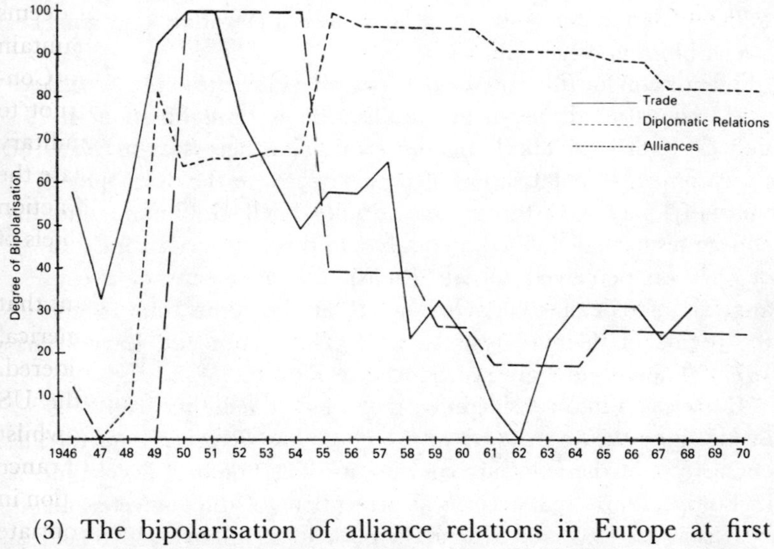


(3) The bipolarisation of alliance relations in Europe at first developed to a lesser degree than trade and diplomatic relations. Indeed the degree of polarisation in the formation of alliances decreased somewhat at the end of the 1940s, then only rose a little until it reached its peak in 1955. However, it subsequently remained at a high level, with a continuous, but relatively small, decrease,

whilst at the same time significant depolarisation occurred in the sphere of trade and diplomatic relations.

(4) The bipolarisation of diplomatic relations in Europe only began in 1950, but was to reach its peak in that same year. Depolarisation began in 1955 — a tendency halted by a slight increase in the degree of bipolarisation in 1965. This relatively low level of bipolarisation in the sphere of diplomatic relations continued in subsequent years.

There are significant differences in processes of polarisation and depolarisation in the economic-trade sphere (and in diplomatic relations) on the one hand and in the sphere of military alliances on the other. This demonstrates that bipolarisation or depolarisation in the sphere of alliances is in no way a necessary precondition for bipolarisation or depolarisation in other spheres. Rather it can be supposed — along with Wall — that changes in polarisation begin in the less formalised and less institutionalised spheres and then spread to the institutionalised spheres. For Europe one can say that the bipolarisation of alliances which stabilise defence policies is a precondition for depolarisation in other spheres of relations. The institutionalisation of regression in the sphere of military and defence policies facilitates integrative relations between blocs in other spheres.

The reason for this may be that perceived threats between antagonistic countries diminish as stabilisation is brought about by alliances. In order to check this supposition it is necessary to relate the development of polarisation in these spheres to the development of mutually perceived threats in Europe. Kjell Goldmann and his colleagues have dedicated themselves to this task, producing a range of data on perceived threats ('tensions') by means of a content analysis of official statements, while at the same time extending the period of their analysis to 1974 (Goldmann and Lagerkranz, 1977). Their results are reproduced in Figures 7.4–5.

If one takes into consideration that which the authors call 'tension' or 'détente' can be equated with high or low perceptions of threats, one arrives at the following conclusions: The graph of developments in Europe shows that reciprocal perceptions of threats were already increasing in 1947 and reached a peak in 1948. In 1948 bipolarisation began to intensify in military alliances and trade policies. In 1949 there was a slight fall in perceived threats which — following a brief rise in 1950 — became more distinct between 1951 and 1953, whilst the polarisation in the sphere of alliances at the same time remained relatively high until 1954–5 (i.e. just below the peak of

Figure 7.4 *European tension and military bipolarisation (standardised scores)*

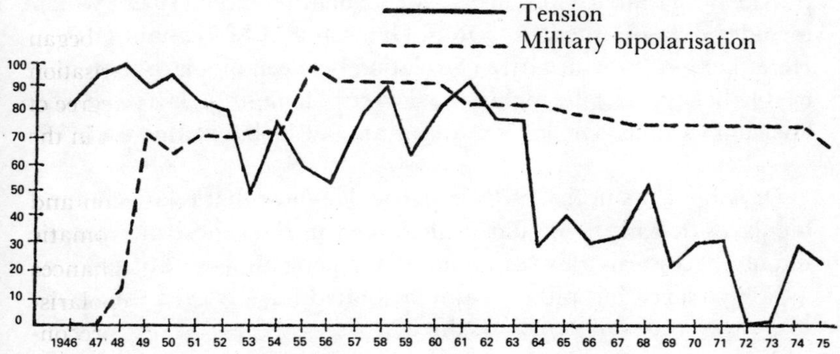


Figure 7.5 *European tension and economic bipolarisation (standardised scores)*

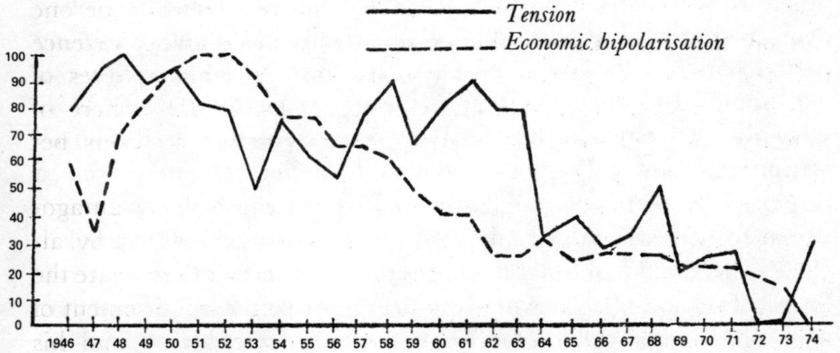


1948–9). Thus polarisation in the sphere of military alliance did not heighten the perception of threats in the first phase of the Cold War; rather the reverse might be argued; and the bipolarisation of defence policies facilitated the subsequent diminishing of perceived threats. The decade between 1954 and 1964 is characterised as one of periods of various changing combinations: heightened perceptions of threats with low degrees of bipolarisation and fewer perceived threats with a high degree of bipolarisation. This complex relationship points to the fact that bipolarisation in the military sphere and in the sphere of alliances could indeed heighten the perception of threats in the short term. If, however, after the crisis in defence policies the system is stabilised through alliances, the degree of perceived threats may decrease.

Additional evidence for the period between 1948 and 1963 is provided by Raimo Väyrynen's independent research (1973), which includes data on interaction from Gamson and Modigliani (1971). Here there is also a negative correlation between bipolarisation and hostile behaviour; 'the higher the degree of alliance polarization the less conflict behavior both in European and global setting and vice versa' (p. 164).

Developments in the 1970s in particular show that relatively high bipolarisation in the military sphere and in the sphere of alliances did not necessarily raise or maintain the perception of threats to, or at, a high level, but rather that it facilitated (or was even conducive to) a lower level of perceived threats.

As to the relation between polarisation or depolarisation in economic and trade policy and perceived threats, it has been argued that, for the period up to 1970, the two mutually reinforced each other. However, even during this period the two tendencies often developed in opposite directions — especially in the relatively long period between 1957 and 1963. An increase in perceived threats corresponded to depolarisation in the sphere of trade, whilst there were also phases when (e.g. 1951–2), conversely, increased bipolarisation in trade policy corresponded to a decrease in perceived threats. It is worthy of note that after 1970 perceived threats, which began to decrease in the mid 1960s, reached their lowest level in 1972, whereas the gradual depolarisation of trade did not reach its lowest level until 1974, when the degree of perceived threats had once again begun to increase. So it cannot be said that a spiral-like structure of reciprocal reinforcement existed. It follows that at the height of the Cold War a pattern of the development of the Cold War in Europe existed which was marked by a high degree of bipolarisation in all spheres of interaction (military alliances, trade and diplomatic relations) and a relatively high degree of perceived threats. In the transitional phase in Europe a tendency towards depolarisation set in (albeit often interrupted) in the sphere of trade and diplomatic relations, whilst the degree of bipolarisation in the sphere of alliance-making remained relatively high. Perceived threats developed in waves, the peaks reaching the level of bipolarisation in the sphere of alliances. The pattern of détente in Europe is characterised by the fact that only bipolarisation in the sphere of alliances remained at a relatively high level. Relations between blocs in the sphere of trade and diplomacy increased steadily and developed a greater intensity than before the Cold War. The perception of threats tended to diminish and reached its lowest level in 1972–3.

In contrast to this European pattern, in the international system depolarisation in the sphere of alliances corresponded roughly, and with a certain time-lag, to depolarisation in the sphere of trade and diplomatic relations. Since (as Wall has also established) the process of polarisation in Asia conforms to the *international* pattern, whilst in the Middle East in the 1960s a split occurred between polarisation in the sphere of alliances and polarisation in the sphere of trade policies along the lines of the *European* pattern, one should be careful not to treat one pattern as 'normal' and the other as a deviation. Neither should too great a value be placed on the statistical differences between the international and the European patterns. In the sphere of European alliances after 1956 a gradual depolarisation can also be identified which progressed slowly, but steadily (i.e. without the fluctuations that occurred in other spheres). Thus it can be said that developments in the international system and in Europe tended to follow the same direction, the only notable difference being between the levels of depolarisation in the sphere of alliances in the international system as a whole and in Europe. This arose because of an important event in 1961 — more precisely it was created by the fact that the advance of depolarisation between 1960 and 1961 was greater in the international system than in Europe. This statistical fact can be explained by two non-European events affecting depolarisation at the same time, — China's withdrawal from her alliance with the Soviet Union and the entry of many new African nations into the international system (without their entering into alliances). After this turning-point in 1961, a correlation is once more established between the gradual depolarisation of alliance relations in the international system and Europe. Depolarisation continued in both, albeit slowly and with small steps. Thus the comparison between the pattern in the international system and that in Europe is important in three aspects.

(1) At the height of the Cold War bipolarisation in the sphere of trade policy was greater than in the sphere of alliances both in the international system and in Europe.

(2) After 1953–4 bipolarisation in that area, both in the international system and in Europe, was greater than bipolarisation in trade policy which had started to decline. Since then the degree of bipolarisation in the sphere of alliances has remained higher than in the sphere of trade policies, both in the international system and in Europe.

(3) In the phase of détente depolarisation developed without changing these characteristics of the pattern, i.e. the degree of polarisation is still higher in the sphere of alliances than in the sphere of trade policies. The gradual depolarisation in the sphere of alliances internationally resulted from the decisive depolarisation brought about by the events of 1961 which had little or no connection with the conflict between the two poles of power. No similar abrupt and deep scission has occurred in the process of depolarisation in the sphere of alliances in Europe. There were hiccups as a result of France's withdrawal from the integrated military system of NATO (1966) and of the crumbling of the alliance between Greece and Turkey in South–eastern Europe (1974–5). Otherwise the pattern in Europe during the phase of détente is characterised by the fact that beneath a relatively stable and only gradually weakening bipolarisation in the sphere of alliances, relations between the systems increased and that, in contrast to the height of the Cold War, bipolarisation in the sphere of trade relations was essentially lower than in the sphere of alliance and defence relations both in the international system and in Europe. The regressive solution to conflict dominated European policies with regard to alliances, whilst in the non-military spheres integrative elements between blocs gained ground.

## The Relation between Bipolarisation and Bipolarity

It could be presumed that the reason for the greater stability in the patterns of polarisation in the sphere of alliances in Europe, despite the decrease (albeit fluctuating) of reciprocal perceptions of threats in the phase of détente, lay in the increase of Soviet Power, which in turn was reflected in the alliances formed between the European states. By comparing patterns of polarisation with the development of polarity based on power potentials (see above) the following picture emerges.

Universal bipolarisation during the Cold War occurred under conditions of international unipolarity (with the United States as the pole of power) and European unipolarity (with the Soviet Union as the pole of power). A balanced bipolar structure was only created in Europe by America's policy of stabilisation in Western Europe and by the Atlantic Alliance. A bipolarity of the power potential internationally emerged only when the Soviet Union's power grew; and then it developed into a strategic parity of both poles of power (symmetric bipolarity). This precarious balance would have been threatened by any fundamental depolarisation in the sphere of alliances in Europe. This substantiates the view, apparently held by the majority of governments in both the East and the West, that only a gradual and reciprocally balanced reduction of bipolarisation in the sphere of European alliances is compatible with European and international security. Without an American commitment in Europe strategic and political instability could be predicted — the more so since actual divergencies of interests between West European countries and the United States on the one hand and between East European countries and the Soviet Union on the other would continue. This is to say that an extensive integrative solution to conflict is, for the time being, an unrealistic goal.

The link between bipolarity and bipolarisation is also instructive on the level of the global nation-state system. The fact that once the war had ended there was first a unipolar allocation of power (including America's atomic and strategic monopoly) and then an unbalanced bipolarity was decisive in creating competition between the main antagonists in the East–West conflict. Russia strove to protect herself from American domination and then to rise to the position of a Great Power of equal status. The conflict of power politics and ideology, which reached crisis point from time to time (see below), led to the universal bipolarisation of East–West relations. The most dangerous expression of this conflict between the Super Powers was the so-called arms race, particularly in the area of nuclear weapons.

Such a statement of course neither says anything about who was, or is, the initiator, of and pace-maker in, the 'arms race' nor does it explain arms processes (see the summaries of Krell, 1976, and Forndran, 1977, pp. 146 ff). New analyses of correlation produced by R. Väyrynen (1973) have come up with no clear answer, but have corrected assumptions previously held.

One cannot discern just one side as actively and continuously initiating increases in military expenditure. However, it may be said that by a narrow margin the United States reacted to changes in military expenditure in the Soviet Union and the USSR played a slightly more important role in initiating expenditure (pp. 87 f.). In the nuclear sphere the United States clearly had the initiative — but the construction and explosion of the first atomic bomb took place within the context of the war against the Axis Powers and not in the context of the East–West conflict. Later series of tests show neither side as the initiator of a cycle of action and reaction; American initiatives in individual weapons' systems (strategic bombers, tactical nuclear weapons and MIRV technology) are contrasted with Soviet initiatives in other weapons (ICBM technology, ballistic-missile defence systems and fractional-orbiting bombardment systems).

The finding that growing political détente usually brought with it an increase, rather than a decrease, in efforts for arms is seen by Väyrynen as confirmation of the growing significance of domestic factors (p. 172).

Similarly, though for different reasons, the theory of 'autism' (Senghaas) or 'dual pole arms autism' (Gantzel, 1972b) emphasises the *Innenleitung* (i.e. the domestic determination) of the arms race. A domestic political basis for an arms policy is seen especially in the so-called military-industrial complex (see also Medick, 1975, and the ingenious criticism by K-Peter Stratmann, 1973). Other scholars dispute the fact that there *is* an arms race — at least in the latest phase of the development of strategic weapons. For example, Albert Wohlstetter (1974 and 1976) has shown that in the 1960s and 1970s the US budget for strategic weapons was considerably reduced (see Fig. 7.6). Wohlstetter argues that this development — the rapid rise of the American strategic budget after the Korean War and the fall in the 1960s and 1970s whilst the Soviet Union's strategic budget was rising continually — contradicts the thesis of a spiralling strategic arms race (see also the controversial documentation in nos. 16 and 20 of *Foreign Policy*).

None of these different interpretations contradicts the analysis of the development of polarisation sketched here, that the Soviet Union has pursued a policy of creating a counterbalance in power by increasing power both at home and abroad (and especially by increasing her potential strategic powers), whereas in Europe the United States has created a counterweight to Russia's superiority and otherwise aimed at asserting her supremacy throughout the world. Recently both sides, the Soviet Union and the United States, have officially acknowledged the principle of approximate balance; however, at the same time they have both actually shown a tendency to strive for superiority. Agreements to limit strategic weapons (see more on this below) try to regulate competition at the level of strategic parity. However, a freeze is not to be expected.

The dynamic link between bipolarity and bipolarisation in the

Figure 7.6 *The Combined US Strategic Offense and Defense Obligational Authority*

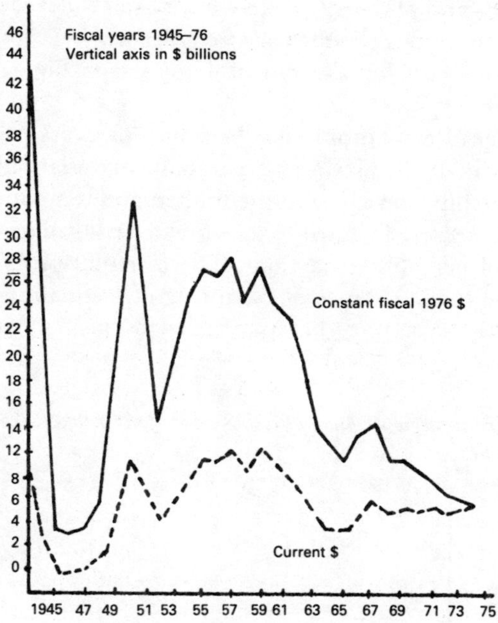


*Source*: Wohlstetter, 1976, p. 198.

East–West conflict confirms the main assumptions of the so-called balance-of-power theory (see Link, German edition, Ch. 1). In view of the sharp antagonisms, bipolarisation was an expected consequence of the distribution of power potentials between the main global contenders in the East–West conflict. It began after the unipolar allocation of power potentials in favour of the United States. Unipolarity was reduced and bipolarity created by Russia increasing her power to strike back both at home and abroad (i.e. by the creation of an opposite pole). The initial imbalance of this bipolarity was gradually reduced until a balanced bipolarity existed at the strategic level, characterising the phase of détente. The achievement of strategic parity has reduced the possibility of an 'open' conflict, i.e. of a military 'solution' to the East–West conflict. The balance of power potentials between East and West may have been an important, albeit an inadequate, precondition for the implementation of the policy of détente at the end of the 1960s and the beginning of the

1970s and ought to remain important for its continuation in the future (see Goldmann, 1974). The 'objective' reason for the crisis of détente at the end of the 1970s may have been the fact that calculations of relative strategic nuclear strength for the 1980s predicted a relative superiority for the Soviet Union (see Fig. 7.7; see also Collins, 1978).

The danger already prophesied by some observers (see Slocombe, 1971; Adomeit, 1973) now appears to have materialised — that the Soviet leadership, conscious of the limited and temporary superiority of the USSR, are inclined to take greater risks in order to extend the radius of her military actions. The essential problem in peace policy lies in the avoidance or balancing of inequalities in terms of strength without setting the spiral of arms production in motion (arms control).

Figure 7.7 *The strategic situation after US counterforce retaliation — day-to-day alert*

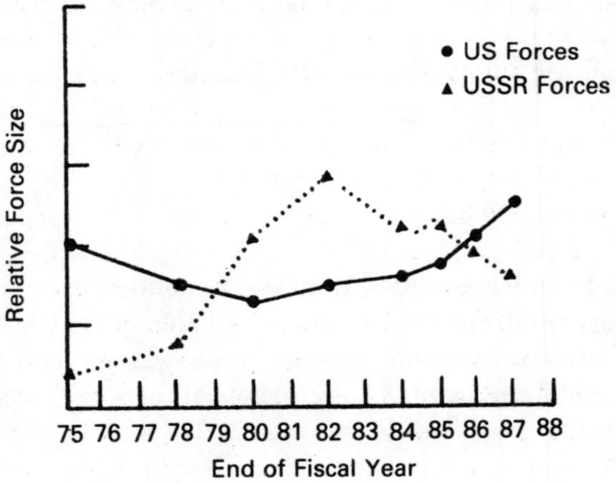


*Source*: US Secretary of Defense, Annual Report, Fiscal Year 1980, published in Ellsworth and Adelman, 1979, p. 150.

# 8 *The Development of Alliance Structures*

In view of the importance of the bipolarisation in the sphere of alliances in the development of the East–West conflict, it is necessary to take a closer look at these relations. Statistics and graphs reflect actual organisational decisions on policies taken from both global and regional perspectives of the East–West conflict. In the structuring of international relations after 1947, states were able to use the provisions of the UN Charter referred to above as a 'reserve security system', namely the right of collective self-defence (Article 51), and to combine this with provisions on regional organisations as well as the exceptions for regional arrangements directed against former enemy states (Article 53, § 1). Both the conclusion of alliances and the survival of the UN Organisation, that is to say its adaptation to the new structure, were facilitated by the fact that such reserve provisions were created in 1945 against the eventuality that co-operation between the Great Powers might fail.

As Figures 7.2–3 show, the tendency to conclude bipolar alliances was global. However, it found its most clear-cut expression in Europe. Uncertainty about the future internal order of societies and nations in Europe and about that between the European nations after the war, promoted competition between the Great Powers for influence which was subsequently regulated by a system of alliances and counteralliances (see Holsti *et al.*, 1973).

## Eastern Europe

In Eastern Europe alignment through the policy of allied blocs and the formal institutionalisation of Soviet hegemony and domination were at first expressed in a tightly woven net of bilateral treaties of friendship, co-operation and mutual assistance between the Soviet Union and Czechoslovakia (1943), Yugoslavia (1945), Poland (1945), Rumania (1948), Hungary and Bulgaria (1948) as well as between individual countries in Eastern Europe.

Political treaties were supplemented by agreements on economic and military aid and long-term trade agreements. At the same time political conformity was enforced internally — where necessary by methods similar to coups d'état ( as in February and March 1948 in Czechoslovakia). This network of agreements, adapted to altered circumstances in the 1960s and 1970s, formalised political and economic links with the hegemonic power, strengthened relations between members of the hegemonic sphere (an integrative solution to conflict), primarily with reference to territorial disputes (see, e.g., Czechoslovakia's border disputes with Poland and Hungary) and diminished relations with the West (regression of relations). Consequently, in the beginning, the formation of a Soviet bloc had a continental character. The globalisation of Soviet foreign policy was the result of co-operative agreements with seven Afro-Asian countries at the beginning of the 1970s (Meissner, 1979). The multilateral approach to treaties began in the economic sphere and was actually a reaction to the institutionalisation of economic co-operation in Western Europe (EEC) and to attempts at renationalisation, most clearly demonstrated by Yugoslavia's withdrawal from the Soviet sphere of domination (1948). In January 1949 the Council for Mutual Economic Aid (CMEA or Comecon) was set up by the Soviet Union, Poland, Czechoslovakia, Hungary, Rumania and Bulgaria (Albania joined CMEA in February, but was expelled in 1962 because of her pro-Chinese line. The German Democratic Republic became a member in 1950, Mongolia joined in 1962 and Yugoslavia has been a quasi-associate since 1964) (see Kaser, [2]1967; Uschakow 1971; Hoensch, 1977). The CMEA introduced co-ordination between the economies of Peoples' Democracies, which at the height of the Cold War was clearly undertaken from the point of view of arms-production policy and orientated towards the Soviet Union's hegemonic policy. The organisational conditions for institutionalised co-operation were created by charter only in 1960, in reaction to the founding of the EEC; and on this basis the 'development of socialist economic integration' was finally made operational in the 1970s with the enactment of the so-called Complex Programme (1971). This integrative development came up against considerable political and economic resistance (see Knirsch, 1972). It is, however (in contrast to the phase of autarky in the 1950s), linked with a principle of opening up trade with the West.

The most important characteristics of this new eco-political pattern are:

- intensified multilateral co-operation within CMEA;
- a rise in trade between some countries of CMEA with Western nations (see Knirsch, 1978);
- simultaneous globalisation (the accession of Cuba in 1972 and Vietnam in 1978 and co-operative agreements with Iraq, Mexico, Laos and Angola); and
- negotiations between CMEA and the EEC (see Schulz, 1975 and 1977).

In the end, economic integration has been hindered rather than helped by the Soviet Union's superiority and position of power (see Bräker, 1976).

In the military sphere it was not until the conclusion of the Warsaw Treaty on friendship, co-operation and mutual assistance between the USSR, Albania (who withdrew between 1962 and 1963), the German Democratic Republic, Poland, Rumania, Czechoslovakia and Hungary that Soviet hegemony was institutionalised multilaterally and extended by bilateral agreements on the stationing of troops. The Joint High Command (under the supreme command of the Soviet Union) and the Political Advisory Committee are the two organs of integration. The main aims of multilateralism were, and are, the integration of the military potential of the German Democratic Republic (in parallel to the Federal Republic of Germany joining NATO) and the formalisation of the Soviet Union's leading position in the East–West conflict. This process is correctly described through reference not to Article 53, § 1, but to Article 51 of the UN Charter. The regressive element in the Warsaw Treaty Organisation is most predominantly expressed in Article 7, whereby member countries undertook 'to participate in no coalition or alliance or to conclude no treaty whose aims conflict with those of the Pact.' The tremendous significance which multilateralism had for the Soviet Union as a means of securing her domination became clearly visible with the military intervention in Hungary in 1956 and in Czechoslovakia in 1968. This showed that the Soviet Union not only exercised a determining influence (hegemony) with the help of her military alliances, but also exercised domination (*Herrschaft*). The Brezhnev doctrine of the limited sovereignty of socialist countries (see Meissner, 1969) reflects this state of affairs.

In the phase of détente, direct bilateral negotiations between the USSR and the United States were of central importance. They are rooted in the common interest in arms control and in the non-proliferation of nuclear weapons. The respective treaty agreements have not created a condominium; nevertheless they have resulted in integrative links which modify regression between the two main antagonists in the East–West conflict. The Warsaw Treaty Organisation is the political instrument of the USSR for retaining control of these bi- and multilateral negotiations with the West and with NATO (CSCE and MBFR) and for avoiding the destabilisation of alliances — a policy threatened by tendencies towards renationalisation (see Meier, 1968; Bromke and Rokowska-Harmstome, 1973; Frenzke, 1975). Since 1969 the Soviet Union has sought to counter this tendency by reorganising the integrative structure of leadership (see Hacker, 1976; Tiedtke, 1978).

## Western Europe

In Western Europe it was Great Britain that first tried to organise co-operation between countries to counter the Soviet sphere of influence (see above). The Dunkirk Treaty of alliance and mutual assistance (1947) was primarily directed against Germany and was thus structured along the lines of the Anglo- and Franco-Soviet alliances of 1942 and 1944 (see Fraenkel, 1954). However, the Dunkirk Treaty was at the same time to serve to crystallize West European co-operation in the context of a growing East–West conflict. It therefore referred not only to the clause concerning enemy states in the UN Charter, but also to the right of collective self-defence (Article 51). Both countries agreed 'to enter no alliance and participate in no coalition directed against either of the two parties.' On Britain's initiative, the Dunkirk Treaty was extended regionally by the Brussels Five Power Convention 'for collective defence and economic, social and cultural co-operation' between Belgium, France, Luxemburg, the Netherlands and Great Britain along the lines of the Rio Treaty of March 1948, with explicit reference to the formation of blocs in Eastern Europe and the founding of the Cominform. It was openly acknowledged to be impossible to form an effective counterbalance to Soviet power without help from the United States, considering the political and economic weakness of West European states and the Soviet Union's superiority in Europe. The leading foreign-policy experts in America were already convinced of this in 1945 (see above). The domestic structure of preference in the United States (see Czempiel, 1966), i.e. the preference for economic relations and the rejection of a policy of military alliances, however, led to attempts to strengthen Western Europe in the economic sector. Secretary of State Marshall had already formulated an offer of American aid for Europe in 1947 and, following the predicted non-participation of the Soviet Union and the countries of Eastern Europe that were Soviet-dominated, this offer was given substance in joint and separate talks between the countries of Western Europe and the United States in a European Recovery Programme, the so-called Marshall Plan (see, e.g., Arkes, 1976). Whilst this policy can be described as traditional in its choice of means, it was highly innovative in its goals. In contrast to the rejection of economic co-operation in Europe between the wars, it aimed at the integration of Western Europe. In general — on analogy with the success of American federalism — European integration was seen as the only chance for the economic and political survival of the war-torn societies of Europe. European integration was especially designed to facilitate Germany's recovery, necessary for the economic health of Western Europe and, by integrating a democratic Germany firmly into a united Europe, at the same time to accommodate French security interests and to prevent the inclusion of Germany in the Soviet sphere of influence (see FR, 1948, II, 71; Link, 1977). Thus the new American policy towards Europe was determined both by general considerations of economic efficiency and by factors that could be ascribed to the East–West conflict.

The founding of the Organisation for European Economic Co-operation (OEEC) in April 1948 fulfilled the minimum demands of the Americans for the co-ordination of West European policy. Further steps towards integration were to follow. Although the United States was not a member of the OEEC, close economic and political links were established between the United States and Western Europe through the allocation of dollar credits, through deliveries of goods and above all through the 'joint decision-making' mechanism for the investment of ERP funds — links which could eventually form the basis of the military alliance (E. H. van der Beugel, 1966).

The founding of NATO (1949) by the United States, Canada and ten West European countries, joined by Greece and Turkey in 1952 and by the Federal Republic of Germany in 1955, was modelled (like the Brussels Pact) on the inter-American regional Treaty of Rio (1948) and followed the guidelines formulated in the Vandenberg Resolution (Senate resolution 239 of 11 June 1948) — namely to circumvent the right of veto of the Great Powers in the Security Council by using Article 51 for a 'progressive development of regional and other collective arrangements for individual and collective self-defence' with active participation by the United States (see Czempiel, 1966). That this regional alliance policy now included the whole Atlantic area was as innovative as the promotion of European integration through the Marshall Plan (when one considers that in the inter-war period the USA had totally rejected a policy of defence links with Europe). However, at the same time the formation of NATO created a latent contradiction between an Atlantic and a European concept (Calleo and Rowland, 1973). It remained latent at first because of the prevailing expectation that a united Europe would pursue a pro-American, Atlantic policy.

At the beginning, NATO had no integrated military organisation. Rather it was a multilateral alliance of mutual assistance with distinctly unilateral decision-making powers in the hands of the United States. Article 5 defined the duties of mutual assistance of member states in the event of an attack thus: 'each of them . . . will assist the Party or Parties so attacked by taking forthwith, individually and in concert with the other Parties, such action as it deems necessary, including the use of armed force, to restore and maintain the security of the North Atlantic area.' Influential forces in Congress and in the American Armed Forces felt it important not to equate the obligation of consultation with the obligation to military action. They feared that a less general formulation would create the danger of interference in America's 'freedom of planning and action with respect to global strategy' (Memorandum of the Joint Chiefs of Staff of 5 Jan. 1949, in FR, 1949, IV. 12).

The distinction between global and regional tasks also meant that from the outset France's desire for a tripartite leadership of America, Great Britain and France within NATO could not be considered. When justifying its need for freedom in decision-making, the US Administration emphasized its global commitments and, whilst conceding that Britain also had such commitments, regarded France primarily as a regional power. Consequently French participation in discussions of strategic global questions was seen as inappropriate (Memorandum of the Director of the Office of European Affairs of 17 Feb. 1949, in FR, 1949, IV. 121).

The transformation of NATO from a classic alliance into a new type of alliance, with jointly planned defence policies, progressed and was accelerated by the loss of China (1949), by the impact of the explosion of the first atomic bomb by the Soviet Union (September, 1949) and in particular by the outbreak of the Korean War (June 1950). This transformation (in which the unilateral elements in the central strategic sphere were not fully eliminated) was closely connected with the decision in September 1950 to rearm the Federal Republic of Germany and to integrate German armed forces (with or without the intermediary of a European army) into NATO whilst at the same time strengthening American ground forces in Europe and designating a Supreme Commander for NATO (see L. W. Martin, 1963, pp. 643ff.).

The American hegemonic position in the multilateral organisation was bolstered by a network of bilateral agreements with individual countries in Europe. From the viewpoint of self-confident European nations this was a necessary evil, tolerable as long as the hegemonic power possessing nuclear deterrents could not be hurt by its opponent in its own territory. This situation changed in the mid 1950s with the development of Soviet intercontinental weapons. New feelings of insecurity generated the debate over greater participation on the part of the countries of Europe within the Atlantic Alliance. The French plan for a tripartite directorate was revived, and its rejection was an important contributory factor to France's eventual withdrawal from military integration (1959–66).

Plans for a multilateral atomic strike force (MLF) failed, as did attempts to set up an independent European defence force (the Fouchet Plan) or to establish Franco-German relations as the basis for an independent European policy (through the Friendship Treaty of 1963). President Kennedy's 'grand design' — the idea of an equal partnership between the United States and Western Europe — was a castle in the air, since its realisation depended on the political unification of Western Europe (see Stanley Hoffmann, 1968).

Despite repeated differences of opinion, the alliance remained relatively stable. The hegemonic power — as an outside élite — promoted the founding of the ECSC (1951) and the EEC as well as Euratom in 1957 (see Etzioni, 1965; and Link, 1972). As the European Community grew stronger and larger, some tensions arose between Atlantic co-operation and European integration which became increasingly relevant within the sphere of economic and trade policies (see the Chicken War and the controversies within GATT) and — following the establishment of European Political Co-operation (1970) — also in the traditional areas of foreign policy. The alliance was not broken up by this, but rather adapted itself.

Meanwhile a dual structure can be discerned in European – American relations which is only blurred by the fact that the countries of Western Europe still remain dependent on the protection of America's nuclear strategy. The Atlantic Alliance balanced the Soviet Union's superiority in Europe, not only facilitating a stabilisation and the beginning of détente in Europe (parallel to corresponding bilateral negotiations between the two hegemonic powers), but actively pursuing this (see the Harmel Report and the Reykjavik Signal; see, amongst others, Haftendorn, 1974). Negotiations between the two military alliances and between the European Community and the Council for Mutual Economic Aid, as well as the strengthening of economic relations between the countries of the West and East, took place despite the central function of stabilisation which now, as before, is exercised by antagonistic alliances and groupings within the context of the East–West conflict.

By 1955 Europe had been stabilised by fully-fledged reciprocal regression, i.e. through a system of alliances and counter-alliances. The superiority of the Soviet Union had been balanced by America's commitments. This new situation created a short phase of détente (semi-détente) during which the neutralisation of Austria was mutually agreed, creating a buffer zone between the two spheres of influence along a stretch of the demarcation line. Conversely, there was still a clear American superiority in the global international system. The Soviet Union could no longer hope to counter the United States' international superiority by extending her influence in Europe, because the demarcation and stabilisation of both spheres of influence in the European region, had been completed. Subsequently competition between the Great Powers was intensified in those regions where stabilisation and demarcation had been less successful.

## Areas Outside Europe

Since the beginning of the Cold War the United States had likewise tried to arrange a reserve security system under its own leadership in areas outside Europe by combining multilateral and bilateral treaties on the basis of Article 51 of the UN Charter, thus organising American hegemony to restrain Soviet influence in place of the collective hegemony of the Great Powers. At the height of the Cold War the leading document on American global policy, NSC-68

(April 1950), very clearly described the global role for which the United States strove in the bipolar system: the United States figured as the centre of power and leadership in the free world with non-Communist countries grouped around her (Etzold and Gaddis, 1978, pp. 385 ff.). As in Europe, the United States favoured the conclusion of multilateral alliances in other regions.

The inter-American treaty on mutual assistance (the Rio Treaty) of 1948 and the Organisation of American States (OAS) of 1948, which was built into the Rio Treaty, was to stabilise Latin America. The Anzus Treaty of 1951 and the South East Asian Treaty Organisation (SEATO) of 1954 were the collective organisations in the Pacific; and the Baghdad Pact (1955), dominated by Great Britain, which was transformed into the Cento-Pact when Iraq withdrew in 1959, included Turkey, Iran and Pakistan and was linked to a system of security agreements between these countries and the United States.

Amongst the many American bilateral treaties the defence pacts with the Philippines (1951), with Japan (1951–2 and 1960), with Israel (1952), with South Korea (1953) and with Taiwan (1954) are particularly worth mentioning.

These multilateral non-European alliances could not, of course, either be protected from erosion or even be 'NATO-ised'. Even in the American *traditional* sphere of influence, Central and South America, the Soviet Union gained a political ally in Cuba. Independent groupings developed (as late as the founding of SELA) which fought for greater independence from the hegemonic power of North America. In countries in Asia and Africa anti-colonial, national liberation movements and social revolutionary groups joined together, making the integration of these countries into a system of alliances orientated towards the East–West conflict difficult, if not impossible. The concept of non-alignment was increasingly pursued in Asia and by the new nations in Africa, who founded the Organisation of African Unity (OAU) in 1963, partly in order to rebuff attempts by the Great Powers to exercise their influence. With the Bandung Conference of 1955 (see Kahin, 1956; Sasse, 1958) the development of loose organisations of the so-called Third World began, which eventually led to the formation of groups of developing nations in the United Nations in the 1960s thus creating the organisational conditions for the politicisation of the conflicting relations between industrial nations and developing countries. The North–South conflict was superimposed on the East–West conflict (see below, Chapter II). Thus America's policy of organising these regions into alliances multilaterally under the banner of the East–West conflict became obsolete — as was demonstrated most clearly by the withdrawal from South Vietnam (1975) and the break up of SEATO in 1977. This, however, clearly did not end competition to secure or to extend influence between the two main powers and between them and the newly developing Great Powers of China. On the contrary, the Soviet Union reinforced her policy of gaining global influence — after achieving parity with the United States — in areas outside Europe using both her own means of power (the Red Navy, the provision of arms and military instructors) and with the help of her allies (e.g. Cuba), in a struggle not only with the United States, but also with China.

The rise of China as a third centre of power (see above) and the withdrawal of this rising power from the Soviet alliance system was the most important change in alliance politics at the beginning of the 1960s.

The differences in ideology and power politics which were partly visible as early as the second half of the 1950s led to open conflict between the Soviet Union and China in the summer of 1960, manifested in the withdrawal of Soviet experts from China and the first major incidents on the Sino-Soviet border. According to Chinese figures, over 4,000 border incidents ensued, eventually escalating in 1969 to the Ussuri Conflict which came to the brink of a nuclear war. (For the international legal and political dimensions of the border conflict and an explanation of Chinese demands for a return of those areas annexed in violation of the Sino-Soviet treaties, see amongs others, Chiu, 1972; Hinton, [2]1972; Heinzig, 1979).

The evolution of an independent Chinese foreign policy, which since the 1970s has attempted primarily to provide a counterbalance against the power of the Soviet Union, produced a new pattern of relations, most apparent in the sphere of trade policy, namely the regression of Sino-Soviet relations and the intensification of relations with 'intermediate zone' countries, predominantly Japan, the countries of Western Europe and Australia (see Holsti *et al.*, 1972, and below, pp. 160–2 on the concept of intermediate zones). In parallel to this, closer relations were sought with the United States, whilst at the same time China became a stronger competitor for influence in the Third World (see DGAP, 1975; Rubinstein, [2]1976; Hsüeh, 1977; Kim, 1979).

The policy of bilateral alliances in areas outside Europe (as opposed to the multilateralism of the past) became the most important structural element in the competition between the Great Powers. At the same time, outside this three-cornered struggle between the Great Powers, multilateral groups came into being in some regions and influenced structures: the Organisation of African Unity (OAU) (see Woronoff, 1970) and the Economic Community of West African States (ECOWAS) (see Onwuka, 1980), the Association of South East Asian Nations (ASEAN) (see Dauth, 1979) and the Economic System of Latin America (SELA) (see Mols, 1978). The relatively simple structure of bipolar alliances of the Cold War period had developed into a much more complex structure which is reflected not only in regional divergencies, but also in differences between forms of action and of relations within each region.

# 9 *The Concretisation of East–West Conflict in Crises*

## *The Behavioural Pattern of Crisis Politics of the Two Super Powers*

Both Great Powers, the United States and the USSR, tried to regulate their conflicting policies of power and order by bloc politics (alliances) and other regressive measures. But this could not and cannot rule out the danger that conflict — intentional or not — could result in war. This danger existed and exists, now as then, if the East–West conflict (a) manifests itself in local or regional crises or (b) is linked with local or regional crises which culminate in an international crisis (for the definition of crises see Phil Williams, 1976, p. 25). The conflict potential, from which both sorts of conflict could develop, was substantial after 1945 — not least because of social upheavals in new nation states. Robert L. Butterworth has identified a total of 247 conflicts of significance to inter-state security policies in the period from 1945 to 1974; of these indeed only 48 (*c.* 19 per cent) were directly and primarily linked with the Cold War, i.e. were disputes between Communist and non-Communist tendencies or groupings. Nevertheless, it is true to say that in many cases there were indirectly mediated links with the East–West conflict. On the one hand, the inclination of one party in a local-regional conflict to ask a Great Power for assistance evokes similar calls for help from the other party to the antogonistic Great Power. On the other hand, the Great Powers tended to use such local conflicts to maintain, or to extend, their own influence, or at least to prevent any increase in the influence of the antagonistic Great Power. Not only the Great Powers, but also medium-sized powers participated in this global struggle for influence; competitive and conflict-orientated disturbances are the order of the day under the conditions of the existing international state system (see Spiegel, 1972, pp. 156 ff.). And the two Great Powers play a large part in these disturbances because of their position of power and their enormous resources. Through their actions they often create a link between local regional conflicts and the East–West conflict; so that the tendency to culminate in a crisis is often heightened. The most serious cases of this development have been the Indo-Chinese and Vietnam War, the Middle East conflict and its warlike escalations, conflicts between India and Pakistan (1965 and 1971) and a series of conflicts in Africa (from the Congo crisis to the conflicts between Somalia and Ethiopia).

The Indo-Chinese Vietnam conflict, the course of which will not be traced here (see the summary and bibliography of K. M. Kreis, in W. Woyke, 1977, pp. 325ff.), began as a regional manifestation of the global tendency towards decolonialisation. It was only transformed into the co-ordinated system of an East–West conflict by the alliance between the Vietnam national revolutionary liberation movement with the socialist countries of the USSR and the People's Republic of China and by American support for French imperial policy at the height of the Cold War. Attempts to find an agreement were specifically undertaken during phases of East–West détente. The first attempt arose out of the Geneva Indo-China Conference (May–June 1954). The truce set a temporary division of North and South Vietnam along the 17th Parallel and general elections for the whole country in 1956. This mixed regressive-integrative policy failed just like the semi-détente (1954–5) on which it rested. The conflict became increasingly violent in the 1960s: on the one hand through North Vietnam's progressive infiltration of South Vietnam which went as far as the dispatch of combat teams, and on the other through massive military support from the United States to South Vietnam with weapons and military personnel (540,500 soldiers in 1969) which went as far as a the bombardment and naval blockade of North Vietnam and the extension of military activities to Laos and Combodia. Active support from the USSR and the People's Republic of China was limited to supplying arms. The readiness to take risks remained surprisingly low in both countries. When, at the beginning of the 1970s, the policy of détente was implemented in Soviet-American and Sino-American relations, despite the escalation of the Vietnam War, a negotiated settlement was made possible. The Paris Agreement of 1973 allowed the Americans to withdraw from a hopeless commitment, but was unable to prevent the Vietnamese Communists from eventually securing domination over the whole of Vietnam by force (1975–6). At the same time the Communists assumed power in Laos and Cambodia. The culmination of Sino-Soviet competition in this region, the opposing power politics of the Association of South East Asian Nations (ASEAN), the 'low profile' of the American presence (the Nixon Doctrine) and Japan's increasing influence characterise the new political situation in South East Asia, which, less than ever before, provides a direct expression of the East–West conflict.

The Middle East conflict also began under the conditions of decolonialisation, particularly with regard to the erosion of the British Empire. The founding of the state of Israel after the departure of the mandate powers (1948) and the struggle of Arab nations and Palestinians against this state transformed the long-standing conflict between Jews and Arabs into a conflict between nations, but did not directly link this to the Cold War. The struggle between the two main antagonists of the East–West conflict reached the Middle East only relatively late and only then — after 1954–5 — essentially dominated the conflict there, especially after the failure of the Franco-British-Israeli Suez adventure of 1956, (see the survey and bibliography of R. Robert in W. Woyke, 1977, pp. 230–5). When the Israeli-Arab conflict reached its climax in war, both Super Powers were careful that support for their current clients should not escalate to a direct American-Soviet confrontation. The United States and the USSR have repeatedly and successfully practised crisis management and the limitation of wars, but, despite some attempts (e.g. the Geneva Middle East Peace Conference), they have not pursued a joint peace policy. Moreover, the United States has tried to establish peace in the Middle East without the co-operation of the USSR. Building on the partial success of Kissinger's diplomacy and following President Sadat's definitive volte-face, a separate peace treaty between Egypt and Israel was concluded (26 March 1979) with the help of American mediation (Camp David, September 1978). This has, however, heightened the conflict between Israel and opposing countries supported by the Soviet Union. The central role played by the Palestinian problem in the Arab-Israeli conflict shows on the one hand that the Middle East conflict, despite links between conflicting regional and global parties, is not a manifestation of the East–West conflict. On the other hand, in view of the commitments of both the United States and the USSR in this region, a peaceful solution to the Middle East conflict is conceivable only within the framework of an understanding between the two contenders in the East–West conflict. Until then there is always a latent danger that the failure of regional crisis management could lead to a direct clash between America and the Soviet Union.

For the global system the most dangerous crises were, and are, those in which the main antagonists of the East–West conflict are the original parties to conflict and clash directly with each other. Four such crises indicate the peak of the Cold War (see Bergeron's graph, 1971, p. 208):

(a) the Blockade of Berlin (1948–9);
(b) the Korean War (1950–3);
(c) the Berlin Crisis (1958–61); and
(d) the Cuban Crisis (1962).

The asymmetrical bipolarity of the international system and the strategic nuclear superiority of one Great Power (the United States) had at this time provided the framework for crisis behaviour (Snyder and Diesing, 1977, pp. 419 ff.). Under the conditions of nuclear deterrence it was irrational to escalate crises or local regional wars to the point of war between the Great Powers; the expected price had become unacceptable. Despite this, in the four crises mentioned above, we have seen a transformation from a risk of crises to a risk of war. The USSR and the United States began to compete in the escalation of the readiness to take risks (Adomeit, 1973, p. 5). Thus American-Soviet crisis management has acquired a central significance. It aimed, and aims, at preventing the outbreak of war or at limiting warlike disputes geographically as well as in choice of goals and the use of means. Put in a nutshell, crisis management (and not the crisis itself, as Glenn Snyder mistakenly formulated, 1972, p. 220) has replaced war between the Great Powers as the manner of solving conflict in the nuclear era and has attained a 'surrogate function' in determining the East–West conflict.

The pattern of the crisis policies of the United States and the USSR has been elaborated in particular in the works of P. C. Fielder (1969), Adomeit (1973) and Phil Williams (1976) (for a theoretical discussion see Thomas C. Schelling, 1960); and the four critical peaks of the Cold War have been sufficiently clarified in many studies to allow a comprehensive evaluation. In all cases the Soviet Union tried to extend her influence beyond the demarcation lines created at the end of the War, whilst the United States resisted this and successfully pursued the maintenance and restoration of the status quo. The crises escalated to the very brink of a direct war between the United States and the Soviet Union, but not beyond.

(a) In the *Berlin Blockade* (1948–9) the Soviet Union used the fiction that 'technical difficulties' were responsible for the breakdown of the Berlin Corridor overland. The United States, as well as Great Britain and France, did not attempt to enforce the overland corridor by military means; instead they reacted by operating the air-lift, which in turn was tolerated by the Soviet Union. The Jessup–Malik agreement essentially re-established the status quo ante.

(b) The *Korean War* (1950–3) was undoubtedly caused with the support and approval of the Soviet Union (see Kalicki, 1975, pp. 25–31), without, however, using her own troops; and the People's Republic of China participated in the struggle (through what were officially described as 'voluntary groups'), only when UN troops, under the American Supreme Command, crossed the demarcation line between North and South Korea (the 39th parallel) and approached the Chinese border. The United States on her side held to the fiction that the UN was the real protagonist and avoided both extending the war into Chinese territory and the use of tactical nuclear weapons (although such threats were made in the spring of 1953 during attempts to establish a cease-fire along the old demarcation line). The war remained limited and likewise ended essentially with the restoration of the status quo ante through the cease-fire agreement of 27 July 1953.

(c) The *Second Berlin Crisis* 1958–61, which began in November 1958 with a Soviet ultimatum demanding the withdrawal of the Western occupying powers and the transformation of West Berlin into a 'free city', escalated in the summer of 1961. Both sides were seriously prepared to risk war; the construction of the Wall (13 August 1961), aimed primarily at halting the flow of refugees, violated the four-power status of the whole of Berlin. The Western Powers refrained from the use of force to remove the wall, but at the same time demonstrated that they were determined to retain their right of access and presence by strengthening their contingents of troops. The presence of the Western allies in Berlin and, with them, the freedom of West Berlin was retained (as well as the West's legal position with respect to the whole of Berlin).

(d) The *Cuban Crisis* (1962), as is well known, brought the most dangerous escalation of the East–West conflict to the very brink of a nuclear war. It was preceded by the extension of Soviet influence through its support for the Castro regime, against which the United States had intervened only indirectly and unsuccessfully (by supporting the Bay of Pigs invasion undertaken by exiled Cubans in April 1961). The decisive act of escalation on the part of the Soviet Union, the secret installation of missile sites on Cuba, was answered by the United States with a naval blockade and the demand for the dismantling of launch pads and withdrawal of the missiles (22

October 1962). The alternative — the destruction of the missile sites, by an American attack — was rejected and the first sign that the Soviet Union was prepared to be reasonable (Khruschev's letter to Kennedy of 26 October) was eagerly seized upon, although an American reconnaissance aircraft was shot down over Cuba the following day. The crisis ended with an agreement on the withdrawal of Soviet missiles in return for an American renunciation of any invasion of Cuba, so that in this case the status quo was also essentially restored. The dismantling of obsolete US missiles in Europe followed a year later and was not part of the official agreement on Cuba (see the exchange of letters between Kennedy and Khruschev published in *Department of State Bulletin*, 19 Nov. 1973, pp. 635-55).

In all four cases the probability of a world war was relatively high. However, the Soviet Union presumably took the initiative in forcing these crises since she initially thought that the risk of war was small.

In 1948 Western democracies (including the United States) were marked by tendencies which, in view of the abnormal geographical position of Berlin, took into consideration a 'straightening of the front line' in order to avoid a military dispute with the Soviet Union in the territory of the former common enemy. In 1949–50 South Korea, after the withdrawal of the occupying forces, was not explicitly included within the American defence perimeter in public statements from General MacArthur and Secretary of State Acheson (Halle, 1967, p. 206) so that the probability of a direct military confrontation with the United States was seen by the Communists to be slight (Kalicki, 1975, pp. 20 ff.). The Soviet Union interpreted the reaction to her ultimatum in November 1958 as signifying that the Western guarantee covered only West Berlin and that a unilateral transfer of Soviet rights in Berlin, or the right of control over the corridor to Berlin to the German Democratic Republic would be treated pragmatically (see the so-called 'Agent' concept of Secretary of State Dulles). Finally the transformation of Cuba into a political ally of the Soviet Union without any decisive resistance allowed the Soviet Union to presume that the development of Cuba as a military base would be possible without risking a nuclear war. (There is no reliable information on the motives and aims that led Khruschev to station medium-range missiles in Cuba. The most probable explanation is that he wanted to counteract American superiority in intercontinental missiles; see Quester, 1970, pp. 233 ff.; Ruehl, 1974, pp. 77 ff.; Allison, 1971.)

Thus in these four crises the Soviet Union had probably calculated the risk as lying below the level of a world war and, when this proved to be false in view of American resistance, corrected her policy in order to avoid over-stepping this level. Conversely the United States also strove to act below this level in her response to the Soviet escalation of crises, and sought to make it easier for the USSR to correct her course. A similar pattern emerged in Sino-American attitudes to war in the 1950s in Korea, Indochina and the Formosa Strait (see Kalicki, 1975).

In this way — as Fielder, Williams and Kaiser concluded independently — cumulative 'behavioural norms' or 'rules' were established and observed on both sides, namely:

to minimise the means of action, i.e. initially to use very tempered means;

to keep open a line of retreat for the opponent and not present the alternatives of 'total war or total capitulation';

not to increase tension beyond a reasonable and controllable limit and to respect the vital interests of the opponent.

Obviously these informal norms of behaviour — as stressed incidentally by Phil Williams (1976, p. 200) — are little more than traditional basic rules of wise diplomacy and statesmanship. However, it is instructive that, contrary to popular opinion, they were carefully observed even during the Cold War. The experience of the threat of war and of joint crisis management promoted the insight amongst the main contenders that, despite insurmountable contradictions, they have a common interest in overcoming and de-escalating crises. In this respect the Cuban crisis of October 1962 is a turning-point — certainly not (as Fielder, 1969, p. 504, has so accurately formulated) because a new technique of crisis management was used (the management of the crisis was indeed very similar to the control exercised in previous crises). The real significance of the Cuban crisis lay in the fact that crisis control came within a whisker of failing. The course of the crisis made both sides aware of the dangers of escalation and of how little room there was for diplomatic error, so that in future neither the Soviet Union nor the United States ran such high risks of escalation. 'It was the political consequences, and not the way the issue was handled, that were important' (P. C. Fielder, 1969, p. 504).

It was not a 'plan', but a political method, that promoted the further development of crisis management and initiated serious negotiations over concrete agreements to avoid confrontation and crises. The policy of a gradual de-escalation in the East–West conflict, introduced by President Kennedy in conjunction with the Soviet Premier and Secretary General Khruschev in the summer of 1963, corresponded to the strategy of gradualism (see Link, German edition, Part 1), the principles of which had already been published by Charles Osgood in 1960 and which were familiar to both Kennedy and his advisers on foreign policy.

The starting-point and impulse of the so-called Kennedy experiment (Etzioni, $^{2}$1970) was the President's speech on the subject of peace to the American University in Washington DC on 10 June 1963.

Kennedy called not only on the Soviet Union, but explicitly on the United States too — his own country and his own citizens — to examine closely their existing attitudes towards the Cold War and towards securing peace and freedom as well as each county's attitude towards the other, and to change them, 'not to see only a distorted and desperate view of the other side, not to see conflict as inevitable, accomodation as impossible, and communication as nothing more than an exchange of threats.' Despite all the differences, both sides had a 'mutually deep interest' in a just and genuine peace which had to be pursued consistently by 'a series of concrete actions and effective agreements which are in the interest of all concerned'. Finally, the President made it known that the (hitherto unsuccessful) Three Power Talks on efforts to suspend the testing of nuclear weapons would shortly be resumed in Moscow, and stated — in a gesture of goodwill — 'that the United States does not propose to conduct nuclear tests in the atmosphere so long as other states do not do so.'

It was unusual and remarkable that this speech was published in full in the Soviet press and thus made known to millions of Soviet citizens. At the time Khruschev welcomed Kennedy's initiative, in a speech and an interview, and gave notice — to a certain extent as a reciprocal gesture — that the production of strategic bombers would be halted. There followed a process of reciprocal gestures and acts of détente which covered the most diverse problem areas:

the conclusion of an agreement (5 August) partially banning atomic testing and its swift ratification by the US Senate while the hearings led to a remarkable mobilisation of Americans in favour of a policy of understanding (81 per cent); an understanding not to station nuclear weapons in space (UN resolution of 19 October);

an agreement (20 June) on establishing a 'hot line' between the centres of government in America and the Soviet Union;

the Soviet Union's renunciation of preventing UN observers from visiting the Yemen and the American renunciation of blocking the readmission of the Hungarian delegation to the UN; and finally

American approval of the sale of wheat, valued at $65 million, to the Soviet Union.

The results were modest, but, they did not have a merely symbolic character. Seen in context (see Etzioni, [2]1970), they confirmed the usefulness of gradualism as a strategy to introduce de-escalation into the East–West conflict. The various domestic, political and international factors which may have caused this process of semi-détente to stagnate have been discussed extensively (see Etzioni, 1968, pp. 160 ff.; Groten, 1977). Because the deliberations of the Soviet leadership are unknown, resistance within America has usually been exaggerated. The fact that the United States at this time still possessed a strategic superiority (see Slocombe, 1971) and that the Soviet Union — contrary to Kennedy's assumptions (see Sorenson, 1966, p. 720) — was not prepared to accept this may well have been more important than internal factors. The process of détente received a new impulse under Kennedy and under Khruschev's successors — after approximate strategic equality had been achieved, and in this context the gradualistic strategy was again used. In the light of this development, hasty judgments are put into perspective. The gradualist presumption that relatively more flexibility is possible within the existing status quo, which has been dismissed as 'short-sighted' by the critical school of peace research (Senghaas, 1969, p. 287), has generally been confirmed, rather than disproved, by the approach of the Nixon–Kissinger Administration (including the fundamental change in Sino-American relations). The breakthrough towards détente did not occur, however, until the Soviet Union was clearly in actual possession of a second-strike capability (see above, Chap. 7, Eastern Europe).

As a provisional summary, it may be said that the Cuban crisis stimulated efforts to defuse regressive conflict regulation (mutual bloc building) by crisis management and to link this with elements of integrative and co-operative conflict regulation (through negotiations and agreements between the blocs, in the sense of antagonistic co-operation). There were earlier and sporadic signs of détente in the Austrian State Treaty (1954–5), at the Geneva Four Power Conference (1955) and at the meeting between Eisenhower and Khrushchev at Camp David (1959). However, the Kennedy experiment was the first attempt at systematic implementation of détente which was subsequently developed further, despite all interruptions. At first, starting with the agreements concluded in the summer of 1963 (e.g. the setting up of the Hot Line and its extensive use during the Arab–Israeli Six Day War in 1967), crisis management was extended informally to a policy of crisis avoidance. Then, linked with the agreement on nuclear policy of 1963 (the Nuclear Test Ban Treaty), regulations on the avoidance of confrontation and crises and on co-operative arms control were negotiated (on this last point see Ch. 10 below).

The informal consolidation of rules governing crises can be identified with two tendencies — as Fiedler (1969) and Buchan (1974), amongst others, have done:

(1) The respect for mutual clearly defined spheres of interest which had determined the behaviour both of the Soviet Union (e.g. at the time of the overthrow of the Arbentz government in Guatemala in 1954) and of the United States (e.g. at the time of military intervention in Hungary in 1956) was henceforward considered to be beneficial. It was more widely held that this policy contributed to a stabilisation in relations and to that extent should be welcomed. The admission of the Hungarian delegation to the UN in 1963 and the fact that the intervention of the USSR and her allies in Czechoslovakia in 1968 led to no more than a short interruption of the US–Soviet arms-control negotiations can be seen as clear indicators of this development. Three years earlier in 1965 the Soviet Union had tolerated American intervention in the Dominican Republic. Finally, in the preliminary stages of the CSCE, the Soviet Union refrained from linking the process of détente in Europe with attempts to oust the United States from Europe. The Helsinki Conference and subsequent conferences give documentary evidence that, on the one hand, the United States is recognised as a component of a stable regional system in Europe, and that, on the other the territorial status quo in Central and Eastern Europe is no longer called into question. The so-called Sonnenfeldt Doctrine indicates that even the Nixon–Ford Administration appreciated true 'organic' political stability in Eastern Europe; 'unorganic, unnatural relations' which rest only on pure military power, were seen as a greater threat to world peace than the East–West conflict (statement of the former Counselor to the US Secretary of State Kissinger at a conference of Ambassadors in London, summarised in a memorandum of 12 February 1976). However, this evaluation was, and

is, highly contentious (see US Congress, United States National Security Policy, 1976).

(2) In regions not clearly aligned, the tendency towards competitive involvements remained but was modified and mitigated by an opposing tendency in the 1960s. That is to say, on both sides there was a gradual development of the common interest in avoiding or decreasing involvement in some regions, or in controlling its effect on relations as a whole (see Fielder):

- in the war between India and Pakistan (1965–6) the United States remained neutral, despite her treaty with Pakistan;

  the Soviet Union, despite her basic pro-Indian views, pursued a policy of mediation (in secret close collaboration with the United States);
- in the Biafran War (1967–70) no link with the East–West conflict was established (contrary to the policy on the Congo in the pre-Cuban period);
- in the Arab–Israeli Six Day War (1967), despite support for the opposing parties from the United States and the USSR, both co-operated in efforts to establish a cease-fire with a subsequent meeting between Johnson and Kosygin in Glassboro;
- in Vietnam the direct and indirect involvement of the United States and the USSR in the war was increasingly found to be a hinderance to continued attempts to achieve global understanding; American-Soviet agreement prepared the way for the Vietnam Treaty of 1973.

Local regional crises, especially the Vietnam War, upset the Super Powers' policy of bilateral détente. However, it is instructive that even shortly after the escalation of the Vietnam War with the mining of the harbour at Haifong, both states went beyond a mere informal management of crises (see Williams, 1976). The joint Soviet–American declaration of 29 May 1972 on the 'Basic Principles of Relations Between the United States of America and the Union of the Socialist Soviet Republics' laid down and formulated co-operative crisis management:

> The USA and the USSR attach major importance to preventing the development of situations capable of causing a dangerous exacerbation of their relations. They will therefore do their utmost to avoid military confrontations and to prevent the outbreak of nuclear war. They will always exercise restraint in their mutual relations, and will be prepared to negotiate and settle differences by peaceful means. Discussions and negotiations on outstanding issues will be conducted in a spirit of

> reciprocity, mutual accomodation and mutual benefit.
>
> Both sides recognize that efforts to obtain unilateral advantage at the expense of the other, directly or indirectly, are inconsistent with these objectives. (see Timberlake, 1978, pp. 28f).

These principles were already predetermined in an agreement on measures to avoid the danger of an accidental nuclear war (30 September 1971) and were reaffirmed in the agreement on the prevention of a nuclear war (see Articles 1 and 4 of the Agreement of 22 June 1973). This did not, however, ensure that they were universally valid and would consistently determine future Soviet and American behaviour.

The harmonious rhetoric of the Soviet–American declaration of principles emphasized unity and skated over actual contradictions. At the same time that both sides were preaching restraint and verbally denouncing efforts to gain one-sided advantages, they were each doing the exact opposite:

- the Moscow Summit Conference coincided with the escalation of American military intervention in North Vietnam;
- a few weeks before the Summit — from 14 to 23 March 1972 — the Prime Minister of Afghanistan, Abdul Zahir, was visiting Moscow; the Soviet leadership pledged not only economic support for Afghanistan (as it had previously done), but also 'political help' (Bräker, 1979); this led directly to a treaty of friendship, concluded after the Communist seizure of power in April 1978, which gave a pseudo-legal basis for the Red Army's intervention in Afghanistan at the end of 1979;
- on 6 April 1972 a friendship treaty was signed by the Soviet Union and Iraq which ensured the further extension of Soviet influence and Soviet bases directly in the Persian Gulf;
- following the Moscow Summit President Nixon travelled to Tehran and committed himself to the provision of massive military support to Iran in order to retain a regional counterbalance to Iraq, who had allied with the Soviet Union after the British withdrawal from Aden (see Szulc, 1978, pp. 282 ff.); when the Shah's regime was overthrown in 1979 the region was destabilised and thus competition of the two powers became critical; it affected the whole relationship of the Super Powers throughout the crisis in Afghanistan (see Chapter 12 below).

Up until then in this phase of détente (both before and after the rules on crisis management had been laid down) there had been no escalation of crises either because the Great Powers thus challenged did not react accordingly or because crisis management was successfully implemented.

The intervention of the Soviet ally Syria on the side of the Palestinians in the Jordan–Palestine civil war in September 1970 was averted partly by reason of American pressure on the Soviet Union and partly by the threat of American intervention. The Soviet Union avoided answering this pressure with increased risk-taking.

The USSR's attempt to circumvent the Kennedy–Khrushchev agreement of 1962 and to expand the Cuban port of Cienfuegos into a base for nuclear submarines in the summer and autumn of 1970 did not escalate into a crisis, as the Soviet Union complied with American objections raised through diplomatic and secret channels: it halted the building programme on 22 October 1970. There was no second Cuban missile crisis.*

During the second war between India and Pakistan in 1971 there were mutual demonstrations of power by the American and Soviet Fleets in the Bengali Gulf. Both sides showed a certain readiness to run risks, but a further escalation between them was avoided. India eventually agreed to a cease-fire — evidently on advice from the Soviet Union.

The naval blockade and mining of the Port of Haifong in May 1972, which directly affected access for Soviet supplies, was not seen as a provocation by the Soviet Union; the USSR and China increased their pressure on North Vietnam to move towards a settlement.

Both Great Powers supported their respective allies in the Yom Kippur War in October 1973, but nevertheless jointly practised crisis management, beginning with Kissinger's visit to Moscow (20 October) and culminating in the jointly proposed Security Council resolution for a cease-fire. When the Soviet Union's readiness to come to the aid of the Egytian Army unilaterally with her own troops became visible, the American strike force was put on red alert (25 October). Against the background of this mutual risk-taking, it was possible to implement the cease-fire in a co-operative spirit and the UN Emergency Force was set up to supervise it.

*The 'discovery' of a Soviet combat unit on Cuba in the autumn of 1979 was not so much an element of an international crisis but rather a by-product of domestic American party politics, intended to influence the simultaneous summit conference of non-aligned states in Havana.

The Cuban–Soviet policy of military intervention in Angola (1975–6) and Ethiopia (1977) was a striking violation of the agreed rules of behaviour. The United States did not, however, take up the challenge; the reasons for this are many, and in the case of Angola have been thoroughly analysed. Not only American resistance at home both on the part of the public and in Congress (due to the trauma of Vietnam and the weakened power of the President as a result of the Watergate scandal), but also, and to a much greater degree, the local situation did not favour an American involvement (see Griffith, 1976).

The behaviour of the Super Powers in crises during the phase of détente in the 1970s in effect also points to the central significance of the framework constituted by power politics. When unilateral advantages can be achieved without hindrance or any risk of a crisis, the agreed rules on behaviour become less effective or are completely ignored, for it is obvious that when there is no likelihood of a crisis arising between the Super Powers the rules on how to avoid crises or of crisis management become irrelevant. The course of crises and the observance of agreed rules depend on the specific situations in power politics and on each side's readiness to risk a crisis (see Adomeit, 1973; Williams, 1976). What is decisive is how effective or ineffective both sides are at deterring each other and how effective or ineffective the balance of power is. This has been borne out during the crisis in Afghanistan (see below).

# 10 *Integrative Elements in the East–West Conflict*

## The Bilateral Détente Policy of the Super Powers

Not only have there been attempts to formalise crisis management and the mechanisms of avoiding crises between the opponents in the East–West conflict, but a network of co-operative agreements has also been established, with the continuance at the same time of a policy of demarcation and deterrence. This allows us to characterise détente as a mingled policy of co-operative, integrative, confrontationist and regressive elements in the regulation of conflict. Seen historically, détente constitutes a second attempt at antagonistic co-operation. The first attempt began because of a common enemy. Following the defeat of the Axis Powers, its advance was wrecked by the extreme imbalance in power relations. The reduction and limitation of political relations and trade (i.e. regression) was the decisive pattern of the Cold War period. The second attempt at antagonistic co-operation developed in a fundamentally different situation compared with that of the first. The following international circumstances were pertinent:

- a balanced bipolarity (equilibrium) between the United States and the USSR at the level of nuclear strategy because both sides had a second-strike capability;
- the reduced imbalance in the allocation of material power potential between the two Super Powers;
- the globalisation of the policy of the USSR (hitherto primarily continental);
- the transformation of the bipolarity of power politics into a tripolarity (although not fully developed) at the non-nuclear level after the Chinese People's Republic had risen to join the group of Great Powers and thus created a competitive triangle: the Soviet Union – China – the United States;
- the superimposition of the North–South conflict on to the East–West conflict.

These structural factors decisively determined the bilateral agreements between the United States and the USSR concluded in the 1970s (a) at the strategic level and (b) in non-military sectors.

### *In the Strategic Sector*

A crucial decision had been taken in 1946–7 against continuing the earlier antagonistic co-operation and towards a move to regressive conflict regulation (the Cold War), since the strategic imbalance excluded co-operation based on parity. When the balance had been redressed, efforts were made to break through to a second stage of antagonistic co-operation in this same sector. The 1968 treaty on the non-proliferation of nuclear weapons, which came into force in 1970, continued the policy of bilateral co-operation between the Super Powers, beginning with the agreement on the partial ban of nuclear tests in 1963 and the 1967 treaty on the non-use of nuclear or mass-destruction weapons in space (see above). At the same time it opened the door to bilateral talks on the limitation of strategic weapons (see the corresponding commitment in the Non-proliferation Treaty). The attempt to stabilise the international system by founding a nuclear club based on the existing hierarchy of Great Powers led to the policy of stabilising relations between the two Super Powers on the basis of approximate strategic parity for which the most suitable method appeared to be 'co-operative arms control' (for the various concepts and goals see Heisenberg, in Forndran and Friedrich, 1979).

Protracted bilateral talks on the limitation of strategic weapons (SALT) had already been started by President Johnson in 1966. These were conceptualised into a broader political framework by President Nixon in the period 1969–72 ('shaping a durable peace') (see Hacke, 1983) and continued by President Ford and President Carter — always in collaboration with Secretary General Brezhnev. This continuity shows that efforts to establish co-operative arms control reflected an interest on the part of both Super Powers which was independent of individual preferences. They were first incorporated into two agreements which have been labelled SALT I (see the detailed study by John Newhouse, 1973):

(a) In the ABM Treaty the United States and the USSR agreed to establish only two anti-ballistic-missile systems (in 1974 the number of possible systems was reduced to only one ABM system) so as to secure mutual vulnerability and to prevent any incentive for a preventive strike. The idea was to maintain a cond-strike capability on both sides.

(b) In the interim agreement, which was at first limited to five years, but eventually extended to the conclusion of SALT II, both sides agreed on a quantitative limit on strategic nuclear offensive arms which allowed the US 1,054 land-based intercontinental ballistic missiles (ICBM) as well as 656 submarine-launched ballistic missiles (SLBM) and the USSR 1,618 ICBMs and 740 SLBMs. An additional protocol permitted the substitution of ICBMs by SLBMs up to a maximum of 44 submarines with 710 missiles for the United States and 62 submarines with 950 missiles for the USSR.

Thus the central problem of how to limit both defensive and offensive weapons in order to maintain a mutually deterrent capability was only solved in a very incomplete way. No agreement could be reached — in view of the American technological advantage — over the equipping of missiles with newly developed multiple independently targetable re-entry vehicles (MIRV) and the settlement of this question was reserved for a new round of SALT. At the Ford–Brezhnev meeting in November 1974 at Vladivostok an agreement was reached on the limitation to 2,400, of the number of nuclear delivery vehicles for intercontinental land- and submarine-based missiles and the number of strategic bombers for both sides; of these not more than 1,320 were to be armed with MIRVs. President Carter's attempt to negotiate a lower level failed.

On the basis of this relatively high level of parity agreed at Vladivostok, the United States and the USSR eventually concluded an agreement in June 1979 to run until 31 December 1985 (SALT II), which laid down the following maximum of strategic nuclear weapon systems (including strategic bombers and bombers armed with cruise missiles or with ballistic ground-to-air missiles with a range of over 600 kilometres) for both Super Powers:

| | |
|---|---|
| Aggregate number of strategic nuclear delivery vehicles — six months after effective date of the treaty | 2,400 |
| Aggregate number of strategic nuclear delivery vehicles, after 31 Dec. 1981 | 2,250 |
| This includes a sub-ceiling MIRVed strategic nuclear delivery vehicles | 1,320 |
| An additional sub-ceiling of launchers of MIRVed ballistic missiles | 1,200 |
| A further sub-ceiling of MIRVed ICBM launchers | 820 |

Both parties to the agreement were free to decide on the composition of their strategic nuclear potential within the framework of these limits (White Paper, 1979, p. 72).

Amongst many further detailed agreements the following provisions are especially important: launchers of light ICBMs were not to be converted into launchers of heavy ICBMs, and cruise missiles with MIRVs having a range of more than 600 kilometres were not to be developed; both sides were allowed to introduce only one new type of ICBM armed with a maximum of ten warheads. In an additional protocol, valid until 31 December 1981, the treaty partners undertook, inter alia, to deploy no mobile ICBM launch systems and no cruise missiles with a range of more than 600 kilometres nor to test or deploy ballistic ground-to-air missiles. Just as in 1972, when the unequal development of new MIRV technology obstructed a long-term qualitative reduction of arms, so in 1979 the new weapon of cruise missiles precluded any comprehensive and long-term regulation, the more so since with this new weapon it was impossible to make an exact distinction between strategic and regional systems. In the same way, the assessment of the new Soviet long-range fighter aircraft, the TU22M (called 'Backfire' in NATO jargon) is disputed. These regional weapons and the Soviet medium-range missile (in particular the SS 20) were excluded from SALT II, neither were they on the agenda for the negotiations in Vienna on the reduction of forces (grey-area arms). Thus SALT II was not concerned with regional disparities and was consciously limited to the stabilisation of strategic parity. Despite the inclusion of a qualitative component, through the limitation on MIRV warheads and through the interim agreements on cruise missiles, the race to acquire technologically more sophisticated arms has in no way been brought under control. The danger that the Soviet Union could knock out the American Minuteman silos in a first strike with her heavy missiles of the SS19 type — after technological improvements increased the accuracy of MIRVs — was countered by allowing the United States to deploy mobile MX missiles. SALT II was the contradictory attempt of both sides to keep open as many strategic options as possible and at the same time mutually to stabilise the 'dynamic balance':

> With its strategic nuclear long-range systems the United States can commit a total of 9,200 nuclear warheads, including more than 5,000 of its invulnerable SLBM arsenal. This demonstrates the assured second-

> strike capability of the United States. The Soviet Union, on the other hand, has 5,000 nuclear warheads. But over 2,600 warheads of this total number are considered to be part of the Soviet ICBM potential whose effectiveness will be upgraded as the fourth-generation missiles are deployed. For the coming years the United States is anticipating numerical parity in warheads for the strategic nuclear systems of both sides. (White Paper, 1979, pp. 102–4)

Proponents of SALT II argued that without it the development of potential strategic nuclear weapons by both Super Powers would increase enormously — and have a destabilising effect. Although SALT II has not been ratified, both sides adhere to its regulations. To this extent SALT II can be regarded as an indication that neither contender seeks strategic superiority for the time being, but rather a stabilisation of the dynamic balance. SALT I and SALT II are the expression of a 'security partnership' (Ruehl) between the two antagonistic world powers, the integrative elements of which are also reflected in the fact that a joint advisory commission for the implementation and continued development of the SALT agreements was set up and is working, and furthermore, in the fact that reciprocal commitments have been undertaken not to disrupt the verification of compliance with the treaty's provision by technological means and to undertake no camouflaging to hinder verification.

Thus, in the 1970s antagonistic co-operation was institutionalised at the strategic level. Even at the very heart of the central 'system of confrontation' (Ruehl), i.e. in the sphere of strategic arms, elements of a 'system of co-operation' were included. The political adaptation of this approach was formulated in the declaration of principle of 27 May 1972 and in two agreements (22 June 1973) on the prevention of incidents on and above the high seas and on the prevention of nuclear wars which formalised the policy of co-operative crisis avoidance and crisis management (see above).

### *In the non-military spheres*

Bilateral agreements on American-Soviet co-operation in the non-military spheres offered groups and individuals in society (especially businessmen) the opportunity of using and extending the room for manoeuvre for transnational integrative links and trade relations under the umbrella of the strategic balance.

The conditions for this were created on the Soviet side by a general opening up of the socialist economies to the world market.

Stalin's theoretical and political maxim of 'the disintegration of the universal world market', of the division into a 'socialist world market' and a 'capitalist world market', which also expressed the structural character of the East–West conflict in the sphere of world economics, was abandoned from the mid 1960s onwards and replaced by the view 'that there is one world market'. Preliminary steps taken at the 23rd Congress of the CPSU in April 1966 had already led to a first wave of East–West economic co-operation (see Wilczynski, 1969), and the conclusion of the ninth Five Year Plan at the 24th Party Congress in March and April 1971 confirmed a new policy 'principle' as binding, i.e. the policy of a reintegration into the world market through long-term economic relations with the 'industrially developed capitalist countries'. At the same time Western Europe's willingness to trade with Eastern Europe increased for economic and political reasons. In the United States at the end of the 1960s there was also a gradual move towards trade with the East. Export controls and credit restrictions were gradually loosened, though not without some relapses (see Goldman, 1975, pp. 49 ff.). The definitive opening up of the Soviet Union at the beginning of the 1970s coincided with a period of prosperity in the West in which exports, as well as the demand for imports, increased. During the recession of 1974–5 markets in the East became even more attractive to firms in the West hoping to secure employment (see below).

The political framework for 'systems of co-operation' was created bilaterally on the occasion of Nixon's visit to Moscow in May 1972, Brezhnev's visit to Washington in June 1973 and Nixon's second visit to Moscow in June and July 1974. From this emerged agreements on co-operation in the area of environmental protection, medical research and public health, the exploration and use of space for peaceful purposes, science and technology, agriculture, the peaceful use of nuclear energy, the study of the world's oceans and transport systems as well as a general agreement on contact, exchange and co-operation, a convention on matters concerning taxation and protocols, on an American-Soviet Chamber of Commerce, on commercial establishments and on questions of the expansion of air traffic (these agreements are collected in Timberlake, 1978). Between the two summit meetings — in October 1972 — both sides signed a trade agreement (settling American claims outstanding since the Lend-Lease Agreement). This agreement was, however, annulled by the Soviet side in 1975 because of the policy of the US Congress which had linked most-favoured-nation treatment to a liberal policy of emigration in the Soviet Union. This left a gap remaining in the otherwise regulated network of functional co-operation. This gap was partly closed by special trade agreements and the agreement on industrial co-operation between America and the Soviet Union also remained in force. Joint commissions, which met at least once a year, assumed responsibility for the implementation of most of the sectional co-operation agreements which were supplemented by a longer-term cultural agreement. All in all, a network of sectional co-operation was thus created which was comprehensively and tightly woven (with only one small flaw) — all areas of society were included, drawing the most important groups in American society (with the notable exception of the trade unions) into a process of exchange and co-operation with the Soviet Union and the countries of Eastern Europe — a development which was consciously pursued by the US Administration (see Nixon, 1973; Nerlich, 1978).

Just how strongly these transnational relations actually became under détente can be documented with the help of a few statistics (see, e.g., Goldman, 1975, and Dörr, 1980).

American exports to the USSR between 1951 and 1955, at the height of the Cold War, amounted on average to approximately $100,000 per year; between 1956 and 1960 they rose to an average annual figure of $11.3 million; after a notable rise in 1961 and a major rise in 1964, the volume of exports fell again in the intervening years only to increase steadily after 1969, reaching an unprecedented level in 1972 and 1973 with rates of increase of 235 and 120 per cent respectively. American imports from the USSR show a similar trend — though starting at a higher level; the annual average between 1951 and 1955 amounted to $16.8 million; between 1956 and 1960, it increased to $21.9 million, declining to $20 million during the period 1961–3; between 1964 and 1968 it shot-up to $42.4 million and between 1969 and 1973 it rose again to $98.3 million (see Fig. 10.1).

A major intensification in the sphere of industrial co-operation followed in the wake of the American-Soviet agreement of 1972 which was not even affected by the failure of the trade agreement. Whilst in the years 1965–7 only four co-operative contracts and agreements on co-operation existed between American companies and the respective ministries of the CMEA countries (Wilczynski, 1969, pp. 379 ff.), by 1975 there were already 389 such contracts of which at least 136 were with the USSR (in 30 cases the country that was party to the contract is unknown) (Stankovsky, in Grünbuch, pp. 297f.; Goldman, 1975, Appendix II).

Along with the growth of trade and co-operative relations there was an increase in communication and tourist traffic (see Fig. 10.2). Thus social activities converted governmental agreements into economic reality. In this way détente experienced support transnationally and within the societies. At the same time, however, there developed an imbalance in the possibilities of controlling these activities. Whereas in socialist countries activities abroad in the respective functional sectors are state activities or state-controlled, groups in American and democratic societies in the West operate with a relatively large degree of freedom and autonomy within the framework of the treaties. This is apparent not only when (as in the spring of 1980) the US Administration strives to cool trade relations for political reasons, but also when official policy desires an increase in trade activity. The Nixon Administration was able to link the conclusion of agreements on sectional co-operation to the whole concept of détente but its practical implementation was difficult to control politically; societal and economic interests develop their own dynamic once they have been set free politically. Thus, for example, those large companies participating in business with the Soviet Union strongly rejected any sort of link between their commercial relations and political matters. As a result, there was hope only for indirect effects, namely that the internal development and foreign policy of the Soviet Union could be influenced through transnational relations between the United States and the USSR, and especially through trade relations, so that interest in a co-operative peace policy would also grow. Whether such expectations are realistic is open to debate (see further discussion in the Excursus below). It is particularly significant for American-Soviet relations that the degree of interdependence (in the sense of relative vulnerability) in the 1970s was still relatively low despite the cementing of relations and joint interests.

Compared with American trade volume in 1973, exports to the USSR amounted to only 1.11 per cent, and imports from the Soviet Union to 0.18 per cent. Of total Russian trade, exports to the United States amounted to 0.62 per cent and imports from the United States was 3.38 per cent. In the same year the exchange of US-Soviet goods accounted for 0.06 per cent of America's GNP and for (an estimated) 0.11 per cent of the Soviet Union's GNP (statistics and data from W. Dörr, Tables A3 and A49; cf. Fig. 10.1).

Figure 10.1 *Exchange of products US–USSR*

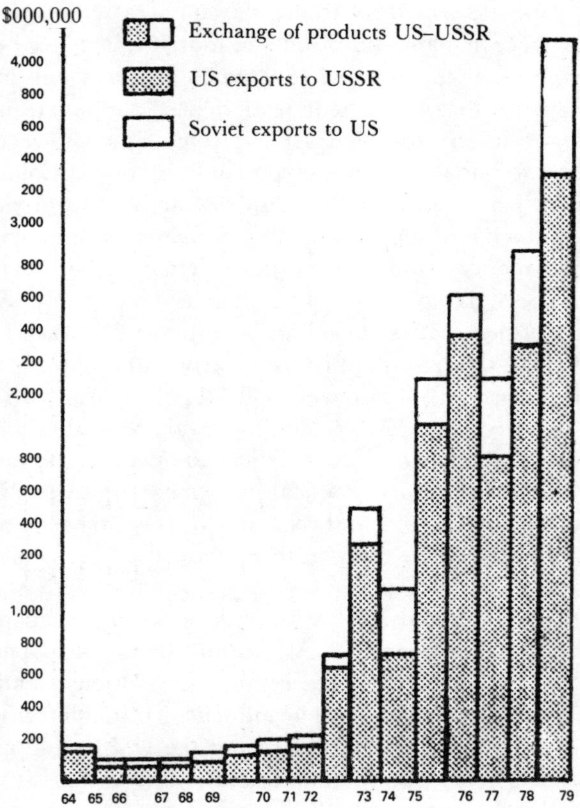


Sources: US Dept of Commerce, *Statistical Abstracts* 1975–9 (1979 data cover only Jan. to Nov.); *Survey of Current Business*, published by US Dept of Commerce, US Bureau of the Census.

Consequently the price of any unilateral withdrawal of co-operation in the economic sector is still relatively low for both sides. In the same way that political détente promoted transnational relations, a renewed intensification of political antagonisms could easily result in regressive transnational relations. Trade restrictions imposed by the United States because of the Soviet invasion of Afghanistan at the beginning of 1980 confirm this supposition (see below, Chapter 12). Only when a higher degree of transnational interdependence is achieved and when this in turn has stabilised the rules of co-operation can it be assumed that a societal and political foundation for the regulation of conflict exists with long-term effects.

That is to say, only the continuation of a lasting détente could gradually create the prerequisites of an integrative solution to the East–West conflict. At present mutual vulnerability through the termination or breakdown of co-operation is of importance only in the strategic nuclear area. For this reason efforts for joint control of

Figure 10.2 *Travel between US and USSR*

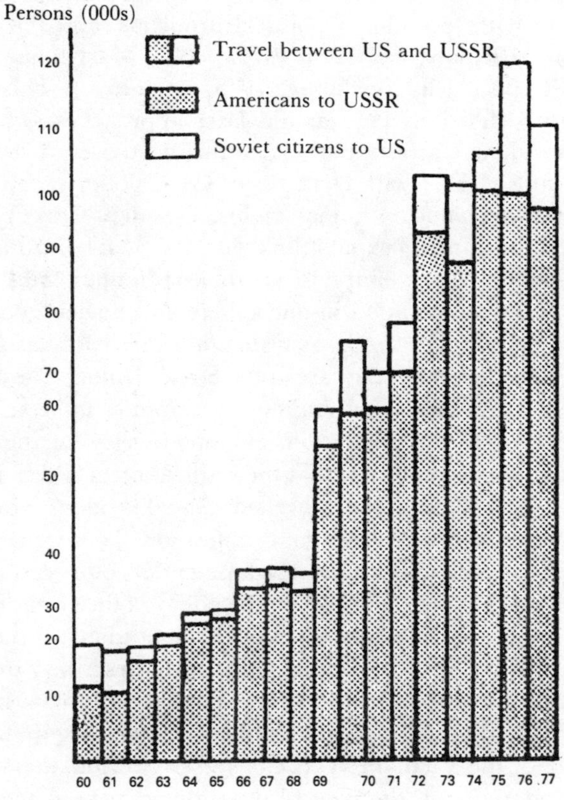


Sources: Americans: *UN Statistical Yearbook*, 1968/78; *Statistical Abstracts* (US Dept of Commerce, 1975–9). (Data for entry into the US, 1974–7, include diplomats' journeys as entries of persons born in the USSR and resident in other countries. The difference from the data for 1960–73 lies between 3,000 and 5,000 annually).

arms have been considered by both sides to be of independent value and the realisation of this has been attempted independently of advances in détente in other areas.

However, the 'linkage' problem arises not only in the linking of co-operation on nuclear strategy with co-operation in the non-military (particularly in the economic) sectors. In a more comprehensive sense the problem is whether, and then how, bilateral agreements on co-operation in the area of strategic policy can be linked conditionally with co-operation in specific regions and conflicts. The Nixon Administration attempted to forge this link and at first wanted to make advances in the SALT agreements dependent on progress with 'prominent political problems' and the Vietnam conflict in particular (see Nixon, 1978, p. 396; Marvin and Bernard Kalb, 1974, pp. 94 ff; Newhouse, 1973, pp. 140 f.). This attempt failed with SALT I in 1972 as did later approaches (when Brzezinski, President Carter's national-security adviser, tried to link advances in SALT II with changes in Soviet policy on Africa). By emphasizing demands on human rights, President Carter managed to avoid establishing an explicit link with the SALT negotiations. A 'linkage' policy, the attempt to create conditional links between agreements on co-operation in one sphere and Soviet 'good behaviour' in others, actually tends, as historical experience has shown, to be counter-productive in the case of the Soviet Union. The control of the nuclear arms race is overridingly a common interest. Accordingly, the Carter Administration felt that in view of the crisis in Afghanistan it was important that the ratification of SALT II should only be postponed, and not cancelled. And President Reagan was willing to observe SALT II without ratification. To say that 'linkage' policies failed is not to deny the development of co-operative bilateralism had, and still has, an effect on the policy of the Great Powers in other regions, since it alters some of the conditions of the general framework. This effect had been pertinently described by Stanley Hoffmann (1979–80) as 'self-linkage'. Thus the Moscow summit of 1972 undoubtedly had a positive influence upon negotiations over the ending of the Vietnam War. Conversely, regional conflicts can block negotiations on the control of strategic arms if they have a negative influence on relations between East and West as a whole, such as the crisis over Afghanistan, for example, has had since the beginning of 1980. Successes or failure of US–Soviet bilateralism, particularly in the central strategic area, advance or obstruct other East–West negotiations. This connection exists particularly in the

European region and in efforts made there for détente.

## Europe and the Multilateralisation of Détente

The Super Powers' bilateral policy of détente at first produced opposing and competing reactions in Europe. At the end of the 1960s, in step with US–Soviet bilateralism, the pattern of bilateral détente developed temporarily between individual countries in Europe; and at the beginning of the 1970s efforts increased to multilateralise European détente policies and to bring about a relationship complementary to the détente between the Super Powers. Recently (1980) Western Europe has striven to protect détente from upsets abroad such as the crisis in Afghanistan.

### *First reactions in Europe and bilateralism*

The Gaullist policy on Eastern Europe and (though to a lesser extent) Rumania's policy towards the West represent the beginnings and the trends of a competing bilateralism which examined ways of overcoming the hegemony of both world powers over Eastern and Western Europe and the division of Europe which resulted therefrom. It was encouraged from time to time by the then opposing Great Powers. The USSR tried to emphasize the practice introduced by de Gaulle, and continued by his successors, of regular consultations at the highest level in joint Franco-Russian commissions as a 'privileged link' (Gromyko). The United States praised the 'practical co-operation' and 'helpful consultations' with Rumania (see Nixon, Report, 1973, p. 92, and G. Fischer, 1972). But the actual distribution of power limited these competing bilateralisms on the part of European countries at a fairly early stage. They were equally limited by the main thrust of the common interests of the two Super Powers which turned the bilateralism of the Great Powers into the determining factor of process of détente (see Vahl, in Schwarz and Meissner, 1979, pp. 227 ff; Braun, 1978).

The opposing reaction at the beginning of the phase of US–Soviet détente was especially influenced by the two Germanies, since they found themselves involved in a 'dual conflict' — a global conflict of systems and a conflict of national identity — with the current global contenders and with their allies (see above). The German Democratic Republic opposed the start of détente because this evoked —

especially under the 'bridge-building' banner of Johnson and Schröder — the danger of isolation and because recognition of her sovereignty as a state had not been made a precondition for the progress of détente (Moreton, 1978). The Federal Republic of Germany opposed the start of détente in so far as the restoration of national unity did not remain a precondition — the Adenauer Government happily developed constructive proposals on the limitation of arms (see the Heusinger Plan), but their realisation was linked to a policy of reunification (Haftendorn, 1974).

At the conference of Foreign Ministers in Geneva (October –November 1955), which concluded the first phase of semi-détente (with the Austrian Treaty of 15 May 1955 and the Geneva Summit Conference of July 1955), the Western Powers had insisted that the question of the reunification of Germany had to be settled before any agreement on disarmament and European security. However, this link was abandoned only four years later at the Geneva Foreign Ministers' Conference (summer 1959) and at the Camp David talks between Khrushchev and Eisenhower (September 1959). From then on the German question was separated from policies on arms control, the centre-piece of Super Power détente. Furthermore, the Berlin problem was taken as an issue separate from the general German problem, with the agreement on special negotiations about Berlin (see End, 1973).

The Adenauer Government sought to delay this development by referring to the commitment to support German reunification given by the Western Allies in the peace contract (Convention on Relations Between the Three Powers and the Federal Republic; see Grewe, 1979; Etzioni, 1965, p. 260). Only when it had been clearly recognised that the Federal Republic of Germany could not link the Super Powers' bilateral approach to détente with political preconditions connected with Germany, did the Erhard–Schröder Government send its so-called peace note (March 1966) and thus gradually begin to implement a 'policy of flexibility' (Schröder). This policy sought to accommodate global détente through bilateral non-aggression treaties without prejudicing a solution to the German question. The Government of the Grand Coalition (December 1966) favoured the priority of détente, as announced in its government statement (see Besson, 1970) — a change clearly emphasized by Foreign Minister Brandt (1967–8).

A new *Ostpolitik* developed out of subsequent negotiations over a 'network of renunciations of the use of force' (Brandt). This was consistently pursued by the Social Democratic–Liberal coalition which at the same time tried to integrate the German Democratic Republic in order to solve the 'special conflict' of Germany or at least to regulate it in the sense of a *modus vivendi*, and in the hope that détente would facilitate a new form of German unity. In practice this meant a conscious transferring of the American programme of détente to policies on the East and on Germany: the thinking behind Egon Bahr's concept of 1963 ('change through rapprochement') was based on a detailed analysis of the Kennedy programme (Kaiser, 1968, p. 90). The proviso on German policy was retained only with regard to the European process of détente and expressed in a kind of 'linking': 'that inter-German relations have to be settled before. . . there can be a conference on security' (Brandt in a speech at the Übersee-Tag in Hamburg on 7 May 1969).

German-Russian, German-Polish and German-German bilateralism, which together with later German-Czechoslovak negotiations made up the Social Democrat–Liberal coalition's policy on the East and on Germany (see Whetten, 1971; Jahn and Rittberger, 1974; Schmid, 1979), ran parallel to US–Russian bilateralism and the competing Franco-Russian bilateralism under the banner of détente. Thus 'détente asymmetrics' (Brandt) were prevented, although this by no means ensured 'complementariness' (Dettke) or compatibility. The fast pace of German *Ostpolitik* and the extent of the FRG's independence in matters of détente already irritated the United States and France. The possibility that German-Soviet, like Franco-Soviet, bilateralism could compete with Great Power bilateralism arose temporarily and was criticised as the start of a 'race between Paris and Bonn to Moscow' (McCloy, 1970, quoted in Link, 1978, p. 161). The idea of a new peace order for the whole of Europe, more or less openly discussed by Bahr and Brandt, appeared to offer the prospect that détente in Europe would remove Europe from US hegemonic leadership and control (see the Bahr memorandum of 1968, published in *Quick*, 27 Sept. 1973). It was only when it had become clear that Germany's *Ostpolitik* essentially accepted the stabilisation of the status quo both currently and in the foreseeable future and that co-operation would be possible only on this basis and within this framework that the complementariness between the legitimisation of the nuclear status quo and the European status quo was substantially established (Duchêne, 1970).

In concrete terms: West Germany's treaties with the East start with 'the situation actually existing in this area' and create a *modus vivendi* between the Federal Republic of Germany and her neighbours in the East on the basis of the territorial status quo — including the Oder–Neisse border and the border between the Federal Republic of Germany and the German Democratic Republic (Article 3 of the Moscow Treaty and Article 1 of the Warsaw Treaty as well as the resolution of the German Bundestag of 17 May 1972). The fact that these treaty arrangements 'did not conflict with' the goal of reunification was stated by the German government in its letter on German unity. However, it was not this declared long-term goal, but the actual existence of two German states, that determined practical politics.

The treaty dealing with the basis of relations between the Federal Republic of Germany and the German Democratic Republic, of 21 December 1972, also accepted the 'historical facts'. Although the fundamental differences between views on the national question were mentioned (in the preamble), a line was drawn between the two German states in order to regulate the German conflict: then followed the recognition of the state authority of the German Democratic Republic, the limitation of 'the jurisdiction of the two states to their own territory' (Article 6) and the renunciation of the claim to represent the other state (Article 4). This at the same time created the precondition for an agreement 'to develop and promote' co-operation between them in various non-military sectors (Article 7). Despite many difficulties and set-backs in German–German relations the actual links between the people of both nations (visits, telephone calls, family reunions, etc.) and trade relations have increased considerably (see materials in the Federal government's report on the state of the nation, 1971, 1972, 1974 as well as Bruns, 1979, and Arndt, 1979). Just as the political organisation in Germany during the Cold War was typical of the regressive regulation of conflict between the Great Powers, the organisation of German–German relations has henceforth been the prototype of détente in the international system. Demarcation and co-operation between clearly defined countries, regression and integration are the elements of the regulation of conflict of détente in inter-German relations and *Ostpolitik*.

The Quadripartite Agreement on Berlin (1971) underlined this fact. Like the treaties with the East it was based on the 'existing situation in the relevant area' and contained typical integrative-regressive elements whereby on the one hand access to West Berlin was guaranteed and 'the ties between the Western Sectors of Berlin and the Federal Republic of Germany will be maintained and developed' and on the other hand 'these Sectors continue to be no constituent part of the Federal Republic of Germany and are not to be governed by it.' The agreement gave a mandate to both states to conclude concrete agreements on post and telephone communications, transit traffic, tourism and travel and the exchange of territory. And the Berlin Agreement was linked (at first by the Federal Republic of Germany and then in turn by the Soviet Union) to the ratification of the treaties with the East. So the way was clear for the American–Soviet Summit conference of May 1972 and for the ensuing agreement (made in Moscow) between Nixon and Brezhnev, to prepare a European conference 'with the aim of broadening European cooperation' (Nixon Report, 1973; see Haftendorn, 1974) — and to negotiate the question of mutual and balanced troop reductions in Europe at a special, smaller conference (MBFR). Thus German *Ostpolitik* paved the way, but it was the two hegemonic powers who, because of their view of common interests, took the decision to 'Europeanise' détente and to convoke two separate (but parallel) conferences (see Haftendorn, 1974, p. 269).

### *Multilateralisation — CSCE and MBFR*

There is only an apparent continuity between these two conferences and discussions in the 1950s and 1960s concerning a European security conference (see the documentation of Schramm, Riggert, Friedel, 1972, and Jacobsen, Mallmann, Meier, 1973; see Haftendorn, 1974). In this earlier phase Soviet demands for the setting up of a European security system were made with reference to the danger of 'revanchism' and 'militarism' emanating from the Federal Republic of Germany. In fact, however, they pursued a dual purpose: 'the liquidation of NATO and the withdrawal of America, on the one hand, and the cementation of the status quo on the other' (Löwenthal, 1967; see Wolfe, 1970, and Wettig, 1972). The attainment of these goals would — in Richard Löwenthal's terminology — have put the Federal Republic of Germany and Western Europe into a 'Finnish situation', i.e. one 'in which the Federal Republic of Germany and Western Europe would neither be occupied, overrun nor Sovietised but, like Finland today, would belong to the Soviet sphere of power, with a Soviet veto on the setting up of governments, with Soviet access to sources of material help and with a corresponding effect on the world-political balance' (p. 347).

In 1967 this perspective may not have been unrealistic in view of the erosion of NATO (with the withdrawal of France from military integration), the American involvement in the Vietnam war and anti-American feelings in Western Europe. By 1972 the situation had altered in important details:

(1) The Federal Republic of Germany had been recognised as a co-operative partner through the treaties with the East: 'The Soviet Union could no longer present European security as a question of defence against the Federal Republic of Germany' (Ruehl, 1974, p. 370).

(2) NATO had seized the initiative in military negotiations (the Reykjavik Signal, 1968); it could no longer be dispensed with (counter-signal of the Warsaw Pact from Tiflis, 1971), but had been recognised as a negotiating power (see Altmeppen, 1972).

(3) The United States (and Canada) were also accepted as components of European security through their inclusion in the CSCE by the Warsaw Pact countries (Budapest Memorandum of 22 June 1970).

(4) A *modus vivendi* in Europe based on the territorial status quo had already been established bilaterally and multilaterally before the conference by the treaties with the East and the Berlin Agreement without any weakening of the Atlantic Alliance or European integration. On the contrary, NATO and the EEC were now poised to pursue an active *Ostpolitik*. European Political Co-operation (EPC) was developed with close links to the new *Ostpolitik* and presented the CSCE with its first task.

(5) The policy of co-operative arms control and functional co-operation between the antagonistic world powers had already led to initial agreements; a multilateralisation was desirable in the very interest of maintaining the Atlantic alliance.

The call for a Conference on Security and Co-operation in Europe in 1972 was, therefore, no longer bound up with the aim of creating an alternative to two systems of alliances. There was no question of a 'Finlandisation'. The starting-point for both leading powers was that the structure of alliances in Europe would continue, with the aim of stabilising them. In Europe in particular, according to the decisive will of the Great Powers, a policy of détente meant détente within the status quo; 'security through agreements' depended on the recognition of the status quo (Ruehl, 1974). However, security was now to be achieved in two ways: through mutual deterrence and through mutual dependencies. In an organisational sense this meant a regulation of conflict which supplemented the regression of the Cold War with new integrative elements. Thus, even from the point of view of the East, the policy of economic co-operation 'with the aim of developing political co-operation between the countries of Europe' (Prague Declaration of Warsaw Pact countries of 31 October 1969) became as important as the policy of renouncing force for the protection of territorial rule. This functionalist aim was also seen as desirable by the West (see Groom, 1975, pp. 30 ff.). Seen in the context of global politics, the agreements to be reached at the CSCE on co-operation throughout Europe were envisaged as an extension and complement to American-Soviet co-operation agreements (Dettke, 1976).

At the preparatory conference of the CSCE in Helsinki, which began in November 1972 and continued until June 1973, an agreement to put economic co-operation on the agenda was achieved relatively quickly in view of the common interest in it which was also shared by neutral and non-aligned countries. The task of 'co-operation in the spheres of economics, science and technology as well as the environment' came in between item 1 of the agenda (questions of security in Europe) and item 3 (co-operation in humanitarian and other areas).

Subsequent negotiations in Geneva which lasted for almost two years filled these three 'baskets' with mutually agreed contents. The compromise which resulted from this 'trans-bloc conference diplomacy' was ceremoniously signed as the 'Final Act of Helsinki' by heads of state and governments from 35 European and North American states on 1 August 1975. This document contained a multilaterally agreed description of a *modus vivendi* in the sphere of territorial and boundary problems which had already been outlined in German treaties with the East. It amounted *de facto* to the legitimisation of the existing spheres of power in Europe, but also included the legitimisation of the role of the United States as a constituent part of European security. The Final Act contains no proposal for an integrative reorganisation of the whole of Europe. It did not succeed in linking recognition of the territorial status quo in Europe to the change of the political status quo, which in any case was never seriously attempted. The Final Act does, however, have aspects which point to the future. Above all, it offered an agreed consensus on a 'measure' by which to judge the behaviour of the CSCE participants in matters of détente and co-operation (Ropers, in *Grünbuch*, 1977). Its practical use is certainly problematical since the general principles, rules of behaviour, guidelines and recommendations present a complex compromise, the individual parts of which are interpreted differently in the context of opposing systems of values and order and given diverse emphases. This is particularly true of Principle VII (respect for human rights and basic freedoms, including freedom of thought, conscience, religion and convictions) and of Basket III (co-operation in humanitarian and other areas). Since there was a parallel interest primarily in the 'institutional stabilisation' of economic relations, the respective agreements in Basket II are less controversial in their interpretation and occupy pride of place (facilitating permanent offices for foreign companies, promotion of projects of industrial co-operation, extension of possibilities for contact and information, arbitration proceedings, principles for harmonising technical standards, methods of scientific co-operation, environmental protection, etc.). Nevertheless, in the short term the CSCE 'had only a marginal effect' on East–West economic relations (see the Excursus). Thus Western companies could now base representatives in all Eastern countries, which had been impossible before (Stankovsky, in *Grünbuch*, 1977, p. 306). Relations between the EEC and the CMEA are as unregulated as they were (see Schulz, 1977), making long-term bilateral agreements on co-operation between individual countries in the East and West (particularly between the USSR and the Federal Republic of Germany and France) more important. The multilateral agreements concluded at Helsinki, however, provide a framework for these. 'Materially the positive elements of the Final Act in the economic sphere can be seen in the fact that they give evidence of the willingness to co-operate and in this way cement mutual trust — an important precondition for long-term economic relations' (Stankovsky). This analysis refers to the internal link which connects Basket II with Basket III and the document on aspects of military and security policy in particular. In this document 'confidence building measures' (notification of military manœuvres, exchange of observers for manœuvres) are explicitly formulated. All the rules of behaviour contained in the Final Act of the CSCE were to reduce ambivalence and insecurity in the expectations of East and West — an aim which can only be achieved gradually with long-term practice and observance (see Kühne, in *Grünbuch*, 1977; Simma and Blenk-Knocke, 1979).

From the point of view of keeping to timetables, it is remarkable that when it was decided in Helsinki to continue multilateral conference diplomacy the date for a second conference was actually adhered to (1977–8) and that this Belgrade Conference ended with the call for a further conference to be held in 1980. There were, however, already signs in the preparatory phase of the Belgrade Conference that even the very limited integrative agreements produced 'conflicts in co-operation' (Jütte, 1977) and had destabilising effects. Civil and human rights movements, which were given a new impulse in the Soviet Union and other East European countries by the Final Act and President Carter's campaign on human rights were perceived as internal and external threats by the ruling élite in the East. As a matter of fact the Western emphasis on the human rights issue was no more than a reminder of jointly undertaken commitments, and not intervention. Despite this, the socialist countries have reacted with increasing repression and demarcation. In other words: a sharpening of antagonisms and a worsening of East–West relations had developed out of the formally agreed unity because there was no substantive understanding and no real agreement on political principles and ideologies. The experience that integrative measures agreed at Helsinki went beyond the actual level of unity between the two antagonistic systems and in the short term increasingly produced a destabilisation, has brought the difficulties of détente to the attention of public opinion (see Hans-Peter Schwarz and Boris Meissner, 1979). The dynamics of a rapprochement have become manifest, but so has the determination of political leaders to keep the dynamics under control. The effect was not to encourage, but to disillusion, and this effect was heightened as increasing domestic political repression found a parallel in arms production and attempts to extend the external influence of the USSR. Instead of trust, a climate of mistrust was produced.

The follow-up conference in Belgrade (October 1977–March 1978) gave no new impulses to détente and no shift in the integrative-regressive mix of relations in favour of a rapprochement, although no fewer than 107 individual proposals were put forward. Rather it evidenced the stagnation of détente. The problem of human rights can be identified as the main bone of contention in the speeches of participants at the conference — indeed, debates on this point led to a confrontation. At the same time they were evidence that 'the international treatment of domestic questions of human rights is not only permissible in law but also — as stated in the Final Act — legitimate from the point of view of détente' (Delbrück, in *DGFK-Jahrbuch*, 1979–80). It is also remarkable that the original consensus in questions of Basket II in the Final Act was stabilised and that in the governments' view the dimension of economic co-operation has become even more significant (Frey and Ruloff, in *DGFK-Jahrbuch* 1979–80).

It is open to debate whether current meetings of experts or (as has often been proposed) the setting up of special conferences to deal with differentiated individual functional problem areas can produce progress. Co-operation in the energy sector, which went to the top of the list of issues worth attention at the end of the Belgrade Conference, would be especially suited to a special conference of this sort, if it were linked to general policy — perhaps with the help of a 'renunciation of economic violence' (Müller, in *DGFK-Jahrbuch, 1979–80*). The agreement to set up a further conference in Madrid in November 1980 kept the conference framework alive and signified a move towards the quasi-institutionalisation of the CSCE (see Williams, 1974); it fixed a definite date at which the results of European détente might be rebalanced. Since both sides indicated their interest in retaining the Madrid Conference despite the crisis of détente, the significance of this forum for a regulated East–West dialogue is demonstrated (see Ropers, in *DGFK-Jahrbuch 1979–80*).

The history of the CSCE has shown that European détente diplomacy depends on the course of détente between the Great Powers. This is even more evident in the case of negotiations over troop reductions in Europe (MBFR) which, following preliminary talks in January 1973, have been conducted in Vienna since October 1973. As yet there is no result, although in the meantime the Soviet side has officially accepted the principle of parity (Joint German-Soviet declaration of 6 May 1978). Leaving to one side the problem of the precise definition of this term, it is open to debate whether a fundamental stabilisation of the military situation in Central Europe is attainable on the basis of the Vienna talks (Ruth, in Forndran and Friedrich, 1979). The area covered, the area of reduction, is limited to Poland, the German Democratic Republic, Czechoslovakia, the Federal Republic of Germany and the Benelux countries (the West also wants to include Hungary):

> Parity of armed forces within this area can be of little positive use from a strategic military standpoint as long as armed forces outside this area are not restricted and continue to be available for fast relocation or political pressure. The MBFR position of the West is, furthermore, still predominantly orientated towards the number of personnel — a figure which since 1973 has changed only very little on the East European side, whilst

the Soviet Union's capabilities, above all in the area of weaponry and equipment, have considerably increased in both quantity and quality. (Schilling, in Forndran and Friedrich, 1979, p. 214).

The geographical area is to be expanded to the whole of Europe by the convening of a conference parallel to the MBFR — (Confidence- and Security-building Measures and Disarmament in Europe) within the framework of the CSCE. It might offer a way out of the conceptual cul de sac of the Vienna Protocol (14 May 1973) and repair the 'innate error' of the MBFR, namely the non-participation of France.

The settlement on strategic parity between the United States and the USSR (SALT I and SALT II) and the continued build-up of Soviet medium-range missiles (SS 20s) have made advances in joint arms control in Europe to balance regional Soviet superiority still more urgent; otherwise — in Western eyes — considerable rearmament was the only alternative. The NATO Council adopted the idea of a 'dual strategy' as its guiding principle in May 1979 and finally decided on it in December 1979. This involved the decision to deploy American medium-range missiles of the Pershing II type and cruise missiles in 1983–4 and at the same time to offer arms-limitation talks. This dual strategy accomodated the complex balance between deterrent and détente. But, at first the USSR refused the offer of negotiations. The intervention in Afghanistan and the decision of the United States not to ratify SALT II worsened prospects for negotiations on strategic weapons in Europe. When the Soviets finally came to the conference table in September 1980, it was the change in American government that caused an interruption in the negotiations; and when the Geneva talks were reopened both sides were unable to find a compromise (see below). Thus, the phase of détente in Europe is characterised by the fact that, whilst multilateralisation has succeeded in regulating co-operation between East and West in the economic sphere, it has failed in the area of military and security policy.

## Excursus: Economic Cooperation and Détente

With reference to the characteristic mix of rapprochement and demarcation in détente it has often been assumed that economic relations between East and West present the most important integrative elements in the regulation of the East–West conflict. Indeed, a process of transnational exchange of material and personnel, of meshing antagonistic societies in the East and West, takes place in this sphere. These processes can, therefore, be regarded as constitutive for both the creation and the continuation of the process of détente. This assumption can be modified and made more precise in the light of events in the 1970s.

In addition to the political developments described above the following data and tendencies must also be considered (see Table 10.3):

(1) *The proportional aspect.* East–West trade (between Western industrial nations and Communist countries in Eastern Europe including the USSR) increased as a proportion of world exports above average in the 1970s, but was still relatively unimportant. In 1978 it amounted to 2.8 and 2.3 per cent.

(2) *The European aspect.* East–West trade is focused on trade between Eastern and Western Europe. East European trade with industrial nations outside Europe accounts for only 0.4 and 0.3 per cent of world exports. Although the growth of the export quota from the East to Western Europe was smaller than that to the United States and Japan in 1978, Western Europe, with 74.4 per cent, still had the greater share of exports from the East, compared with the United States with 11.4 per cent and Japan with 9.9 per cent.

(3) *The aspect of imbalance.* The proportion of trade with the East of total exports and imports accounts for only 4.3 per cent for Western Europe, and only 2.6 and 0.9 per cent for the United States (1978); In contrast, the proportion of trade with the West of total exports/imports account for 26.2 and 36.8 per cent for Eastern European countries (including the USSR), and 27.5 and 36.3 per cent for the USSR.

(4) *The aspect of imbalance.* The contribution of exports to the East to the GNP is 1 per cent for Western industrial nations, whilst the contribution of exports to the West to the GNP is 2-4 per cent for Eastern European countries.

(5) *Complementarity.* East European states (including the USSR) import predominantly investment goods from the industrial nations of the West (44.2 per cent), whereas Western nations import mainly fuel (37.8 per cent) and other raw materials (14.4 per cent) from countries in the East (1977).

(6) *Dependence on economic cycles.* Exports to the East from Western industrial nations (see Table 10.1) rose rapidly in 1972 and 1973 –

Table 10.1 *East–West trade and economic developemnt*

| | 1970 | 1971 | 1972 | 1973 | 1974 | 1975 | 1976 | 1977 | 1978 |
|---|---|---|---|---|---|---|---|---|---|
| Economic development of OECD countries[1] | | | | | | | | | |
| GDP | 3.0 | 3.8 | 5.5 | 6.1 | −3.1 | −0.6 | 5.2 | 3.7 | 3.7 |
| Industrial production | 3.5 | 2.2 | 7.0 | 9.2 | 0.0 | −7.9 | 8.6 | 4.0 | 4.4 |
| Exports from OECD countries | | | | | | | | | |
| to CMEA countries[2] | 7 | 5 | 21 | 21 | 7 | 23 | 6 | −10 | 2.5 |
| to USSR | 5 | −2 | 33 | 22 | 8 | 35 | 10 | −13 | 2.0 |
| (at constant prices) | | | | | | | | | |
| Imports to OECD countries | | | | | | | | | |
| from CMEA Countries[2] | −1 | 6 | 11 | 11 | −12 | −2.5 | 7.5 | −1 | 7.0 |
| from USSR | −8 | 1 | 8 | 24 | −7 | −3 | 9 | 0.5 | 6.5 |
| (at constant prices | | | | | | | | | |

1. Changes (%)
2. Changes against previous year(%)
*Source:* Stankovsky, in *DGFK-Jahrbuch* 1979–80

during the boom; it increased even further during the recession of 1974–5; the rise was smaller in 1974, but by 1975 it was enormous; it began to weaken once more in 1976 and by 1977 the percentage change compared with that of the previous year was strongly negative; in the following year there were again signs of a rise. Exports to the West from East European states reflect developments in the economy even more clearly; they likewise rose considerably in 1972 and 1973, but declined badly by 1974 and 1975; they experienced a temporary high in 1976, whilst the percentage change in 1977, compared with that of the previous year, was negative and in 1978 there was once more a notable rise.

(7) *Long-term orientation.* Between 1972 and 1974 there was a 'boom' in long-term agreements between East European states and companies in the West and in the number of tripartite agreements

between industrial nations in the East and West and developing nations (1975 = 132); in 1973 there were *c.* 600 and by 1974 *c.* 1,000 East–West co-operation agreements; the number then fell somewhat; proportionally Hungary and Poland and the Federal Republic of Germany and France are at the top here.

From this summary it can be seen that there was a sort of explosive expansion in East–West economic relations running parallel to the breakthrough of détente between 1972 and 1974. For example, trade relations between the Soviet Union and market economies in the West — compared with the total Soviet foreign trade — had reached the same level proportionately as in 1946 before the outbreak of the Cold War (see tables in Goldman, 1975, p. 24). If one takes trade-policy indicators as a basis, the second attempt at antagonistic co-operation can be said to have reached the level of the first attempt, but not to have gone beyond it. Transnational relations and economic links have broadened the societal base of support for détente — particularly when they were long term (see point 7 above): An interest in stable East–West relations has developed not only among the Western economic élites which gain advantages from trade with the East, but also among management in the socialist countries. In part, economic élites themselves have actively contributed to the preparation and the introduction of détente and created favourable conditions for the advance of political détente (for Germany's *Ostpolitik*, see Weisert, 1973; Kreile, 1974). However, the enormous expansion in East–West economic relations first began once governments had overcome political obstacles and created new political frameworks. To this extent economic co-operation followed political co-operation. In this respect bilateral agreements between governments were obviously more important than the multilateral declarations of the CSCE. Apparently developments in the economy are even more important than foreign policy and international decision. The expansion of East–West trade ran parallel to a period of prosperity; the 1974–5 recession immediately hit imports from East European countries, whilst exports to the East were restricted more slowly (see points 5 and 6 above). For this reason alone East–West trade is difficult to control politically or to instrumentalise for foreign policy. The corresponding difficulties, referred to above in connection with American-Soviet economic relations, are analogous with East–West economic relations in general.

Although the United States played a leading role in the expansion of exports to the East, Europe is plainly the region in which economic relations between East and West have been most quickly and strongly cemented (see point 2 above and Wilczynski, 1969). Does this fact support the assumption that therefore in Europe (in contrast to American-Soviet relations) favourable preconditions exist for integrative developments between systems and for the establishment of a new political order? Scholars of the functionalist and neo-functionalist schools argue in this way: the form of organisation follows the actual pattern of transactions and functions (Groom, 1975) and political associations develop from economic and societal links (Zellentin, 1970); economic co-operation is said to extend increasingly to other areas and to have the political power to push individual transnational interests into planned co-operation in some spheres; thus 'a new system of military, political, economic and social security' can be superimposed on, and eventually replace, 'the balance of deterrence' (Zellentin). These assumptions and expectations should be judged with scepticism, if for no other reason than that East–West economic relations have an essentially more limited scope (see point 1 above) than relations between Western industrial nations (1978 = 47.5 per cent of world trade) and are even lower than relations between these nations and developing countries (1978 = 15.9 and 16.7 per cent of world exports and imports). The pattern of transactions and functions, which, according to functionalist ideas, create the form of organisation, has too low a profile even in Europe. Furthermore, it is doubtful whether the conditions of integration, which have been developed in analysing West European integration, can be applied (by means of a so-called functional equivalent) to relations between democratic market economies and planned socialist economies. The state managers of the Soviet Union and East European countries can hardly be regarded as 'functional equivalents' to Western industrialists. They are the official representatives and functionaries of a political and socio-economic system with opposing values and aims. In contrast to market economies, in which socio-economic groups have more room for manoeuvre *vis-á-vis* governments, the governments in socialist countries possess the instruments of control to block processes of spill-over which threaten their exercise of power. At present and in the foreseeable future it is hardly likely that 'forms of socialist pluralism' will develop sufficiently (Zellentin, 1970). It has further to be taken into account that the functionalist theory has only been partially confirmed even in the analysis and prognosis of the integration process of similarly structured societies in Western Europe. Evidently, the independent weight of high politics, especially of security policy, has to be considered more carefully even in non-antagonistic co-operation — the more so with respect to co-operation between antagonistic states, particularly since ideological demarcation cannot be without influence on the economic and political spheres. Experience of economic co-operation between the systems in the inter-war period reinforces the question of whether peaceful change can be induced by economic means in relations with closed societies.

The proviso that ideological divisions cannot be overcome by joint economic goals was acknowledged in the original neo-functionalist concept of Ernst Haas (1964): it is central to an evaluation of East–West relations (see Williams, 1976). In the context of power and security politics the imbalance of East–West economic relations (see points 2 and 4 above) and the complementarity of the products of East–West trade (see point 5 above) are of prime importance. The question whether thereby a one-sided dependence has been created in the countries of Eastern Europe is debatable. An answer in the affirmative is supported by the fact that imported technology represents a considerable factor in the growth and development of the countries of Eastern Europe and that these imports are very dependent on the continued provision of credits by banks and governments in the West in view of the complementarity of exchange relations. The vulnerability, i.e. the degree of economic costs and long-term negative effects in the event of a unilateral curb or break in economic relations (regression), would be considerably greater for the countries of Eastern Europe than for Western nations. To be sure, exports to the East have a certain relevance for the employment policies of Western industrial nations. In the United States it is reckoned that exports to the East worth more than $15,000 create one job (Goldman, 1975, p. 276); in total, *c.* 1 per cent of employment in the western industrial nations may be dependent on exports to the East. However, in view of these dimensions, a curb on trade would hardly produce a 'recession caused by a fall in demand' (Müller). To a certain degree, both sides (perhaps the countries of Eastern Europe more strongly than the West) may be said to be interested in stabilising East–West relations. There is a 'limited dependency' — governed by political considerations (Knirsch, 1978 and 1979).

The discussion about indirect opportunities of influence to be gained by Western governments upon the long-term behaviour of socialist governments thus has to differentiate between the domestic or social and foreign policy effects.

The potential effect of a domestic 'liberalisation' of socialist states and societies is regarded as a threat to the position of power held by the respective élites. They therefore make vigorous efforts to prevent this sort of effect, especially since they may well have opened their societies economically to the West to import Western technology in order to avoid otherwise inevitable reforms. From this standpoint the policy of demarcation and repression pursued by the socialist governments can be seen as an attempt to avoid the domestic effects of economic co-operation which they regard as destabilising (see Jacobsen, 1975). Therefore, even if one does not conclude from this a law of the dialectical development of détente (see Williams, 1976), the positive, domestic political effects of East–West economic relations leading to a further rapprochement are clearly limited in Western eyes.

The impact of economic asymmetries on the foreign policy of the socialist ruling élite should likewise not be overestimated as to its extent or its value for détente. Commercial contracts, generally based on economic advantages for both sides, are thus in principle balanced. If one nevertheless assumes, on the basis of the above analysis, that the general economic advantages of economic co-operation are greater for socialist countries and that a willingness for political co-operation is thus promoted, one also has to acknowledge the possible reverse effect on the grounds of logic alone: i.e. that regression in economic relations, intentional or unintentional (resulting from economic cycles), would remove an important impulse towards the continuation of détente in socialist countries. The policy of limited trade embargoes pursued since the beginning of 1980 in reaction to the Soviet invasion of Afghanistan could thus prove to be counter productive.

More important is the unintended impact of the business cycle on East–West trade. The unequal development of exports and imports, heightened by the 1974–5 recession, considerably increased the balance of trade deficit and the debts of countries in Eastern Europe (1978 = $60 billion). In order to restrain them and to overcome the shortage of convertible currency, the Soviet Union moved to curb imports from the West from 1975 onwards and has increasingly pursued a policy of compensatory agreements. This worsened the prospect for Western exports and increased the pressure from Soviet goods in the markets of the Western industrial nations. If a new economic recovery does not occur, conflicts could arise, to threaten détente both domestically and internationally:

> A long-term growth of 3.5 per cent in the West is in no way guaranteed, especially after the . . . oil crisis of 1979. At this rate of growth unemployment will scarcely be reduced. The political pressure to protect jobs from competition from abroad will, therefore, not raise the willingness of Western industrial nations to remove existing trade restrictions; rather the tendency to raise new barriers will increase . . . The positve effect of East–West trade on employment to date (a result of the active trade balance and of the exchange of labour-intensive manufactured goods against raw materials and fuel) would be transformed into a negative effect if the gap in the balance of payments was only slightly closed. However, such a situation would doubtless meet with considerable resistance in the West. Any resulting protectionism against the East would certainly have repercussions in the political sphere. However, it could also lead to individual countries in the East being unable to repay their debts, which would create problems which hardly bear thinking about (Stankovsky, in *DGFK-Jahrbuch* 1979–80).

At the peak of a conflict — as historical experience has shown (see Link, 1970) — the position of debtor countries could be used as the 'weapon of the weaker' (Reichs Chancellor Brüning): the asymmetric dependency would be reversed. In a political crisis no longer the long-term, but rather the short-term, effective dependency of East–West economic relations would be important. At this moment these are unbalanced to the disadvantage of Western nations because of the high proportion of fuel imports from the East to Western industrial nations (see above). This would give the Soviet Union a strategic advantage in the event of tension.

To summarize then, we may draw the following conclusion: In the 1970s an equally strong interest in the stability of long-term economic relations existed and the effects of East–West economic relations on détente were ambivalent. East–West economic relations can support détente and political regulation of conflict: but they can also promote conflict, necessitating the support of political détente for economic co-operation. In this case the regulation of conflict and the stabilisation of economic relations would have to take place for political reasons. However, at the beginning of the 1980s a contrary tendency can be identified, namely that — as in 1946–7 — political tension leads to a regression of economic relations.

The 'reciprocal dependency' (Müller) of long-term stability in economic and political relations between East and West became more obvious during the 1970s. It excludes a successful 'linking', just as much as a unilateral political instrumentalisation of East–West trade. An understanding of reciprocal dependence on stability could, however, create a common interest (perhaps only limited) in the continuation of détente. In other words: as the aim is the creation of long-term stability, a common interest could exist linking the economic and strategic spheres. Long-term stability is an essential goal for the regulation of the East–West conflict both for economic and strategic reasons. If political and strategic stabilisation fails, economic stability is also affected. And if it is correct that the political effects resulting from intensified East–West economic relations should not be exaggerated, then neither should the political effects arising from restricted relations (through an embargo policy) be considered to be very great. The economic sanctions imposed in protest over the Soviet invasion of Afghanistan at the beginning of 1980 are thus of doubtful value, if they are not integrated into constructive crisis management.

## Summary: Détente in the 1970s

The organisation of international relations became more complex during the second phase of antagonistic co-operation than during the Cold War. In both phases (not only during the Cold War) the East–West conflict has to a great extent determined the course of world politics. However, the regulation of conflict has altered. Détente is not aimed at abolishing or 'solving' East–West conflict, but rather at creating a new international framework for its regulation. The 1970s may be characterised as a phase in which the contenders in the East–West conflict sought to develop a mix of demarcation (regression) and co-operation (integration) in the various areas of relations, depending on what seemed appropriate to the situation (see also G. Zellentin, 1976). As empirical analysis has shown, the supplementation of the structure of relations formed by the Cold War through integrative elements has been used very hesitantly and only partially, sometimes bilaterally, sometimes multilaterally. Antagonisms of ideology and power politics and incompatible (or apparently incompatible) tendencies in the context of the East–West conflict contain such a great potential for tension and escalation that a fast shift of these mixed relations in favour of a 'systems of co-operation' is not appropriate. In fact it can lead straight to destabilisation. Too high expectations have proved to be counter-productive for the continuation of détente; they conceal the danger of producing mistrust instead of trust, of leading to disillusionment and of turning into new confrontation or regression. It can be assumed that the uncertainties about the intentions and behaviour of opponents can be subdued only in a long-lasting process of co-operation. Détente moves between the minimum goal of 'controlled relations of mistrust' and the maximum goal of 'trusting relations' (Kaufmann, [2]1973). Here lies the wide field of confidence-building measures — a field which has to be tilled and cultivated according to the specific conditions of the soil. Up to now only a few plots have been cultivated; and the limited successes achieved are now threatened, although not totally destroyed, by the cooling of the East–West climate resulting from the Afghanistan crisis. The reorganisation of international relations in the sense of creating a new type of conflict regulation is a long and contradictory process which — as past experience has shown — is best promoted by a gradualist policy.

Doubtless Super Power bilateralism determined, and determines, this process, especially at the decisive level of nuclear strategy. This dominance of US -Soviet bilateralism, the results of bilateral negotiations in the sphere of nuclear strategy and the difficulties encountered by the multilateralisation of détente have, at the height of détente, nourished the assumption that a 'partial duopoly' (Czempiel) or even a 'condominium' of Super Powers (Jobert) has been created, with serious consequences for Europe and the structure of alliances. According to this thesis, Western Europe has experienced a loss of status (Jobert), resulting from a sort of a second Yalta. The originally central security function of the Atlantic Alliance has been demoted to a mere 'reserve function' (Czempiel) of American security policy. And there has emerged a tendency to dissociate or uncouple West European security from American security (see Nerlich, 1973; Dettke, 1976, with further references).

The empirical analyses of the structures and processes of Cold War and détente, the development of alliances, of behaviour in crises and of the integrative elements in the East–West conflict (Chapters 7–10) do not bear out this assumption. During the phase of détente bipolarity and the bipolarisation of relations between the antagonists in the East–West conflict were merely extended by elements of co-operation. They were not dissolved. And the polarisation of policy in the sphere of alliances was (albeit to a lesser extent) apparently the direct precondition of a far-reaching depolarisation and of integrative, co-operative development in other, non-military areas. It has, however, also been shown that the impact of integrative elements is smaller than has often been assumed.

The stabilisation of alliances has shown itself to be one main condition of political détente. The system of military alliances can be directly understood as an international security system 'within which specific behaviour [aggression and extortion] are excluded, thereby making other [economic] co-operation . . . probable' (Kaufmann, $^{2}$1973, p. 60). Thus the functions of the system have increased in significance and expanded rather than been reduced. This increasing significance can be explained by the fact that, because of the co-operative agreement on strategic nuclear parity in the main weapons system (SALT I and SALT II), the armies and weapon systems in Europe have been made more important also for American security (see the discussion on Euro-strategic weapons). The traditional function of alliances — deterrence and stabilisation through the military organisation of demarcation, which has been expanded at the geo-strategic level — has been supplemented by the integrative function of co-operative arms control and conflict-regulation, a function which necessitates initiative and co-ordination in order to give substance to détente. Whilst information on the internal workings of the Warsaw Pact is insufficient for a well-founded statement (see Tiedkte, in *DGFK-Jahrbuch* 1979–80), it is possible to say of the Atlantic Alliance that it received adequate support for détente from all member states, that it was able to develop détente initiatives and, despite considerable difficulties and continuing irritations, was able to co-ordinate détente in the West in a flexible way, by differentiating roles and sharing work with other bodies such as the EPC (European Political Co-operation) and summit conferences of the Seven or the Four (see the studies of Holsti *et al.*, 1973). In contrast, it appears to be much more difficult for the Alliance to react to the crisis of détente with a joint strategy.

As an immediate result of our analysis it can be said generally that détente aims at calming, regulating and transforming the East–West conflict into peaceful competition, through arms limitation, through control agreements in the military sphere and through integrative processes in other areas. This corresponds with the following characteristic pattern of relations:

- closest relations at all levels and in all areas between European and American countries and societies;

- a comparatively low level of relations between the two alliances in the military sphere;
- many closer relations between the nations and societies of both alliances in non-military spheres.

The détente of the 1970s provides documentation that a gradual approximation to this pattern can be realised despite all difficulties. The developments at all three levels were linked together and could mutually influence one another. Military agreements can promote closer economic relations, and conversely closer economic and cultural relations can favour confidence-building measures in the military sphere. In the future also the maintenance and strengthening of relations between the Atlantic and West European nations and societies — the regulation of competition between them and the co-ordination of their policies — can be said to be the precondition of a balance between East and West. In the same way, conversely, the development of a 'more organic' relationship between the Soviet Union and her allies in Eastern Europe could be very helpful for the stabilisation of détente. By the end of the 1970s it became clear that détente had not yet become an irreversible process. At the beginning of the 1980s after the intervention of the Red Army in Afghanistan, the continuation of détente openly came under strain. This means that alternative patterns for the regulation of conflict have to be considered without a satisfactory answer being immediately available.

# 11 *East–West Conflict and North–South Conflict*

## *The State of the International System*

In the 1960s and 1970s, alongside the East–West conflict, a further structural world conflict emerged — the so-called North–South conflict. Its origins and development, and the strategies of conflict regulation have been analysed with the aid of the conflict theory presented above and in connection with the theory of decolonialisation (Zartman, 1976). Since the results have been published elsewhere (Link and Tücks, 1985), the following presentation will be limited to a summary.

In general, the North–South conflict is about the structure of world order in the political and economic spheres — with changing emphases emerging with the passage of time. The long-term tendency towards the global implementation of the nation-state principle had clashed with the tendency to maintain imperial and colonial structures as early as in the inter-war period and did so to an even greater extent after the Second World War, with the great thrusts of decolonialisation coming in 1955 and 1960. Territorial or national sovereignty and self-determination in all spheres (in politics, the economy and culture, at the domestic, as well as at the international, level) against imperial domination and the global predominance of industrial nations was, and is, the political core of the structural antagonism between the First and Third Worlds. In the spheres of economics and trade policies, seen as ideal types, the tendencies of market economies and free trade clash with the tendencies of control, planning and intervention. This impinges not only on domestic structure, but also on that of international order (see Heiduk, 1973).

In the process of political decolonialisation those structural principles of territorial sovereignty and autonomy were finally implemented world-wide which had formerly been established in Europe by the Peace Treaty of Westphalia in the seventeenth century and then replaced, in the wake of imperialist expansion overseas, by the principle of colonialist imperialism. Anti-colonialism at first produced only partial conflicts — conflicts which concerned the respective empires or imperial regions. Tensions escalated in parts to bloody wars of independence (in Indonesia, Indochina, Algeria, Guinea-Bissau, Mozambique, Angola). The parties in these conflicts were neither totally the 'North' nor the 'South', but rather individual liberation movements in the colonies on one side and the respective colonial empires on the other. However, once many of the former colonies or mandate territories had become independent states, they created a coalition relevant to power politics by unifying their positions both within and outside the United Nations. The United Nations increasingly developed as an important forum for negotiations and also as an international agent to be used by liberation movements as a coalition partner (see, e.g., Delbrück, 1973).

In the 1960s and 1970s, the process of political decolonialisation accelerated tremendously with the dissolution of empires and the creation of more than 100 new sovereign states. With few exceptions, this process has now been completed (see Modelski, 1972, pp. 119ff., and Ansprenger, [2]1973). This result alone marks a radical change in the structure of the international system. The new nations of the Third World have organised themselves into a group (the Organisation of Non-aligned States and the Group of 77; see Willetts, 1978, Matthies, 1979), to become a collective quasi-agent. They are demanding that the organisation of domestic economics and the new organisation of international relations (especially in the economic sphere) take account of these developments. The overall tendency towards decolonialisation found its organisational expression in the creation of a collective counterweight and has become important for world politics. Partial conflicts have in principle fused into a global conflict which directly concerns the organisation of international relations. This new quality was reached at the beginning of the 1970s. In the same period, critical tensions in the East–West conflict were relaxed by détente, so that the tensions in the world-economic order were made more obvious.

In the course of the regulation of conflict between East and West and North and South far-reaching changes have occurred in the structure of international relations (i.e. with regard to structural principles and the arrangement of states).

Most importantly, the principle of national or territorial decentralisation was implemented globally in opposition to the principle of colonial, imperial domination. The resulting extreme fragmentation of the international system into more than 150 nations had two main consequences.

(a) The relative superiority of both the United States and the USSR has been considerably strengthened. Because of their sheer size, their economic potential and the stage of their development, they are — as is increasingly true of the Chinese People's Republic — the 'natural' Great Powers in a fragmented system of nations, to whom the task of leadership falls, whether they like it or not.

(b) The demands made upon the organisation and control of this fragmented world have increased immensely. The formal fragmentation has been accompanied by an actual interlocking. Global communications and interactions have created an extremely complex web of relations. Thus international regime-building has become more necessary and at the same time more difficult than ever. Serious divergencies in power and development and ideological antagonisms militate against an organisation of international relations which would be accepted by all nations as legitimate.

The opposing tendencies and interests which lie at the heart of both world conflicts, and the various attempts to regulate conflict have led to a range of changes in the groupings between nations in the course of time — which is the second important aspect of the change in the international structure.

In the 1920s and 1930s the traditional competition between the Great Powers was still predominant. However, the East–West conflict and its regulation had already begun to influence international groupings during those decades — at first through the exclusion of the Soviet Union from, and then its integration into the League of Nations and into the community of nations. The United States and the USSR were already the main contenders, with opposing views on world order in the inter-war period and, as such, were prototypes for future developments. The Hitler–Stalin pact brought together those states that were striving for a new ordering of international relations based on policies of race or class into an 'unholy' alliance against the representatives of the traditional order of nations and empires. But this arrangement lasted only two years. The opponents in the East–West conflict were then gradually forced into a new conflict configuration with the Axis Powers and into a policy of a military conflict resolution which created the antagonistic co-operation of World War II between the democratic countries of the West and the socialist Soviet Union. It was to be continued on the basis of the UN concept of integration in peacetime. The projected degree of organisation did not, however, correspond to the actual mix of antagonistic and joint interests. Once the threat that had united them despite all differences disappeared in 1945, the ideological and political antagonisms between East and West regained greater importance. The difference in power of the two main contenders was so enormous that the realisation of the concept of integration would indeed have meant the subordination of the weaker (the USSR) to the stronger (the United States). Instead of joint control over global politics on the part of the Great Powers, which would have amounted to the co-operative supremacy of the United States, bipolar systems of alliances were formed as signs of a regressive policy. Spheres of influence were established which followed the rules of establishing a balance of power. This tendency occurred throughout the world, but was found most persistently in Europe. The general characteristic of state groupings in Europe was the bipolarisation of alliances, both during the Cold War and during phases of détente. The continued need to establish the balance of power in the areas of national security explains its unusual continuity — despite the fact that, in the economic sphere, new groups were formed (such as the creation and strengthening of the EEC in particular). The system of alliance and counter-alliance has created a clear demarcation of spheres of influence and thereby stabilised security policies. On this basis more intensive exchange relations in the various functional areas might then be developed.

In regions outside Europe, the bipolarisation of alliances has been only partially and temporarily successful. The North–South conflict, which is at heart a continual and all-embracing process of decolonialisation, had from the very outset and to an ever-increasing extent modified (and been superimposed on) the structure of the East–West conflict in regions outside Europe, and vice versa. The collective self-organisation of the Third World, the Organisation of Non-aligned States, has defined itself on the one hand in relation to the main contenders and alliances of the East–West conflict as 'non-aligned'. It attempts to adopt a position outside the configuration of conflict of bipolar alliances. On the other hand, it is defined as an informal, anti-colonial alliance wedded to the development policies which constitute a collective counterweight to the group of industrial nations that dominates the world economic order even after the fall of the colonial empires. The demand for the establishment of a New International Economic Order is an attempt to reduce critical tensions between the antagonistic tendencies of the First and Third Worlds by using the concept of integrative regulation of conflict (see Sauvant and Hasenpflug, 1977; Senghaas,

1977; Fishlow *et al.*, 1978; Hansen, 1979).

It is important to note that both structural world conflicts, East–West and North–South, present two different configurations of conflict. However, both conflicting tendencies bear upon the organisation of global international relations. Whereas in the 'West' and 'South' the dominant tendency is to separate the two conflicts as much as possible, the 'East' pursues an opposing policy.

Communist-socialist countries and theorists maintain on the one hand that the demands of the developing nations are directed exclusively at the former colonial powers or the 'neo-colonialist' countries in the West. On the other hand, they try to establish a conceptual and practical link between the two conflicts and their present main contenders by interpreting decolonialisation as part of the Second World's 'anti-imperialist struggle'. Accordingly the socialist countries are seen as the natural allies of the Third World in the joint struggle against 'imperialism' and 'colonialism' or 'neo-colonialism' (see Alimow and Stchetinin, 1975). The axis of the North–South conflict is to a certain extent shifted to coincide with the axis of the East–West conflict. Those Western analysts who regard the dispute with the Third World as an international class struggle, indirectly accept this approach. However, the Communist approach has not been adopted by the Third World apart from a few exceptions (such as Cuba and Vietnam). The Third World has rather pursued the reverse policy — forming an informal, anti-colonial alliance based on development policy outside the Cold War competition between the Great Powers. As a rule the countries of the Second World vote with Third World states in the United Nations on questions of development policy and often on those of world politics, thus creating a united front against First World countries. However, the demands of the Third World for the transfer of resources and the restructuring of international economic order are increasingly directed towards the socialist industrialised nations also. Demands for practical contributions to the development of the Third World and for the restructuring of international economic order and trade are also made to the Second World. The vast majority of developing countries do not identify their interests with the 'socialist camp' and reject a binding political or military alliance with the USSR as much as with her opponent, the United States.

A new situation has been created by the competition in power politics and ideology between the Chinese People's Republic and the USSR. This intra-socialist struggle has culminated in conflict, but not because the two opponents represent incompatible tendencies on the principles of how to structure international relations. Both powers retain internationalism based on their class politics and revolution. They interpret each other's policy as a deviation and an attempt at imperial domination (hegemonism). The conflict is about the faithfulness to principles and about international alignment.

Before breaking with the USSR, Mao Tse-tung, like Stalin, promoted the 'Two Camps' theory: socialism vs. imperialism; according to him, no intermediary position and no third path was possible (Mao , 1949, in Kim, 1979, p. 75). Similarly the United States and her allies in that phase also saw the conflict with the Chinese People's Republic as an ingredient in the East–West conflict (see Kalicki, 1975); and it took them some time to react to the changes that had already begun in Chinese politics by the end of the 1950s. Since then, Chinese Communists have gradually, and with different variations, formulated and established the theory of an intermediate zone, initially in order to separate themselves from both Super Powers. Their new international structural model is based on the hypothesis that there are four main contradictions in the present situation in world politics:

(1) the contradiction between oppressed nations, on the one hand, and imperialism and social imperialism, on the other;

(2) the contradiction between the proletariat and the bourgeoisie in capitalist and revisionist countries;

(3) the contradiction between imperialist and social-imperialist countries and between imperialist countries;

(4) the contradiction between socialist countries, on the one side, and imperialism and social-imperialism, on the other.

Correspondingly four zones are seen to have been established in the world system:

(1) the zone of the Super Powers (American imperialism and Soviet social-imperialism);

(2) the zone of socialism (with the People's Republic of China as the prime example of a socialist state);

(3) the first intermediate zone of developing nations (the Asian, African and Latin American countries); and

(4) the second intermediate zone made up of 'specific larger capitalist countries in the East and West'.

By linking the first intermediate zone and the socialist zone the theoretical world model is finally reduced to three zones:

(1) the zone of both imperialistic and social-imperialistic Super

Powers;

(2) the intermediate zone of the countries of Europe, plus Canada and Japan;

(3) the Third World, including China (see amongst others Kim, 1979, pp. 76f.; Bechtoldt, [2]1969).

Thus the original equation of socialism, anti-imperialism and anti-colonialism has been restored in theory; although henceforward not the Soviet Union, but the People's Republic of China is considered the leading power, while emphasizing, like the Soviet Union, that she wishes to make no claims to domination: 'China is a socialist country and a developing country. China belongs to the Third World . . . China is not a Super Power nor will she ever seek to be one' (Teng, 1974, quoted in Yahuda, 1978, p. 242). However, in general, this model of world politics is regarded as a transitional configuration until socialism has been implemented on a world scale by revolutionary means. The revolutionary force of developing countries is seen to be propelling the wheel of history in this direction, 'combating colonialism, imperialism and particularly the super-powers'. 'Victory in the world-wide struggle against hegemonism and victory in the international proletariat's struggle for Socialism and Communism are identical as far as fundamental interests are concerned' (*People's Daily*, 1 November 1977, quoted in Yahuda, 1978, p. 269). Consequently the struggle against the Super Powers, and eventually against the Super Power that, from the Chinese standpoint, poses the greatest direct threat, is justified ideologically as revolutionary socialism. This means that a link is being forged between the two axes of conflict, East–West and North–South, a mirror-image of the Soviet attempt at 'linking' already discussed. The socialist-imperialist Soviet Union is declared to be the main opponent both of Western democratic industrial countries and of the Third World. Because it is imperative to form a counterweight, the United States becomes a desirable partner, just as the Soviet Union, during the SALT negotiations, tried to win over the United States to an anti-Chinese policy even to the extent of tolerating a nuclear attack on the People's Republic of China (see Newhouse, 1973, p. 188; *New York Times*, 2 July 1973). The more, in the wake of the Sino-American rapprochement of 1972, the Super Power America is drawn into an anti-Soviet counter-group, the more the three-zone model is actually transformed into a bipolar model: a concept of containment *à la chinoise*.

Admittedly all this concerns not so much a description of reality as an idea of international order and a political programme whose chances of realisation are unknown. Whilst the four-zone model is characterised by the recognition of the structural significance of Super Power bipolarity and by the compatibility of the concept of a (first) intermediate zone of Asian, African and Latin American countries with the views of the Organisation of Non-aligned States, neither the three-zone model nor its bipolar reduction corresponds with developments in the Third World. The Organisation of Non-Aligned States explicitly seeks to avoid any involvement in the East–West confrontation between the Super Powers, and it is no accident that the Chinese People's Republic is not a member of the Organisation of Non-Aligned States or of Group 77. Like the contrasting Soviet concept, the Chinese attempt to fuse the axis of the North–South conflict with that of the East–west conflict gains the immediate assent of those politicians in the West who view the problems of the Third World from the standpoint of conflict with the Soviet Union and its global policy and who thus advocate a Sino-American 'proto-alliance' (Robinson, 1978) to restrain Soviet expansionist policy. The US Administration has in practice acted along these lines in recent years. The advocates of a coalition of containment with the Chinese People's Republic purposely overlook the fact that the Chinese principle of proletarian internationalism and the long-term goal of realising the principle of class politics in global terms are incompatible with Western ideas. China's Communists do not want to stabilise world order; they wish to revolutionise it (see e.g. Bechtoldt, [2]1969; Näth, 1978; Opitz, 1980).

If we turn our attention away from theoretical, programmatic concepts, in which ideological goals and current political tactics are inextricably mixed, and concentrate instead on actual international configurations and groups of nations, we find a more complex and richer picture than that of the patterns and models sketched above. As we have shown in detail, a bipolar grouping at the highest level of nuclear strategy remains the decisive structural characteristic of the state system, and American superiority has been dismantled in favour of an approximate balance between the two Super Powers. If we look at the total distribution of power potentials, however, a tripolarity developed in the 1970s — the People's Republic of China joined the group of Great Powers on the strength of her economic potential (which has still not been fully mobilised). There is also the potential of gaining a nuclear second-strike capability over one of the Super Powers, namely the USSR.* But the prospect of catching up with either of the Super Powers in the foreseeable future is slim.

Below the level of nuclear policies, characterised by bipolarity and a gradually developing tripolarity, countries and groups of countries have specific relations to one another according to the issue and region; and they establish various multipolar configurations, with some changes and overlap.

In general political terms we can distinguish the three Great Powers of the United States, the USSR and the People's Republic of China (combined with their current bi- and multilateral alliances) and the informal alliance of the Organisation of Non-Aligned States. In the sphere of world economic and trade policy we have the OECD states, the Group of 77, the socialist countries (led by the Soviet Union) and the Chinese People's Republic. At the regional level we have numerous groupings (the EEC, CMEA, ASEAN, OAS, LAFTA, SELA, the Arab League, OAU, ECOWAS, etc.) and cartel-type groups (OPEC, OAPEC).

The relations between these states and groupings produce configurations of competition and conflict which are to some extent interlocked and reciprocally interrelated:

- the bipolar formation of competition and conflict between the Super Powers and their alliances (the East–West conflict);
- the bipolar formation of competition and conflict between industrialised and developing countries, between the First and Third Worlds (the North–South conflict); and
- many multipolar formations of competition and conflict between Great Powers, medium powers and/or regional groups (with changing combinations according to the issue and region), under which the power triangle USSR–PRCh–USA in Asia, and gradually on a global scale, is the most important multipolar formation.

This complex structure of international relations restrains foreign policy to a considerable degree, and even the actions of the two Super Powers. No single country, no group of countries and neither of the two Super Powers can achieve a stable international order of peace unilaterally. Stability or instability, and the survival of civilisation in the long run, depend essentially on whether, and how, the opponents in both structural world conflicts accomplish a regulation

---

*Multistage intercontinental ballistic missiles (ICBM) with a range of between 3,000 and 3,500 miles were successfully tested and deployed in 1976; since then ICMBs with a range of 8,000 miles may also have been deployed (IISS, *The Military Balance, 1979–1980*, p. 59).

of their competing and conflicting relations; on whether the Super Powers in particular succeed in reducing critical tension, as well as respecting other countries and groupings as independent regional factors of order and allowing them to participate in a regionally and functionally differentiated world order.

East–West détente and parallel attempts at an integrative regulation of the North–South conflict were, and are, steps taken in that precise direction even if they have at present entered a cul de sac.

Within the situation after the Second World War, when expectations linked to the concept of integrative peace were too high and thus contained the seeds of failure of that concept (see above), expectations on both sides have been unrealistically high during the phase of détente. Both the Soviet Union and the United States have been disappointed with détente since they expected too much and hoped for incompatible results (see Wagner, 1980). In both cases the central problem was, and is, how to regulate the competition for security at the nuclear level (Baruch Plan 1946 and SALT II 1979–80) as well as at the conventional level through the redressing of regional imbalance. Furthermore, there is a certain analogy to be drawn between the crisis of antagonistic co-operation after the Second World War and the current crisis of détente even with regard to the events that triggered off the crisis. In both cases the struggle for power in one and the same region (see Agwani, 1978) was, and is important. The integrative concept failed in Iran in 1946–7 (see above), and in 1980 it appears to have failed in Afghanistan — partly because of the Iranian crisis. Finally, both in 1947 and 1980 the change in East–West relations was signalled by the spectacular pronouncement of an American doctrine on foreign policy related to the Middle East and the Gulf region.*

This is as far as the analogy goes, because the present situation is fundamentally different vis à vis power structures. The Soviet Union, once a continental power, has become a global Great Power with land and sea bases all over the world (see map in SIPRI Yearbook, 1972, annex). The Soviet Navy sails on every ocean (see map, Fig. 11.1).

*The Truman doctrine (12 Mar. 1947) was a direct response to threats against Turkey. However, the Gulf region and the Indian Ocean were regarded as the goal of Soviet efforts towards expansion (see above, Ch. 6). The Carter doctrine (23 Jan. 1980) stated: 'An attempt by any outside force to gain control of the Persian Gulf region will be regarded as an assault on the vital interests of the United States of America. And such an assault will be repelled by any means necessary, including military force'.

Figure 11.1 *Regional distribution of the US and Soviet navies (1974)*

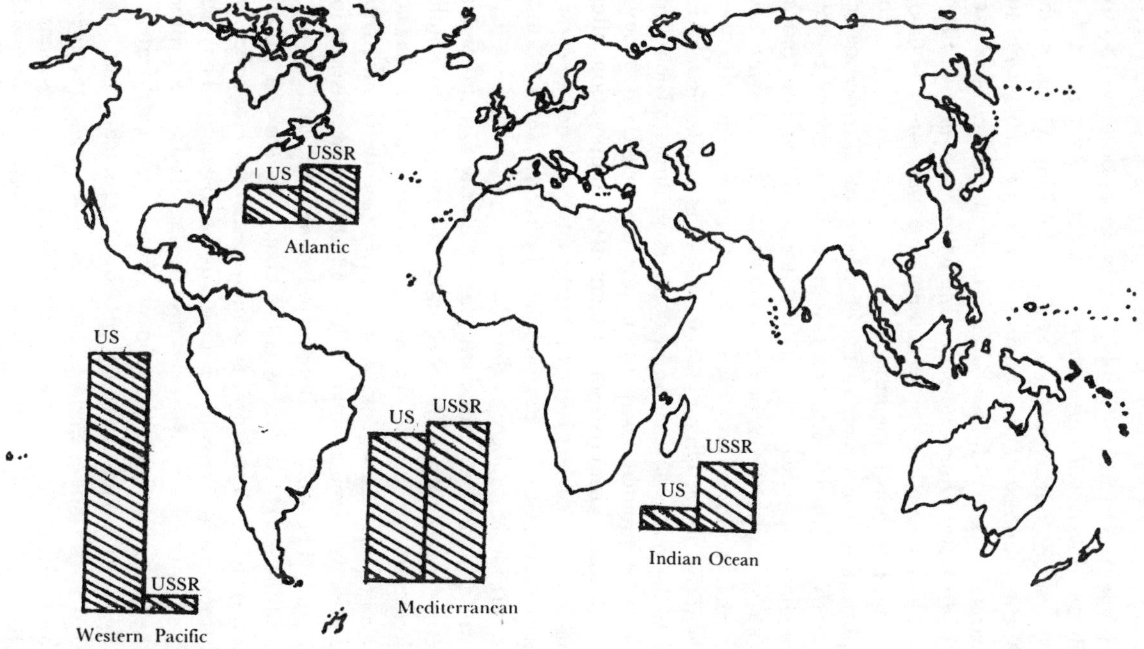


*Source*: Collins, 1978, p. 188.

In place of the United States' nuclear monopoly or superiority, an approximate strategic balance has been reached, shifting slightly in favour of the Soviet Union by the end of the 1970s. By the end of the 1980s (once American and NATO rearmament becomes effective) it is predicted that it will shift once more in the United States' favour. In this situation our hypothesis applies (see Link, German edition, Ch. 1), that in phases shortly before or after the achievement of an approximate balance the probability of open conflict or of extreme crises is greatest. Thus a considerable willingness to take risks and the tendency to exploit opportunities for expansion was to be expected and has indeed begun.

Opportunities for the expansion of spheres of influence are offered particularly in Third World countries because of the social, political and religious upheavals there. The local or regional parties in conflict seek support from one or other of the Great Powers according to their political and ideological affinities. The direct intervention of the Soviet Union in Afghanistan is to some extent simply a link in the chain of development which begins under these conditions of heightened competition between the Great Powers in regions outside Europe. However, it also signifies a qualitative turning-point, because it is the first time since the end of World War II that the Soviet Union has intervened directly, and with military means, outside her sphere of domination.

Continuity can be seen in the fact that the Great Powers are competing for influence in local and regional power vacuums or turbulences, particularly when the region is important for the supply of raw materials and for strategic security (see Bertram, 1979).

Détente was unable to change this fact; it was unrealistic to expect it to do so. The only meaningful question was, and is, by what means influence is exerted: whether crises are avoided by mutual restraint or whether at least crisis management is intensified within the framework of détente or peaceful coexistence. The rhetoric employed in the joint US–Soviet declaration of May 1972 appeared to point in this direction (see above). However, it was contradicted not only by official statements of the Soviet leadership that 'peaceful coexistence' did not exclude 'support for liberation movements' in the Third World, but also by the actual policy of both Super Powers (see above).

In the course of increased competition between the Great Powers in regions outside Europe during the phase of détente the Soviet Union has had both successes and failures — that is to say, the balance has in no way tipped in favour of the USSR.

The USSR and her Eastern allies have without doubt appreciably increased their economic and military links with the Third World. Economic aid between 1973 and 1975 was concentrated in Turkey (26 per cent), Afghanistan (18 per cent), India (14 per cent) and Pakistan (11 per cent), whereas military aid was centred in the Middle East (US Congress, *The Soviet Union and the Third World*, 1977). However, the political effects up to the mid 1970s were marginal, or even completely counter-productive (see Rubinstein, $^{2}$1976). The expulsion of Soviet advisers from the Sudan (1971) and from Egypt (1972) mark the most notable failure of this phase, the seriousness of which was further underlined by Egypt's eventual switch to the American camp in 1976. In contrast to this, the Soviet Union and her ally Cuba succeeded in 1975–6 in helping the pro-Soviet party (the MPLA) in the Angolan civil war to power and in stabilising the regime through massive indirect and direct military intervention (with 15,000 to 20,000 Cuban soldiers). In Mozambique the formerly successful People's Republic of China was ousted by Soviet and Cuban competition. Since 1977 the pro-Soviet regime of Mengistu in Ethiopia has been heavily supported by Cuban forces and Soviet military advisers both internally and externally, in the struggle against Somalia and the Eritrean Liberation Movement. However, at the same time the Soviet Union lost Somalia, including the Port of Berbera, built by the Soviets, which from now on is at the United States' disposal. The Communist seizure of power in South Yemen and Afghanistan in 1978 was a strategic gain for the Soviet Union which cannot yet be fully evaluated. The Soviet–Vietnamese link is more important because it is prejudicial to both American and Chinese influence in the Asian region. The forcible integration of Cambodia into the Vietnamese sphere of influence weakens the Chinese position; at the same time, however, Chinese military intervention against Vietnam in February and March 1979 has made the vulnerability of the Soviet ally more obvious.

Taken together, the United States and her allies in Africa, Asia, Latin America and the Middle East have, as before, an essentially greater number, and a denser network, of political and military agreements and bases than the USSR and her allies (see IISS, *The Military Balance*, 1979–80). Soviet attempts to extend the Soviet sphere of influence outside Europe were not, therefore, always successful either before or during the phase of détente and should not be exaggerated in an international comparison. Doubtless Soviet gains were already a strain for the continuation of détente before 1979–80. However, in the period between the Cuban missile crisis and the crisis in Afghanistan there was no reciprocal policy of taking risks, no direct escalation of crises between the Super Powers. Crisis management has functioned as 'rehearsed' since 1963 (see above). By and large the Soviet Union has not been very successful in exploiting local crises in the Third World.

# 12 *Conclusions and Prospects*

This brief look at North–South conflict and at local and regional conflicts in the Third World has shown that the East–West conflict is not the only conflict configuration in international politics. However, it still dominates world politics because the main contenders are the two Super Powers. International politics in this day and age are shaped — as the empirical analysis has illustrated — by the various attempts to regulate it, i.e. attempts to reduce critical tensions in the international system by improving or 'cooling' international relations through integration or regression or through various mixtures of the two. The difficulty has been, and is, in finding an appropriate mixture for changing the relations between common and opposing interests. At the level of practical politics, countries or their governments have employed methods of trial and error. Thus phases of predominantly integrative regulation of conflict and phases of more regressive regulation have superseded each other in waves. The curves of bipolarisation and depolarisation in the various spheres of relations have been described above (Ch. 7).

If political events are arranged as points on a graph defined by demarcation (regression) and co-operation (integration) and the peaks of critical situations and détente are joined, a wave-like curve emerges (see Cline, 1977, pp. 164 f). Phases of regressive regulation of conflict include (in vastly differentiated forms) the period of military intervention and non-recognition (1918–33) as well as the period of the Hitler–Stalin Pact (1939–41) and are then characterised by the Berlin Blockade (1948–9), the Korean War (1950–3), the crisis in Hungary (1956), the second Berlin crisis and the Cuban missile crisis (1961–2), the Czechoslovakian crisis (1968) and now the crisis in Afghanistan (1980 onwards). Between these phases lie periods of integrative co-operative regulation of conflict in lesser and greater degree. Their peaks are marked by the establishment of diplomatic relations (1933), the antagonistic war coalition (1941–5), the bilateral meeting at Camp David (1959), the semi-détente of 1963 and the bilateral and multilateral summit meetings in Moscow (1972), Washington (1973), Moscow (1974), Vladivostok (1977) and Helsinki (1975).

As was shown in Chapter 10 above, the phase of détente politics in the first half of the 1970s was characterised by the introduction of integrative elements into the regulation of the East–West conflict through a mixture of delimitation and co-operation which varied according to the sphere of relations and according to regions. The main conditions of this policy were an approximate balance of power and stability in the sphere of alliances. The policy was implemented by co-operative measures in balance control, extended and supported by economic and cultural co-operation.

Recent developments in the East–West conflict, apparent since the end of the 1970s, are characterised by a different style of conflict regulation compared with détente. There is a greater emphasis on confrontationist and regressive elements in conjunction with unilateral action. This change in the regulation of conflict has come about because the conditions have changed. And as the foundations have shifted, the whole structure has begun to sway.

This shift has involved changes in: (1) the strategic balance; (2) trade relations; (3) competition in regions outside Europe; and (4) the situation in the two alliances. These aspects will now be discussed to provide some conclusions and a look forward.

## Changes in the Strategic Balance

In the history of the East–West conflict, the emergence and eventual recognition of an approximate balance (strategic parity) was a new development after decades of American superiority. The fact that this new balance was in principle unstable and difficult to control could scarcely have been surprising to observers who do not scorn insights gained from historical experience. Policies based on preserving the balance of power have, at least in modern history, never been pursued more than temporarily, whether for longer or shorter periods (Dehio, [3]1974). The attempt to maintain such a policy in the long term requires considerable concerted efforts, particularly in view of the fact that no common values exist. There is also the problem that some policies conducted by one power are not regarded as legitimate by the other. The policy of balance therefore always contains the ingredients for upsetting that balance. It is directed towards preventing a potential opponent from achieving superiority. It conceals the ever-present temptation to maintain or attain a balance that favours one's own side, i.e. to preserve or to extend (even if only slightly) a position of superiority which opponents in turn will try to prevent. A balance-of-power policy — including a policy that seeks a balance through arms control — does not, therefore, suspend competition for power; rather it exists inside the competition. All this is further complicated by the fact that balance or superiority in general and in individual sectors is difficult to measure and scarcely definable in any objective way (see Marshall, 1982). As a result, perceptions become increasingly important.

American calculations, which at the end of the 1970s perceived a relative Soviet superiority on the strategic, nuclear power level, have been decisive for the latest developments in the East–West conflict. American projections expected this superiority to emerge most markedly at the beginning of the 1980s (see above, pp. 95f.). According to estimates of the political groups that attained power after Reagan's election to the presidency, it was feared that the carefully negotiated compromise on arms-control policy of SALT II would not produce the 'cementing of strategic stability', as claimed by parties to the treaty, but rather engender toleration of Soviet superiority (see Czempiel, 1982).

In addition there has been the clearly recognisable tendency on the part of the Soviet Union to attain a European strategic superiority through the continuous build-up of SS-20s. Chancellor Helmut Schmidt publicly pointed out this problem at an early stage, but it was not considered at SALT II 'despite repeated European, especially German, recommendations to the contrary' (Schmidt). According to remarks made by West Germany's Foreign Minister Genscher in the Bonn Cabinet, Carter and Brezhnev discussed medium-range missiles 'briefly in the lift' in Vienna (Cabinet Meeting, 25 Feb. 1981, quoted in *Der Spiegel*, 23 (1983), p. 20).

As has been mentioned above, it was only in December 1979 that NATO first attempted to reduce the Soviet Union's strategic superiority in Europe with its two-track decision and the idea of co-operative arms control. In contrast, the Reagan Administration has advanced along the traditional path in the context of intercontinental relations. Its policy has been aimed at 'reversing the negative trend in the balance of military strength' with the help of unilateral arms measures. Negotiations were to follow later. This meant that unilateral rearmament to overcome the actual or presumed imbalance had priority over diverse attempts to initiate arms-control negotiations (INF negotiations reopened on 30 Nov. 1981; START negotiations began on 29 June 1982).

The successes to date and the future effects of the modernisation of the American weapons system are undoubtedly remarkable. Nevertheless, according to the estimates of the US Administration, a balance of military power has not yet been reached. Therefore the demands of the peace movement for an arms freeze at current levels both in the East and in the West are dismissed with the argument that this would be to recognise Soviet superiority. It would also remove any inducement for arms control on the part of the Soviet Union. The 'rebuilding of the foundation of our military strength' is to be the 'precondition of a strengthened and purposeful foreign policy' (Reagan address to American legion, 22 February 1983, in *Amerika Dienst*, 2 March 83) and at the same time the inducement for an agreement in arms control negotiations of a military balance at a lower level. Some observers regard present circumstances as favourable because the Soviet Union may be interested in an agreement if faced with the prospect of uncontrolled American rearmament (Hyland, 1982–3, p. 11).

The stationing of the first American Pershing II and Cruise missiles in Western Europe led the Soviet Union to leave the negotiating table on arms control policy in Geneva. Only the framework of the CSCE and MBFR has been maintained; the follow-up conference in Madrid was successfully concluded in September 1983; and a new Conference on Confidence- and Security-Building Measures and Disarmament in Europe was planned and begun in January 1984 in Stockholm. However, only after the confirmation of Chernenko's position as new General Secretary of the CPSU and after the re-election of President Reagan did both sides agree 'to enter into new negotiations, with the objective of reaching mutually acceptable agreements on the whole range of questions concerning nuclear and outer space arms on 22 November 1984' (*New York Times*, 23 Nov. 1984).

In official statements both Super Powers reveal that the ideologically-based belief in superiority is weakening in favour of an emphasis on balance-of-power politics. However, the contradiction between Soviet claims concerning the existing balance and the actual military situation is evident, at least in Europe. The offer to reduce the number of SS 20s to the level of French and British missiles is an indirect admission that at present there is an imbalance in favour of the Soviet Union (see the after-dinner speech by General Secretary Andropov on the occasion of Honecker's visit on 3 May 1983, *Europa Archiv*, 10 (1983), p. D280). By now the Soviet

Union must have realised that this change in the strategic balance in Europe will be redressed by the NATO rearmament programme and that imbalances in some areas of intercontinental strategic forces will likewise be redressed or even be shifted in the United States' favour. In this situation the Soviet Union has been anxious to maintain the greatest possible margin of power and to keep alive the non-military elements of détente politics in Europe. In resorting to claims that an approximate balance already exists in Europe, the USSR has emphasized the joint interests of European states in continuing détente irrespective of conflicting structural concepts (see Oudenaren, 1982). Although this Soviet argument was undoubtedly intended to promote misunderstanding between Western Europe and the United States under the slogan of a European community of interests, 'a partnership of détente', it also offered a positive starting-point. A reduction in SS-20s could be introduced as a bargaining counter in return for American concessions in the negotiations on intercontinental strategic weapons. A compromise on the joint definition of approximate balance is one alternative. If it were to materialise, the essential preconditions for a new policy of détente would be met.

The alternative would be to succumb to the temptation not only to prevent unilaterally the superiority of one's opponent whilst at the same time purporting to support a policy of balance, but also to strive for superiority over the opponent. Developments in weapon technology have increased this temptation on both sides. Because the USSR and the United States are building up the potential of their forces to hold the balance, and are including the option of fighting a war in their doctrine of deterrence so that, should deterrence fail, they can still win a nuclear war, the basis for a common definition of approximate balance is undermined. The attempt to regulate conflict through war is threatening to become reality — a novel development since the invention of nuclear weapons.

There are indications of this kind of thinking in Soviet and American discussions on strategy. The evidence for this comes e.g. from the originally highly secret, but leaked, Pentagon study 'Fiscal Year 1984–1988 Defense Guidance' which is orientated towards a strategy of victory (*New York Times* 30 May 1982). Finally the research and development of programmes for defensive weapons in space, undertaken by both the United States and the USSR, could, if linked to offensive weapons, become the basis for an aggressive policy (see Herrmann, 1983).

These dangerous developments are supported in the United States and in the USSR wherever and in so far as ideologically-based concepts of 'friend or foe' take over, and begin to determine actions. In the USSR such thinking results from the conviction that peace can be accomplished only through the global victory of socialism and the overthrow of imperialism. This view generates the need to pursue the revolutionary process 'by changing global power relations in favour of peace and socialism' (A. Nikonov, quoted in Geierhos, 1980, p. 152). This corresponds to the tendency in the United States to expect peace to come about only through the defeat of Communism. Instead of emphasizing a minimum of common interests, the differences between the systems of democracy and Communism which reflect the irreconcilable tendencies in the East–West conflict are being elevated to the position of sole determinant of East–West relations. Only a 'change in the Soviet system itself' is said to be able to create a common basis. Therefore the Soviet system 'has to be confronted with unremitting pressure and failures in such a way that in a *political* sense it looses its ability to survive and thereby becomes open to fundamental change' (Ermarth, 1982, p. 141; see the critique of Oye, Lieber and Rothchild, 1983).

The vital question is whether the option of victory for one side or the other can be excluded by the unilateral building up of a balance of power or by a co-operative policy on arms control. Political reason speaks for the second approach. John Steinbruner indicated in 1982 that even the solution of the most dangerous problem of the day — the vulnerability of the strategic command structure by 'decapitation' in a pre-emptive strike — can be solved only through an explicit bilateral understanding, which appears to be impossible without a constructive stabilisation of political relations between the United States and the USSR (Steinbruner, 1982). The success of the new comprehensive arms-control negotiations depends on American-Soviet willingness to co-operate in other spheres.

Finally, as to Europe and the European balance, many, including none other than Henry Kissinger, pose the question as to whether it is absolutely necessary to have regional European balance in addition to the intercontinental strategic balance (see *Der Spiegel*, 40, 1983, p. 156). Proposals put forward by political scientists are also aimed in this direction — for example the proposal of Ernst-Otto Czempiel (1983) of accepting a gradualist strategy of disarmament 'by acknowledging the disproportionate advantange' of the Soviet Union within *Europe* in order to encourage the Soviet Union to disarm. The West would in this way 'consciously take a risk' in Europe to further the large aim. But the risk would be limited. In military terms those SS-20s remaining after reduction would be 'more than covered by American submarine-launched missiles and by submarines under the command of NATO.'

This proposal disregards the fact that an armed conflict cannot be uncoupled from the general conflict and that military conflict has to be integrated into the anatagonistic relations as a whole — in the sense of a 'comprehensive picture of conflict'. The military superiority of the Soviet Union in Europe would have dire consequences both regionally as well as globally (because of the significance of Western Europe) in view of the fact that military advantages are politically important and can be used politically. Past experience leads one to speculate that the proposed strategy would not remove the danger of military conflict. On the contrary, it would make it politically effective by creating asymmetry and by promoting destabilisation. On the other hand, a symmetrical stabilisation in the military sphere — as the experience of semi-détente and détente has shown — could also stabilise the political sphere. Under conditions of intercontinental parity and a global balance, an approximate regional European balance also seems necessary for a genuine policy of détente. If one renounced the idea of regional balance in Europe, one would either concede a politically useful advantage to the Soviet Union or unwillingly support the arguments that maintain that American strategic superiority is necessary because the Soviet Union possesses regional superiority (Gray and Brennan, 1982, p. 535). An imbalance in Europe would also preclude a joint agreement on a strategic balance.

## The Reappraisal of Trade Relations

With changes in the military balance there has been an increasing tendency to question the connections and links that have developed in the non-military sphere during the period of détente. Whilst in the 1970s economic trends and the debts of the CMEA states affected East–West trade for economic reasons, the new element in the present development of the East–West conflict is that politics affect trade.

Although President Reagan has conceded that efforts to re-establish a balance do not exclude 'productive relations' between the

United States and the USSR, the sanctions imposed because of the Soviet intervention in Afghanistan and the threat of intervention in Poland point to a far-reaching regression in non-military relations. In the past few years the United States has withdrawn from more than fifty American–Soviet agreements. For example, the United States has not extended the agreement as to co-operation in the exploration of space which expired in May 1982. The sole exception has been the resumption of grain exports for domestic political reasons. Within NATO the minimum demand is for a tightening up of the COCOM list and of credit conditions. Internally (e.g. in the Pentagon study mentioned above) a maximum concept envisages a trade boycott. It is based on the view that the trade policy of the West must exercise the greatest possible pressure on the Soviet economy. In present circumstances East–West interdependence is not considered to be an asset. In the US view there is a danger that Western Europe is heading for dependence on the Soviet Union as a result of co-operation with the East (see Link, 1982–3; Roosa, Gutowski and Matsukawa, 1983).

In contrast, the Europeans take the view that the maintenance and extension of trade relations with Eastern Europe during a period of competition for the creation of a military balance could limit the possible damage of East–West relations. 'Protective' security should be extended by 'co-operative' security (Mertes, 1983), and by a conscious use of integrative elements of conflict regulation as a stimulus. The assumption is that 'deterrence can be effective only when there are incentives' (Bialer, 1983, p. 550). The former government in West Germany operated on these lines and the present government is maintaining this continuity: 'Bonn judges it to be advantageous that agreement has been achieved in Vienna [at the meeting of Foreign Ministers] to continue to pursue political contacts and co-operation in the long term' (*FAZ* 21 Oct. 1983).

The fact that economic co-operation between the CMEA states (including the Soviet Union) and individual West European countries depends on long-term agreements between governments and is put into practice in long-term projects such as the controversial natural-gas pipe-line project, has been interpreted by K. Goldmann (1981–2) in the context of his stabilisation theory. Goldmann argues that stabilising elements are necessary in order to allow economic interdependence to affect politics in a way that enables the continuation of détente. In Western Europe, and especially in West Germany, this sort of effect has already been seen. On the other hand, this stabilising element has played no role in US policy because trade relations with the East continue to be minimal. This is also why it would be wrong to have too great expectations. Relations between the main contenders — as Frei and Ruloff have also clearly shown — dominate the development of East–West relations.

## Heightened Competition in Regions Outside Europe

Heightened competition between the Great Powers in regions outside Europe has doubtless had destabilising effects. However, this is not a new phenomenon of the post-détente phase. As we have shown, it was already visible during détente. The Soviet Union has never interpreted the 'code of conduct' of 1972 in the same way as the United States. The United States doubtless practised restraint and pursued a vacillating policy for some time, though more for domestic reasons than out of regard for a code of conduct in foreign policy. At all events, once the Soviet Union attained a position as a global power, the non-inclusion of regions outside Europe in attempts at integrative conflict regulation has been an essential cause of the failure of détente. To a certain extent Soviet actions outside Europe served as a prism in the United States through which the Soviet Union was observed and her policy as a whole assessed. Meanwhile the Soviet Union evaluated American attitudes towards the People's Republic of China as being aimed against Super Power détente (see Link, 1982). Following the Soviet invasion of Afghanistan, the United States has again responded to Soviet challenges in the Third World, especially in the Gulf region and in Central America (Nicaragua, Grenada). At the same time a tendency towards biased interpretation and over-reaction has emerged in the Reagan Administration's policy towards developing nations. Conflicts in these regions are primarily interpreted in the light of the East–West conflict. The decision to deny any positional gain to the Soviet Union has been upgraded to a strategy of horizontal escalation (see the Pentagon study mentioned above). However, readiness to take risks has hardly increased in concrete political terms. If one can believe Charles William Maynes (1982), in Soviet circles there is also an awareness that unrest in countries of the Third World might get out of control and is not, therefore, entirely to the advantage of the Soviet Union. The traditional strategies of limiting spheres of influence or of excluding countries or regions from competition between the Great Powers are — as Wilhelm Grewe (1980) has argued so impressively — now, as before, best suited to furthering stabilisation.

The greatest problem facing this strategy is the position of the People's Republic of China. Arbatov, the Soviet expert on America, warned as early as 1978 that if a Sino-American axis were forged, 'then there would be no place for détente, not even to a limited degree' (*International Herald Tribune*, 11 Nov. 1978). The US Administration's latest decision to provide the Chinese People's Republic with strategically useful technology points in the direction of classifying China as an anti-Soviet ally in the East–West conflict, although one always has to be aware of the ups and downs of Sino-American relations. If this classification is correct, the possibility of an understanding on conflict regulation between the United States and the USSR is reduced.

## Changes Within the Two Alliances

Changes that have occurred in the alliance systems of both East and West are closely linked to the changes already discussed.

In the countries of Eastern Europe and the Warsaw Pact the effects of détente and internal economic difficulties have evinced a change which has unleashed centrifugal tendencies (see Hyland, 1982–3, p. 8). The costs of control have been high for the hegemonic power, the USSR: 'The situation in Eastern Europe has in fact increasingly become an uncomfortable burden which has cost the Soviets much of the influence which they still have on Communist parties abroad and which, on the other hand, threatens détente with Western Europe' (Bialer, 1983, p. 545).

To date, the Soviet Union has not been prepared to transform her domination over Eastern Europe, based on military and ideological power, into a 'more natural and organic' hegemonic relationship (Sonnenfeldt). Consequently she sees herself forced to maintain her dominance by military means or (as in the case of Poland) with the threatened use of such means. Thus the demarcation of alliances has, at least up to now, been preserved, albeit with some difficulty. At the same time this situation has delayed, or completely prevented, any reduction in the polarisation in the political sphere and the development of trade between the systems. In the long term real stabilisation is possible only if internal reforms can be linked to economic co-operation with the West. Détente has turned out to be destabilising to the Eastern bloc because East–West trade has become a substitute for essential reforms. Détente can, however, also promote stabilisation, if it is combined with internal reforms. Such evolutionary stabilisation could be in the interests of the East as well as of the West (see Bornstein *et al.*, 1981).

Ironically, America's policy of sanctions has (unintentionally) increased Poland's dependence on the Soviet Union and, as the 37th Council Meeting of the CMEA (19–20 Oct. 1983) showed, has strengthened the forces in CMEA that urge closer co-operation under Soviet leadership. They argue that one would thus become 'unassailable vis-à-vis all attempts at extortion at the hands of imperialism' (Honecker, quoted in *FAZ*, 21 Oct. 1983; see also Spielman, 1982–3). Because of the economic and political difficulties experienced in Eastern European countries there is admittedly hardly a realistic chance of reaching any 'qualitatively new level' of economic integration. At the same time the Soviet Union's move into areas outside Europe presents the countries of Eastern Europe with the problem of how far, and at what costs, they are to, or are able to, participate in this global policy.

In the countries of Western Europe and NATO the destabilisation in the Gulf region and the ensuing US policy of sanctions, with which the countries of Western Europe reluctantly complied, also generated additional tensions. A fundamentally new situation was created by the fact that West European security was threatened as a consequence of the East–West conflict, not only in Europe, but in the Gulf as well. Whereas the specific problem of apportioning tasks in conflicts outside Europe could be cleared up relatively quickly internally, the general problem of defining a new strategy towards the Soviet Union has produced far-reaching differences of opinion. In the phase of détente, despite all disagreement over individual questions, a basic consensus existed on the actual policy of détente. In contrast, geo-political differences and divergent interests have emerged in the wake of the new American–Soviet confrontation and have led to dissent between the United States and Western Europe. These differences have also produced an outbreak of sharp disagreement within the Western democracies. As a consequence of its illusory peace policy, the peace movement in Western democracies generally questions the policy of deterrence and the essential conditions for effective détente, namely a military balance. Dissent between the governments of Western Europe and the United States concerns 'merely' the specific shape of the deterrent and the assessment of economic co-operation, which during détente had a flanking and supporting function. At the economic summit conference in Versailles and in the Bonn NATO declaration of 10 June 1982 a makeshift compromise was reached between the American and European approaches. The compromise was eventually annulled by America's unilateral extension of embargoes and (once the measures were again revoked on 13 Dec. 1982) a new agreement was reached at the Williamsburg summit which was never fully implemented. This shows the ups and many downs in the internal debate. An exaggerated policy of regression on the part of the United States would become a dangerous burden and would even bring about the political destabilisation of the alliance. This is particularly relevant with regard to the Pentagon's plan to impose a trade boycott and to push for horizontal escalation. It promoted the idea, already expressed in the NATO Council in 1981, of applying military countermeasures in Europe in the event of Soviet intervention in the Gulf region. This would — as Fritz Ulrich Fack rightly remarked in *Frankfurter Allgemeine Zeitung* (8 June 1983) — 'theoretically mean that for the first time the classic doctrine of the Western alliance was abandoned according to which an attack by the enemy leads to a response [in the region] where the attack is taking place.' The fact that Defense Secretary Weinberger officially withdrew his support of this concept, so dangerous for the countries of Western Europe, and especially for West Germany, has led to a certain stabilisation within the alliance.

There are two ways in which the danger of 'uncoupling' has been, or may become, relevant for the future of Western Europe in the alliance. On the one hand, the danger of an uncoupling from the American deterrent existed in the event that the second half of the NATO two-track decision was not implemented and if the Soviet Union were to retain her strategic potential to blackmail Europe. With the stationing of Pershing II and Cruise missiles, this danger has diminished.

The other danger of 'uncoupling' arises from the fact that a war that is limited to Europe is conceivable. This new development has had a consequence which has been pertinently discussed by Michael Howard (1982–3). He wrote that it is often assumed that the threats, against which American protection was requested, now exist only in the fevered imagination of our protectors; that the American presence in Western Europe no longer gives protection, but is a threat in itself.

External deterrence and domestic support for such security policy, 'reassurance and deterrence', which belong together, are thus drifting apart. The remedy proposed by Howard has in the meantime also been advocated by various advisory groups, namely to do everything to reduce Western European dependence on American nuclear weapons by intensifying its own defence capability as far as this is possible militarily, socially and economically (see the ESECS European Security Study, 1983). The strengthening of European co-operation may be the only promising concept for stabilising the alliance, a stabilisation which we know from past experiences of détente is, together with an approximate balance, of central importance to a policy of détente in the East–West conflict.

This analysis of current tendencies in the development of the East–West conflict gives rise to warnings both against the comforting illusion of a total solution to conflict through co-operation as well as the chilling illusion of overcoming conflict through the so-called 'victory strategy'. Neither position is tenable on a political, or even on an ethical, level (see Rendtorff, 1982). A regulation of East–West conflict which adequately reflects a common interest in survival as well as incompatible ideas of structural order stands between the two extremes. And since political, military and economic conditions do not remain constant, but, on the contrary, are subject to change, new efforts must be made time and time again to find out which conflict regulation best suits the current situation.

Purism is out of place in politics. Limitations and demarcations have to be supplemented by forms of interaction and partial integration. However, whichever relationship is sought between these elements in political practice, an agreement over the limitation of influence and the demarcation of spheres of interest will not be possible as a 'classical' dictate of the Great Powers, but will have to be agreed with the countries in the regions concerned. Only their sovereign and equal right of participation and free consent make it possible to legitimise such agreements. Regional powers have to be respected as central factors of the international order. Regional groupings can increase the bargaining power of medium-sized and smaller countries and their capacity to act in a structurally important way, thereby ensuring that their interests will be adequately considered. These quasi-institutionalised inter-regional relations such as the co-operative relationship between the EEC and regional groupings in Africa, Asia and Latin America (see Hasenpflug,

1979), provide sensible starting-points and a concrete basis for a regionally differentiated world order. In the end, a limit to the struggle between the Great Powers and the maintenance of such understandings cannot be expected from verbal agreements between the Great Powers, but only from the existence and practical political effect of power-based groupings of medium-sized and smaller nations or regional organisations. The political, social and economic stability of the countries of the Third World and their regional combinations is thus an essential component in the regulation of the struggle between the Great Powers.

In the final analysis, the contest between countries and ideologies will not be settled globally or regionally, but at best will be transformed into a 'co-operative competition' or into a 'competition through co-operation' (Stanley Hoffmann, 1965, p. 157). The stabilisation of power between East and West through a regulation of conflict, which along with elements of demarcation contains enough elements of integration and co-operation, is in the end also the essential precondition of the security necessary for an integrative reörganisation of worldwide economic and political relations in which the socialist countries must take an active part (see the Brandt Commissions' proposals).

No one can say whether such a restructuring of international relations will succeed. But if it is to succeed, it can only do so by avoiding a world war and only through peaceful change based on compromise. The necessary condition for this is an approximate global and regional balance in security which has to be supplemented by efforts towards integrative conflict regulation. The main tasks of a peace policy are mutually dependent. They are to structure international relations so that opportunities for aggressive actions are restricted, or even excluded, and to promote co-operation in competition (see the Introduction). The extent of such successful forms of international organisation can be measured by the degree of common interests and goals which again will vary regionally and fundamentally. In global terms, it is still relatively low in comparison with the serious antagonisms. However, a minimum of common interests and goals, the universal interest in securing survival, does exist and has to gain political realisation.

While there is a regressive element in the imperative to form a balance of power, the 'imperative of non-reggression' (Stanley Hoffmann, 1978, p. 242) corresponds with the tendency to maintain or to strengthen the elements of an integrative and co-operative regulation of conflict. Both imperatives belong together and have to be linked. The practical political elimination of one in favour of the other leads either to catastrophe or to a Utopia far removed from reality. In the present world situation a 'mixed constitution' (*regimen mixtum*) is the adequate form of organisation for international relations. It is not only necessary, but also possible, to extend and to link both imperatives. The rationale for this is to be found in the joint interest in securing individual and national survival in a decentralised system of states in which otherwise deep antagonisms exist and where terrible destructive potentials are available.

In the light of experience gained over decades in the development of both structural world conflicts and the regulation of conflict, Harold Lasswell's warning (1946) formulated in the transitional phase from antagonistic co-operation to the Cold War is more valid than ever: 'If . . . world organisation lags behind the level which is capable of being achieved by political skill at any particular time, humanity will remain under the shadow of atomic disaster.'

The shadow of a nuclear catastrophe lengthens in times of international crises in which the Super Powers are involved. The challenge today is to use political skills to prevent that regulation of conflict achieved in the 1970s from being abandoned and the quasi-order of détente from being revised in a regressive way. Only then will new opportunities arise for a careful strengthening of common interests and goals, a gradual enhancement of international compromise and the further development of the global organisation of international relations according to the respective levels of common interests and goals.

# *Bibliography*

Acheson, D., *Present at the Creation* (New York 1970).
Adler-Karlsson, G., *Western Economic Warfare 1947–1967* (Stockholm 1968).
Adomeit, H., *Soviet Risk-Taking and Crisis Behaviour: From Confrontation to Coexistence?* (London 1973).
Agwani, M. S., *The Politics in the Gulf* (New Delhi et al. 1978).
*Akten zur deutschen Auswärtigen Politik* (*ADAP*), 1918–1945 (Göttingen 1966).
Alimow, J. I., and W. D. Stschetinin, *Die Legende von der Einteilung der Welt in reiche und arme Nationen* (Berlin 1975).
Allison, G. T., *Essence of Decision, Explaining the Cuban Missile Crisis* (Boston 1971).
Altmeppen, H., 'Entspannungsinitiativen von NATO und Warschauer Pakt seit 1966'. *Beiträge zur Konfliktforschung*, 2 (1972), 65–96.
Ansprenger, F., *Auflösung der Kolonialreiche* (Munich [2]1973).
Arkes, H., *Bureaucracy, the Marshall Plan, and the National Interest* (Princeton, NJ 1972).
Arndt, C., 'The Effects of Détente on the Two German States', *West European Politics*, 2 (1979), 237–45.
Aron, R., *The Imperial Republic* (Englewood Cliffs, NJ 1974).
Arons, R. and E. Jahn, 'Vom Kalten Krieg zur Entspannung', in C. Bielfeldt et al., *Frieden in Europa?* (Reinbek 1973), pp. 88–130.
Barringer, R. E., *Patterns of Conflict* (Cambridge, Mass. 1972).
Bechtoldt, H., *Chinas Revolutionsstrategie* (Freiburg [2]1969).
Bergeron, G., *La guerre froide inachevée* (Montreal 1971).
Bergström, L., 'What is a Conflict of Interest?', *Journal of Peace Research*, 7 (1970), 197–218.
Bernstein, B. J., *The Atomic Bomb. The Critical Issues* (Boston and Toronto 1976).
——, 'The Uneasy Alliance: Roosevelt, Churchill, and the Atomic Bomb, 1940–1945', *Western Political Quarterly*, 29 (1976), 202–30.
——, and A. J., Matusow, eds., *The Truman Administration* (New York 1966).
Bertram, C., 'Die Dritte Welt in der Ost-West-Politik' (MS 1979).
Besson, W., *Die Außenpolitik der Bundesrepublik* (Munich 1970).
Beugel, E. H. van der, *From Marshall Aid to Atlantic Partnership* (Amsterdam 1966).
Bialer, S., 'Die Sowjetunion und der Westen in den achtziger Jahren', *Europa-Archiv*, 18 (1983), 539–50.
Bishop, D. G., *The Roosevelt–Litvinow Agreements. The American View* (Syracuse, NY 1965).
Black, C. E., ed., *Challenge in Eastern Europe* (New Brunswick, NY 1954).
Blakeslee, G. H., 'Negotiating to Establish the Far Eastern Commission 1945', in R. Dennett and J. E. Johnson, eds., *Negotiating with the Russians*

(World Peace Foundation 1951).
Bornstein, M., Gitelman, Z., and W. Zimmerman, eds., *East–West Relations and the Future of Eastern Europe* (London et al. 1981).
Boulding, K. E., *Conflict and Defense* (New York 1967).
Bracher, K. D., 'Kritische Betrachtungen über den Primat der Aussenpolitik', in *Faktoren der politischen Entscheidung*, ed. G. A. Ritter and G. Ziebura (Berlin 1963), pp. 115 ff.
——, *Europa in der Krise. Innengeschichte und Weltpolitik seit 1917* (Frankfurt a.M. etc. 1979).
Bräker H., 'Aspekte des Konzeptionswandels in der wirtschaftlichen Zusammenarbeit und Integration Osteuropas', *Moderne Welt. Jahrbuch für Ost-West-Fragen*, 1976, pp. 343–69.
——, *Die sowjetische Iran-und Afghanistan-Politik* (Cologne 1979).
Braun, A., *Romanian Foreign Policy since 1965* (New York *et al* 1978).
Braunthal, J., *Geschichte der Internationale*, Vols. 1 and 2 (Berlin and Bonn [3]1978).
Bromke, A., and T. Rokowska-Harmstone, eds., *The Communist States in Disarray 1965–1971* (Minneapolis 1972).
Bruns, W., *Deutsch-deutsche Beziehungen* (Opladen [2]1979).
Buchan, A., *The End of the Postwar Era — A New Balance of World Power* (London 1974).
Bühl, W. L., ed., *Konflikt und Konfliktstrategie* (Munich 1972).
Bull, H., *The Anarchical Society* (London and Basingstoke 1977).
Burton, J. W., *Systems, States, Diplomacy and Rules* (Cambridge 1968).
——, *World Society* (Cambridge 1972).
Butterworth, R. L. (with E. Scranton), *Managing Interstate Conflict, 1945–74* (Pittsburgh, Pa. 1976).
Byrnes, J. F., *Speaking Frankly* (Westport, Conn. 1947).
Calleo, D. P., and B. M. Rowland, *America and the World Political Economy* (Bloomington and London 1973).
Chiu, H., *The People's Republic of China and the Law of Treaties* (Cambridge, Mass. 1972).
Churchill, W. S., *The Second World War*, Vols. I–VI (London etc. 1948 ff.).
Claude, I. L., *Power and International Relations* (New York 1962).
——, *Swords into Plowshares* (New York [3]1964).
Cline, R. S., *World Power Assessment 1977* (Boulder, Colo. 1977).
Cohen, B. J., *The Question of Imperialism* (New York 1973).
Collins, J. M., *Imbalance of Power* (San Rafael, Cal., and London 1978).
Coser, L. A., *The Functions of Social Conflict* (Glencoe, Ill. 1956).
——, 'The Termination of Conflict', *Journal of Conflict Resolution*, 5 (1961), 345–53.
Cox, A. M., *Russian Roulette: The Superpower Game* (New York 1982).
Crossman, R. H. S., 'Reflections on the Cold War', *Political Quarterly*, 22 (1951), 7–15.
Czempiel, E.-O., *Das amerikanische Sicherheitssystem 1945–1949* (Berlin 1966).
——, 'Frieden und Konflikt in den internationalen Beziehungen', in H. Haftendorn *et al.*, eds., *Theorien der Internationalen Politik* (Hamburg 1975) pp. 83–113.
——, ed., *Amerikanische Aussenpolitik im Wandel* (Stuttgart et al. 1982).

——, 'Nachdenken über Nachrüsten', *Merkur*, 5 (1983), 530–9.
Dahrendorf, R., *Soziale Klassen und Klassenkonflikt in der industriellen Gesellschaft* (Stuttgart 1957).
Dauth, J., 'Asean', *Aus Politik und Zeitgeschichte*, 1979, B 8, pp. 31–46.
Davis, L. E., *The Cold War Begins* (Princeton, NJ 1974).
Dawson, R. H., *The Decision to aid Russia 1941* (Chapel Hill, NC 1959).
Dehio, L., *Gleichgewicht oder Hegemonie* (Krefeld $^{3}$1974).
Delbrück, J., 'Selbstbestimmung und Dekolonisation,' in U. Scheuner und B. Lindemann, eds., *Die Vereinten Nationen und die Mitarbeit der Bundesrepublik Deutschland* (Munich and Vienna 1973), pp. 69–108.
——, ed., *Völkerrecht und Kriegsverhütung* (Berlin 1979).
Dennett, R., and J. E. Johnson, eds., *Negotiating with the Russians* (World Peace Foundation) 1951.
Dettke, D., *Allianz im Wandel* (Frankfurt 1976).
Deutsch, K. W., *The Analysis of International Relations* (Englewood Cliffs, NJ $^{2}$1978).
Deutsche Gesellschaft für Auswärtige Politik (DGAP), Forschungsinstitut, ed., *Die Aussenpolitik Chinas* (Munich and Vienna 1975).
*DGFK (Deutsche Gesellschaft für Friedens- und Konfliktforschung)- Jahrbuch 1979–80*, ed. W. Graf von Baudissin, J. Delbrück, K. Koppe, P. Knirsch, W. Link and N. Ropers (Baden-Baden 1980).
——, *1982–83*, ed. Vorstand der Deutschen Gesellschaft für Friedens- und Konfliktforschung (Baden-Baden 1983).
Domes, J., and M. Näth, *Die Aussenpolitik der Volksrepublik China* (Düsseldorf 1972).
Dörr, W., 'Wandlungsprozesse in der amerikanischen Aussenpolitik gegenüber der Sowjetunion 1961–72' (MS, Trier 1980).
Duchêne, F., 'SALT, die Ostpolitik und die Liquidierung des Kalten Krieges', *Europa-Archiv*, 25 (1970), 639–53.
Eakins, D. W., 'Business Planners and America's Postwar Expansion', in D. Horowitz, ed., *Cooperations and the Cold War* (New York and London 1969).
Easton, D., *A Framework for Political Analysis* (New York 1965).
Ellsworth, R. F., and K. L. Adelman, 'Foolish Intelligence', *Foreign Policy*, 36 (Autumn 1979), 147–59.
End, H., *Zweimal deutsche Aussenpolitik* (Cologne 1973).
Ermarth, F. W., 'Die globale Projizierbarkeit sowjetischer Macht und die strategischen Erfordernisse ihrer Eindämmung,' in U. Nerlich, ed., with F. Bomsdorf, *Die Einhegung sowjetischer Macht* (Baden-Baden 1982), pp. 109–41.
ESECS-European Security Study, *Wege zur Stärkung der konventionellen Abschreckung in Europa: Vorschläge für die 80er Jahre* (Baden-Baden 1983).
Etzioni, A., *The Hard Way to Peace: A New Strategy* (New York 1962).
——, *Political Unification* (New York et al. 1965).
——, *The Active Society* (London and New York 1968).
——, 'Das Kennedy-Experiment', in E. Krippendorff, ed., *Friedensforschung* (Cologne and Berlin $^{2}$1970), pp. 393–412.
Etzold, T. H. and J. L. Gaddis, eds., *Containment* (New York 1978).
Falk, R. A., *A Study of Future Worlds* (New York 1975).
Faul, E., 'Hitlers Über-Machiavellismus', *Vierteljahrshefte für Zeitgeschichte*, 2

(1954), 344–72.
Feis, H., *1933: Characters in Crisis* (Boston and Toronto 1966).
——, *Churchill–Roosevelt–Stalin. The War They Waged and the Peace They Sought* (Princeton, NJ 1967).
Feld, W. J., *Nongovernmental Forces and World Politics* (New York et al. 1972).
Fielder, P. C., 'The Pattern of Super-Power Crises', *International Relations*, 3 (1969), 498–510.
Fink, C. F., 'Some Conceptual Difficulties in the Theory of Social Conflict', *Journal of Conflict Resolution*, 12 (1968), 412–60.
Fischer, A., ed., *Teheran–Jalta–Potsdam. Die sowjetischen Protokolle von den Kriegskonferenzen der 'Großen Drei'* (Cologne 1968).
——, 'Kollektive Sicherheit und imperialistischer Krieg', *Saeculum*, 28 (1977), 419–31.
Fischer, F., *Griff nach der Weltmacht* (Düsseldorf 1967).
Fischer, G., 'Rumania', in A. Bromke and T. Rakowska-Harmstone, eds., *The Communist States in Disarray 1965–1971* (Minneapolis 1972), pp. 158–179.
Fishlow, A., Diaz-Alejandro, C. F., Fagen, R. R., and R. D. Hansen, *Rich and Poor Nations in the World Economy* (New York et al. 1978).
*Foreign Relations of the United States* (= FR) (Papers Relating to . . .), 1919ff., Washington 1934ff.
Forndran, E., 'Die Dynamik des gegenwärtigen Rüstungsprozesses', in K. Kaiser and K. M. Kreis, eds., *Sicherheitspolitik vor neuen Aufgaben* (Frankfurt 1977), pp. 143–219.
Forndran, E., and P. J. Friedrich, eds., *Rüstungskontrolle und Sicherheit in Europa* (Bonn 1979).
Fraenkel, E., 'Regionalpakte und Weltfriedensordnung', *Vierteljahrshefte für Zeitgeschichte*, 2 (1954), 34–54.
Freeland, R. M., *The Truman Doctrine and the Origins of McCarthyism* (New York 1972).
Frenzke, D., *Rumänien, der Sowjetblock und die europäische Sicherheit* (Berlin 1975).
Freye, A., *Nazi Germany and the American Hemisphere 1933–1941* (New Haven, Conn. and London 1967).
Fucks, Wilhelm, *Formeln zur Macht* (Stuttgart 1965).
Gaddis, J. L., *The United States and the Origins of the Cold War, 1941–1947* (New York 1972).
——, *Strategies of Containment: a Critical Appraisal of Postwar American National Security Policy* (New York et al. 1982).
Galtung, J., 'East–West Interaction Patterns', *Journal of Peace Research*, 3 (1966), 146–76.
——, 'A theory of Peaceful Co-operation', in J. Galtung, ed., *Cooperation in Europe* (Oslo 1977), pp. 9–20.
Gamson, W. A., and A. Modigliani, *Untangling the Cold War* (Boston 1971).
Gantzel, K. J., 'Internationale Faktoren der·Rüstungsdynamik im Ost-West-Konflikt', in Hessische Stiftung Friedens- und Konfliktforschung, *Mitteilungen*, No. 4. (Frankfurt 1972), pp. 4–60.
——, 'Zu herrschaftssoziologischen Problembereichen von Abhängigkeitsbeziehungen in der gegenwärtigen Weltgesellschaft', in D. Senghaas, ed., *Imperialismus und strukturelle Gewalt* (Frankfurt 1972), pp. 105–20.

——, Kress, G., and V. Rittberger, eds., *Konflikt–Eskalation–Krise* (Düsseldorf 1972).
Gardner, L. C., *Architects of Illusion*, (Chicago 1970).
——, Schlesinger, A., and H. J. Morgenthau, *The Origins of the Cold War* (Waltham, Mass. 1970).
Gardner, R. N., *Sterling-Dollar Diplomacy* (London [2]1969).
Gaulle, Charles de, *Mémoires de Guerre. L'Unité 1942–1944* (Paris 1956).
Geierhos, W., *Das Kräfteverhältnis* (Lüneburg 1980).
George, A. L., ed., *Managing U.S.–Soviet Rivalry* (Boulder, Colo. 1983).
Geyer, D., *Die Sowjetunion und Iran* (Tübingen 1955).
Gimbel, J., *The Origins of the Marshall Plan* (Stanford, Cal. 1976).
Goldman, M. I., *Détente and Dollars* (New York 1975).
Goldmann, K., 'Bipolarization and Tension in International Systems', *Cooperation and Conflict*, 7 (1972), 37–63.
——, *Tension and Détente in Bipolar Europe* (Stockholm 1974).
——, 'Change and Stability in Foreign Policy: Détente as a Problem of Stabilization', *World Politics*, 34 (1981–2), 230–66.
——, and J. Lagerkranz, 'Neither Tension nor Détente', *Cooperation and Conflict*, 12 (1977), 251–64.
Görtemaker, M., *Die unheilige Allianz* (Munich 1979).
Gosovic, B., *UNCTAD — Conflict and Compromise* (Leiden 1972).
Gray, C. S., and D. G. Brennan, 'Gemeinsame Interessen als Grundlage für Rüstungskontrolle', in U. Nerlich, ed. with F. Bomsdorf, *Sowjetische Macht und westliche Verhandlungspolitik im Wandel militärischer Kräfteverhältnisse* (Baden-Baden 1982), pp. 511–40.
Grewe, W. G., *Rückblenden 1976–1951* (Frankfurt a.M. et. al. 1979).
——, 'Machtvergleiche in der Weltpolitik', in H. Kohl, ed., *Der Neue Realismus* (Düsseldorf 1980), pp. 69–91.
Griffith, W. E., ed., *The Soviet Empire: Expansion and Détente* (Lexington and Toronto 1976).
Groom, A. J. R., 'The Functionalist Approach and East/West Cooperation in Europe', *Journal of Common Market Studies*, 13 (1975), 21–60.
——, and P. Taylor, eds., *Functionalism — Theory and Practice in International Relations* (London 1974).
Groten, H., *Friedensforschung — Anspruch und Praxis* (Baden-Baden 1977).
*Grünbuch zu den Folgewirkungen der KSZE*, DGFK-Veröffentlichungen, 3, ed. by J. Delbrück, N. Ropers and G. Zellentin (Cologne 1977).
Haas, E. B., *Beyond the Nation-State* (Stanford 1964).
——, *The Uniting of Europe* (Stanford [2]1968).
Hacke, C., *Die Ära Nixon-Kissinger 1969–1974. Konservative Reform der Weltpolitik* (Stuttgart 1983).
Hacker, J., 'Der Warschauer Pakt', in D. Geyer and B. Meissner, eds., *Sowjetunion, Völkerrechtstheorie und Vertragspolitik (Osteuropa-Handbuch)* (Cologne 1976).
Haftendorn, H., *Abrüstungs- und Entspannungspolitik zwischen Sicherheitsbefriedigung und Friedenssicherung* (Düsseldorf 1974).
——, ed., *Theorie der Internationalen Politik* (Hamburg 1975).
Hagemann, M., *Der provisorische Frieden* (Erlenbach-Zürich and Stuttgart 1964).

Halle, L., *The Cold War as History* (New York 1967).
Hansen, R. D., *Beyond the North–South Stalemate* (New York *et al.* 1979).
Hasenpflug, H., ed., *Die EG-Aussenbeziehungen* (Hamburg 1979).
Heiduk, G., *Die weltwirtschaftlichen Ordnungsprinzipien von GATT und UNCTAD* (Baden-Baden 1973).
Heinzig, D., 'Der sowjetisch-chinesische Grenzkonflikt', *Berichte des Bundesinstituts für ostwissenschaftliche und internationale Studien*, 17 (Cologne 1979).
Herring, G. C., Jr., 'Lend-Lease to Russia and the Origins of the Cold War, 1944–1945', *Journal of American History*, 56 (1969), 93–114.
Herrmann, R., 'ABM in den achtziger Jahren', *Aus Politik und Zeitgeschichte*, 1983, B 15–16, 32–46.
Herz, J. H., *International Politics in the Atomic Age* (New York 1959).
Herz, M. F., *Beginnings of the Cold War* (Bloomington and London 1967).
Hess, G. R., 'The Iranian Crisis of 1945–46 and the Cold War', *Political Science Quarterly*, 89 (1974), 117–46.
Hewlett, R. G., and O. E. Anderson, Jr., eds., *The New World, 1939/1946* (Pennsylvania 1962).
Hildebrand, K., *Deutsche Aussenpolitik 1933–1945* (Stuttgart et al. 1971).
——, 'Innenpolitische Antriebskräfte der nationalsozialistischen Aussenpolitik', in *Sozialgeschichte heute*, Festschrift für Hans Rosenberg zum 70. Geburtstag, ed. H.-U. Wehler (Göttingen 1974), pp. 635–51.
——, 'Hitlers "Programm" und seine Realisierung 1939–1942', in G. Niedhart, ed., *Kriegsbeginn 1939* (Darmstadt 1976), pp. 178–224.
Hillgruber, A., *Hitlers Strategie* (Frankfurt 1965).
——, 'Der Faktor Amerika in Hitlers Strategie 1938–1941', *Aus Politik und Zeitgeschichte*, 1966, B 19, 3–21.
——, *Kontinuität und Diskontinuität in der deutschen Aussenpolitik von Bismarck bis Hitler* (Düsseldorf 1969).
Hinton, H. C., *The Bear at the Gate* (Washington, DC $^2$1972).
Hiscocks, R., *The Security Council* (London 1973).
Hoensch, J. K., *Sowjetische Osteuropa-Politik, 1945–1975* (Kronberg and Düsseldorf 1977).
Hoffmann, S., *The State of War* (New York et al. 1965).
——, *Gulliver's Troubles or the Setting of American Foreign Policy* (New York 1968).
——, *Primacy or World Order* (New York et al. 1978).
——, 'Muscle and Brains', *Foreign Policy*, 37 (1979–80), 3–27.
Holsti, K. J., *International Politics* (Englewood Cliffs, NJ 1967).
Holsti, O. R., Hopmann, T. P., and J. D. Sullivan, *Unity and Disintegration in International Alliances* (New York et al. 1973).
Hopkins, R. F. and R. W. Mansbach, *Structure and Process in International Politics* (New York et al. 1973).
Howard, M., 'Reassurance and Deterrence: Western Defense in the 1980s', *Foreign Affairs*, 61 (1982–83), 309–24.
Hsüeh Chün-Tu, *Dimensions of China's Foreign Relations* (New York 1977).
Hull, Cordell, *Memoirs* (New York 1948).
Huntington, S. P., 'Transnational Organizations in World Politics', *World Politics*, 25 (1972–3), 333–68.
Hyland, W. G., 'Clash with the Soviet Union', *Foreign Policy*, 49 (Winter

1982–3), 3–19.

IISS (The International Institute for Strategic Studies), *The Military Balance 1979–1980* (London 1979).

*Die Internationale Politik*, Jahrbücher des Forschungsinstituts der Deutschen Gesellschaft für Auswärtige Politik, 1956–7ff. (Munich and Vienna 1961ff.)

Jacobsen, H. D., *Die wirtschaftlichen Beziehungen zwischen West und Ost* (Reinbek bei Hamburg 1975).

Jacobsen, H. A., *Nationalsozialistische Aussenpolitik 1933–1938* (Frankfurt and Berlin 1968).

——, Mallmann, W., and C. Meier, eds., *Sicherheit und Zusammenarbeit in Europa* (KSZE), Vols. 1 and 2 (Cologne 1973 and 1978).

Jahn, E., and V. Rittberger, eds., *Die Ostpolitik der Bundesrepublik* (Opladen 1974).

Jankowitsch, O., and K. P. Sauvant, eds., *The Third World without Superpowers. The Collected Documents of the Non-aligned Countries*, I-IV (Dobbs Ferry, NY 1978).

Jegorow, W. N., *Friedliche Koexistenz und revolutionärer Prozess* (Berlin 1972).

Jervis, R., *Perceptions and Misperceptions in International Politics* (Princeton, NJ 1976).

Jones, J. M., *The Fifteen Weeks* (New York 1955).

Junker, D., *Der unteilbare Weltmarkt* (Stuttgart 1975).

Jütte, R., 'Europäische Friedensstruktur', in A. Grosse-Jütte and R. Jütte, eds., *Entspannung ohne Frieden* (Frankfurt 1977), pp. 148–72.

Kahin, G. M., *The Asian-African Conference, Bandung, Indonesia, April 1955* (Port Washington, NY and London 1956).

Kaiser, J. H., 'Crisis Management', in G. Picht and C. Eisenbart, eds., *Frieden und Völkerrecht* (Stuttgart 1973), pp. 623–39.

Kaiser, K., *German Foreign Policy in Transition* (London et al., 1968).

——, and H. P. Schwarz, eds., *Amerika und Westeuropa* (Stuttgart and Zürich 1977).

Kalicki, J. H., *The Pattern of Sino-American Crises* (London 1975).

Kanet, R. E., ed., *The Soviet Union and the Developing Nations* (Baltimore 1974).

Kaser, M., *Comecon. Integration Problems of the Planned Economies* (London $^{2}$1967).

Kaufmann, F. X., *Sicherheit als soziologisches und sozialpolitisches Problem* (Stuttgart $^{2}$1973).

Kautsky, K., 'Nationalität und Internationalität', *Ergänzungsheft zur 'Neuen Zeit'*, No. 1, 1908.

——, 'Der Imperialismus', *Die Neue Zeit*, 32 (1914), 908–922.

——, *Nationalstaat, imperialistischer Staat und Staatenbund* (Nuremburg 1915).

Keohane, R. 0., and J. S. Nye, eds., *Transnational Relations and World Politics* (Cambridge, Mass. 1971).

——, and ——, *Power and Interdependence* (Boston and Toronto 1977).

Kim, S. S., *China, the United Nations, and World Order* (Princeton, NJ 1979).

Kipp, J. W., 'Détente Politics and the U.S.–USSR Military Balance', in D. W. Sheldon, ed., *Dimensions of Détente* (New York et al. 1978), pp. 196–216.

Knapp, M., ed., *Die deutsch–amerikanischen Beziehungen nach 1945* (Frankfurt 1975).

Knight, J., 'American Statecraft and the 1946 Black Sea Straits Controversy', *Political Science Quarterly*, 90 (1975), 451–75.

Knipping, F., *Die amerikanische Russlandpolitik in der Zeit des Hitler–Stalin–Paktes, 1939–1941* (Tübingen 1974).

Knirsch, P., 'Bemühungen um eine Wirtschaftsintegration in Osteuropa', *Europa-Archiv*, 27 (1972), 21–32.

——, 'Interdependence in East-West Economic Relations', in Organisation for Economic Cooperation and Development, ed., *From Marshall Plan to Global Interdependence* (Paris 1978), pp. 135–67.

Kolko, G., *The Politics of War* (London 1968).

Kolko, J. and G., *The Limits of Power* (New York et al. 1972).

Korpi, W., 'Conflict and Balance of Power'. *Acta Sociologica*, 17 (1974), 99–114.

Kraus, R., *Die Imperialismusdebatte zwischen Vladimir I. Lenin und Karl Kautsky* (Frankfurt 1978).

Kreile, M., 'Ostpolitik und ökonomische Interessen', in E. Jahn and V. Rittberger, eds., *Die Ostpolitik der Bundesrepublik* (Opladen 1974), pp. 71–94.

Krell, G., 'Zur Theorie der Rüstungsdynamik im Ost–West–Konflikt', *Politische Vierteljahresschrift*, 17 (1976), 437–73.

Krippendorff, E., *Die amerikanische Strategie* (Frankfurt 1970).

Kuklick, B., 'The Division of Germany and American Policy of Reparations', *Western Political Quarterly*, 23 (1970), 276–93.

Larson, T. B., *Soviet-American Rivalry* (New York 1978).

Lasswell, H. D., 'The Interrelations of World Organization and Society', *Yale Law Journal* 55, (1946), 890–909.

Legvold, R., 'The Super Power Rivals: Conflict in the Third World', *Foreign Affairs*, 57 (1979), 755–78.

Lenin, W. I., *Der Imperialismus als höchstes Stadium des Kapitalismus* (1917, Berlin 1951).

Levin, N. G., Jr., *Woodrow Wilson and World Politics* (New York 1968).

Link, W., *Die amerikanische Stabilisierungspolitik in Deutschland 1921–32* (Düsseldorf 1970).

——, *Das Konzept der friedlichen Kooperation und der Beginn des Kalten Krieges* (Düsseldorf 1971).

——, 'Die Rolle der USA im westeuropäischen Integrationsprozess', *Aus Politik und Zeitgeschichte*, 1972, B 14, 3–13.

——, *Procedures and Outcomes of Détente Policy* (Washington, DC 1974).

——, 'Zielperspektiven in der amerikanischen Deutschlandpolitik in der frühen Nachkriegszeit', *Zeitgeschichte*, 5 (1977), 2–12.

——, *Deutsche und amerikanische Gewerkschaften und Geschäftsleute 1945–1975. Eine Studie über transnationale Beziehungen* (Düsseldorf 1978).

——, 'Die Konkurrenz der beiden Weltmächte im Zeichen stagnierender Entspannung', *Die Internationale Politik*, 1977–8 (Munich and Vienna 1982).

——, *Die neueren Entwicklungen des Ost-West-Konflikts. Konstanten und Veränderungen* (Veröffentlichungen der Deutschen Gesellschaft für Politik-

wissenschaft (DGFP), Heft 1) (Cologne et al. 1984).
——, 'Die amerikanische Deutschlandpolitik 1945–1949', in Göttinger Arbeitskreis, ed., *Die Deutschlandfrage und die Anfänge des Ost-West-Konflikts 1945–1949*, Studien zur Deutschlandfrage, Vol. 7 (Berlin 1984), pp. 7–23.
——, and W. J. Feld, eds., *The New Nationalism* (New York et al. 1979).
——, and P. Tücks, *Der Nord–Süd–Konflikt und die Zusammenarbeit der Entwicklungsländer* (Berlin 1985).
Löwenthal, R., 'Der Einfluss Chinas auf die Entwicklung des Ost-West-Konflikts in Europa', *Europa-Archiv*, 22 (1967), 339–50.
——, 'Freiheit der Eigenentwicklung', in *Aussenpolitische Perspektiven des westdeutschen Staates, Vol. I, Das Ende des Provisoriums* (Munich and Vienna 1971), pp. 11–18.
——, 'Vom Kalten Krieg zur Ostpolitik', in R. Löwenthal and H. P. Schwarz, eds., *Die Zweite Republik* (Stuttgart [2]1974), pp. 604–99.
Luard, E., *Conflict and Peace in the Modern International System* (Boston 1968).
Maddox, R. J., *The New Left and the Origins of the Cold War* (Princeton, NJ 1973).
McNeill, W. H., *America, Britain and Russia* (New York 1953).
Marshall, A. W., 'Rüstungskonkurrenz: Der Stand der Analyse', in U. Nerlich and Bomsdorf, eds., *Sowjetische Macht und westliche Verhandlungspolitik im Wandel militärischer Kräfteverhältnisse* (Baden-Baden 1982), pp. 491–510.
Martin, B., *Friedensinitiativen und Machtpolitik im Zweiten Weltkrieg 1939–1942* (Düsseldorf 1974).
Martin, L. W., 'The American Decision to Rearm Germany', in H. Stern, ed., *American Civil-Military Decisions* (University of Alabama Press 1963).
Marx, Karl, *Die Frühschriften*, ed. Siegfried Landshut (Stuttgart 1953).
Mastny, V., *Russia's Road to the Cold War* (New York 1979).
Matthies, V., 'Die Bewegung der Blockfreien', *Aus Politik und Zeitgeschichte*, 1979, B 37, 35–46.
Mayer, A. J., *Political Origins of the New Diplomacy, 1917–1918* (New Haven 1959).
——, *Politics and Diplomacy of Peacemaking* (New York 1967).
Maynes, C. W., 'Old Errors in the New Cold War', *Foreign Policy*, 46 (Spring 1982), 86–104.
Medick, M., 'Das Konzept des "Military-Industrial Complex" und das Problem einer Theorie demokratischer Kontrolle', in V. Berghahn, ed., *Militarismus* (Cologne 1975), pp. 347–77.
Meier, V. E., *Neuer Nationalismus in Südosteuropa* (Opladen 1968).
Meissner, B., *Die 'Breschnew-Doktrin': das Prinzip des 'proletarisch-sozialistischen Internationalismus' und die Theorie von den 'verschiedenen Wegen zum Sozialismus'; Dokumentation* (Cologne 1969).
——, 'Spezifische Wandlungen im Ostpakt-System', *Aussenpolitik*, 30 (1979), 279–300.
Mertes, A., 'Friedenserhaltung — Friedensgestaltung', *Europa-Archiv*, 7 (1983), 187–96.
Messelken, K., *Politikbegriff der modernen Soziologie* (Cologne and Opladen 1968).

Millis, W., ed., *The Forrestal Diaries* (New York 1951).
Mitrany, D., *The Functional Theory of Politics* (1943 — London 1975).
Modelski, G., *Principles of World Politics* (New York and London 1972).
Mols, M., 'SELA — das jüngste lateinamerkanische Koordinations instrument', *Berichte zur Entwicklung in Spanien, Portugal und Lateinamerika*, 3 (1978), 14–30.
Moore, B., Jr., *Soviet Politics — The Dilemma of Power* (Cambridge, Mass. 1951).
Moran, H., 'Foreign Expansion as an "Institutional Necessity" for U.S. Corporate Capitalism', *World Politics*, 25 (1972–3), 369–86.
Moreton, E. N., *East Germany and the Warsaw Alliance: The Politics of Détente* (Boulder, Colo. 1978).
Morgenthau, H. J., *Politics among Nations* (New York 1948).
Mortimer, R. A., *The Third World Coalition in International Politics* (New York 1980).
Müller, H., *Energiepolitik, Nuklearexport und die Weiterverbreitung von Kernwaffen.* HSFK (Hessische Stiftung für Friedens-und Konfliktforschung)-Report (Frankfurt 1977).
Näth, M.-L., *Strategie und Taktik der chinesischen Aussenpolitik* (Hannover 1978).
Nerlich, U., 'Die Einhegung des Nuklearkrieges', *Europa-Archiv*, 28 (1973), 669–78.
——, 'Die amerikanisch-sowjetischen Beziehungen', *Die Internationale Politik, 1970–72* (Munich and Vienna 1978), pp. 187–230.
Neuhold, H., *Internationale Konflikte — verbotene und erlaubte Mittel ihrer Austragung* (Vienna and New York 1977).
Newhouse, J., *Cold Dawn. The Story of SALT* (New York etc. 1973).
Niclauss, K., *Die Sowjetunion und Hitlers Machtergreifung* (Bonn 1966).
Niedhart, G., 'Der Bündniswert der Sowjetunion im Urteil Grossbritanniens 1936–1939', *Militärgeschichtliche Mitteilungen*, 2 (1971), 55–67.
——, *Grossbritannien und die Sowjetunion 1934–1939* (Munich 1972).
Nixon, R., *U.S. Foreign Policy for the 1970's. A Report to the Congress*, 3 May 1973.
Nolte, E., *Deutschland und der Kalte Krieg* (Munich and Zürich 1974).
Nye, J. S., 'Transnational Relations and Interstate Conflicts: An Empirical Analysis', *International Organization*, 28 (1974), 961–96.
——, ed., *The Making of America's Soviet Policy* (New Haven and London 1984).
Offner, A. A., *American Appeasement. United States Foreign Policy and Germany 1933–1938* (Cambridge, Mass. 1969).
Onwuka, R. I., *Development and Integration in West Africa. The Case of ECOWAS* (University of Ife, Nigeria 1980).
Opitz, P. J., 'Prinzipielle Grundlagen und strategische Grundlinien der Aussenpolitik der Volksrepublik China', *Politische Studien*, 31 (1980), 51–62.
Organization for Economic Co-operation and Development, ed., *From the Marshall Plan to Global Interdependence* (Paris 1978).
Osgood, R. E., and R. W. Tucker, *Force, Order, and Justice* (Baltimore 1967).
Oudenaren, J. van, 'Die sowjetische Politik in Europa und die Rolle von

Rüstungskontrollverhandlungen', in U. Nerlich and F. Bomsdorf, eds., *Sowjetische Macht und westliche Verhandlungspolitik im Wandel militärischer Kräfteverhältnisse* (Baden-Baden 1982), pp. 237–75.

Oye, A., R. J. Lieber, and D. Rothschild, eds., *Eagle Defiant. United States Foreign Policy in the 1980s* (Boston and Toronto 1983).

Paterson, T. G., 'The Abortive American Loan to Russia and the Origins of the Cold War, 1943–1946', *Journal of American History*, 56 (1969), 70–92.

Polonsky, A., *The Great Powers and the Polish Question 1941–1945* (London 1976).

Popper, K. R., *Of Clouds and Clocks. An Approach to the Problem of Rationality and the Freedom of Man* (St. Louis, Miss. 1965).

Quester, G. H., *Nuclear Diplomacy* (New York 1970).

Range, W., *Franklin D. Roosevelt's World Order* (Athens 1959).

Ratchford, B. U., and W. D. Ross, *Berlin Reparations Assignment* (Chapel Hill, NC 1947).

Rauschning, H., *Gespräche mit Hitler* (Zürich etc. 1940).

Rendtorff, T., 'Friedensethik — ein Weg zur Wiederent deckung der politischen Struktur militärischer Rüstung', in U. Nerlich and Bomsdorf, eds., *Sowjetische Macht und westliche Verhandlungspolitik im Wandel militärischer Kräfteverhältnisse* (Baden-Baden 1982), pp. 541–59.

Rivera, J. H. de, *The Psychological Dimension of Foreign Policy* (Columbus, Ohio 1968).

Robinson, T. W., 'Détente and the Sino-Soviet-U.S. Triangle', in D. W. Sheldon, ed., *Dimensions of Détente* (New York et al. 1978), pp. 50–83.

Rölling, B. V. A., *Einführung in die Wissenschaft von Krieg und Frieden* (Neunkirchen 1970).

Roosa, R. V., Gutowski, A., and M. Matsukowa, eds., *Ost-West-Handel am Scheideweg. Ein Sonderbericht für die trilaterale Kommission* (Hamburg 1983).

Rosecrance, R., *International Relations: Peace or War?* (New York *et al.* 1973).

Royen, C., *Die sowjetische Koexistenzpolitik gegenüber Westeuropa* (Baden-Baden 1979).

Rubinstein, A. Z., ed., *Soviet and Chinese Influence in the Third World* (New York $^{2}$1976).

Ruehl, L., *Machtpolitik und Friedensstrategie* (Hamburg 1974).

Ruffmann, K.-H., *Sowjetrussland 1917–1977* (Munich $^{7}$1977).

Sasse, H., *Die asiatisch-afrikanischen Staaten auf der Bandung-Konferenz* (Frankfurt a.M. 1958).

Sauvant, K. P., and H. Hasenpflug, eds., *The New International Economic Order* (Boulder, Colo. 1977).

Schelling, T. C., *The Strategy of Conflict* (Cambridge, Mass. 1960).

Schmid, G. *Entscheidung in Bonn: Die Entstehung der Ost- und Deutschlandpolitik 1969/1970* (Cologne 1979.)

Schmiederer, U., 'Systemkonkurrenz als Strukturprinzip der internationalen Politik', *Internationale Beziehungen als System*, PVS-Sonderheft 5 (1973), 309–346.

Schmitter, P. C., 'Three Neo-Functional Hypothesis about International Integration', *International Organization*, 23 (1969), 162–6.

Schramm, F. K., Riggert, W. G., and A. Friedel, eds., *Sicherheitskonferenz in Europa 1954–1972* (Frankfurt 1972).

Schröder, H.-C., *Sozialismus und Imperialismus* (Hanover 1968).
Schröder, H.-J., *Deutschland und die Vereinigten Staaten 1933–1939* (Wiesbaden 1970).
____'Zur Genesis des Kalten Krieges', *Neue Politische Literatur*, 21 (1976), 488–506.
Schröder, P. W., 'Quantitative Studies in the Balance of Power', *Journal of Conflict Resolution*, 21 (1977), 3–22 and 23–74.
Schulz, E., *Moskau und die europäische Integration* (Munich and Vienna 1975).
____, *Die Ostbeziehungen der Europäischen Gemeinschaft* (Munich and Vienna 1977).
Schumpeter, J. A., 'Zur Soziologie der Imperialismen', in J. Schumpeter, *Aufsätze zur Soziologie* (Tübingen 1953).
Schwarz, H.-P., and B. Meissner, eds., *Entspannung in Ost und West* (Cologne et al. 1979).
Schwarzenberger, G., *The Dynamics of International Law* (Abingdon 1976).
Senghaas, D., *Abschreckung und Frieden* (Frankfurt a.M. 1969).
____, *Rüstung und Militarismus* (Frankfurt a.M. 1972).
____, *Gewalt — Frieden — Konflikt, Essays zur Friedensforschung* (Hamburg 1974).
____, *Peripherer Kapitalismus* (Frankfurt a.M. 1974).
____, *Weltwirtschaftsordnung und Entwicklungspolitik, Plädoyer für Dissoziation* (Frankfurt 1977).
____, ed., *Imperialismus und strukturelle Gewalt* (Frankfurt a.M. 1972).
Senghaas-Knobloch, E., *Frieden durch Integration und Assoziation* (Stuttgart 1969).
Sherwin, M. J., *A World Destroyed* (New York 1975).
Simma, B., and E. Blenk-Knocke, eds., *Zwischen Intervention und Zusammenarbeit* (Berlin 1979).
Simmel, G., *Soziologie* (1908) (Berlin [4]1958).
Simson, W. von, *Die Verteidigung des Friedens* (Munich 1975).
Singer, D., and Melvin S., *The Wages of War 1816–1965* (New York 1976).
Singer, K., 'The Meaning of Conflict', *Australasian Journal of Philosophy*, 27 (1949), 145–70.
____, 'The Resolution of Conflict', *Social Research*, 16 (1949), 230–45.
____, *The Idea of Conflict* (Basle and Tübingen 1973).
SIPRI (Stockholm International Peace Research Institute), *World Armaments and Disarmament, Yearbook 1972 ff.* (Stockholm et al. 1972 ff.).
Slocombe, W., *The Political Implications of Strategic Parity* (London 1971).
Smith, R. F., 'American Foreign Relations 1920–1942', in B. J. Bernstein, ed., *Towards a New Past* (New York 1968), pp. 232–62.
Smith, Tony, 'Changing Configurations of Power in North–South Relations since 1945', *International Organization*, 31 (1977–8), 1–27.
Snyder, G. H., 'Crisis Bargaining', in C. F. Herrmann, ed., *International Crises* (London 1972).
____, and P. Diesing, *Conflict among Nations* (Princeton, NJ 1977).
Soell, H., 'Weltmarkt-Revolution-Staatenwelt', *Archiv für Sozialgeschichte*, XII (1972), 109–84.
Sorensen, T. C., *Kennedy* (Munich 1966).
Spiegel, S. L., *Dominance and Diversity* (Boston 1972).

Spielman, R., 'Crisis in Poland', *Foreign Policy*, 49 (Winter 1982–3), 20–36.
Sprout, H. and M., *The Ecological Perspective on Human Affairs* (Princeton, NJ 1965).
Spulber, N., *The Economics of Communist Eastern Europe* (New York and London 1957).
Spykman, N. J., *America's Strategy in World Politics* (New York 1942).
Steinbruner, J. D., 'Nuclear Decapitation', *Foreign Policy*, 45 (Winter 1981–82), 16–28.
Steinert, M. G., and H. Kapur, 'New Configurations of Power in International Relations', in Institut universitaire des hautes études internationales, ed., *Les Relations internationales dans un monde en mutation* (Geneva 1977), pp. 123–61.
Stent, A., *From Embargo to Ostpolitik. The Political Economy of West German–Soviet Relations 1955–1980* (Cambridge, Mass. etc. 1981).
Stratmann, K.-P., 'Vom Autismus kritischer Friedensforschung', *Aus Politik und Zeitgeschichte*, 1973, B 40, 3–22.
Sumner, W. G., *Folksways* (Boston 1911).
Szulc, T., *The Illusion of Peace: Foreign Policy in the Nixon Years* (New York 1978).
Tiedtke, S., *Die Warschauer Vertragsorganisation: Zum Verhältnis von Militär- und Entspannungspolitik in Osteuropa* (Munich 1978).
Timberlake, C. E., *Détente, A Documentary Record* (New York et al 1978).
Thompson, J. M., *Russia, Bolshevism, and the Versailles Peace* (Princeton, NJ 1967).
Triepel, H., *Die Hegemonie* (Aalen ²1974).
Tucker, R. W., *The Inequality of Nations* (New York 1977).
Uibopuu, H.–J., *Die sowjetische Doktrin der friedlichen Koexistenz als Völkerrechtsproblem* (Vienna 1971).
United Nations, Department of International Economic and Social Affairs, Statistical Office, ed., *Statistical Yearbook* (New York 1948 ff.).
US Congress, House of Representatives, *United States National Security Policy vis-à-vis Eastern Europe (The 'Sonnenfeldt Doctrine')*, Hearings before the Subcommittee on International Security and Scientific Affairs, 94th Congress, 2nd Session, 12 April 1976 (Washington, DC 1976).
US Congress, House Committee on International Relations, *The Soviet Union and the Third World*, 95th Congress, 1st Session (Washington, DC 1977).
US Department of Commerce, ed., *Statistical Abstracts of the United States* (Washington, DC 1975ff.).
Uschakow, A., *Der Ostmarkt im Comecon* (Baden-Baden 1972).
Värynen, R., 'Militarization, Conflict Behavior and Interaction', Tampere Peace Research Institute, *Research Reports*, No. 3, 1973.
——, 'Zur Dynamik des Unfriedens in Europa', in A. Gross-Jütte and R. Jütte, eds., *Entspannung ohne Frieden* (Frankfurt 1977), pp. 60–7.
Vandenberg, A. H., Jr., ed., *The Private Papers of Senator Arthur H. Vandenberg*, (Boston 1952).
Venkataramani, M. S., 'Manganese as a Factor in Indo-American Relations', *Indian Quarterly*, 14 (1958), 135 ff.
Vukadinovic, R., *Non-Aligned Countries and Détente* (Belgrade 1979).
Wagner, W., 'Das Ost-West-Verhältnis nach der sowjetischen Invasion in

Afghanistan', *Europa-Archiv*, 35 (1980), 135–46.
Wall, R. G., *The Dynamics of Polarization* (Stockholm 1975).
Wallensteen, P., *Structure and War* (Stockholm 1973).
Walters, F. P., *A History of the League of Nations* (London 1952).
Waltz, K. N., 'Conflict in World Politics', in S. L. Spiegel and K. Waltz, eds., *Conflicts in World Politics*. (Cambridge, Mass. 1971), pp. 454–74.
——, 'Theory of International Relations', in *Handbook of Political Science*, vol. 8, ed. F. I. Greenstein and N. W. Polsby (Reading, Mass. 1975), pp. 1–85.
Watt, D. C., *Too Serious a Business* (Berkeley and Los Angeles 1975).
Weingartner, T., *Die Aussenpolitik der Sowjetunion seit 1945* (Düsseldorf 1973).
Weisert, H., *Die Ausübung von auswärtiger Gewalt durch Privatpersonen*, Diss. jur. (Tübingen 1973).
Wendt, B.-J., *Economic Appeasement* (Düsseldorf 1971).
Wettig, G., *Europäische Sicherheit* (Düsseldorf 1972).
Whetten, L. L., *Germany's Ostpolitik* (London et al. 1971).
White Paper 1979, *The Security of the Federal Republic of Germany and the Development of the Federal Armed Forces*, Published by the Federal Minister of Defence on behalf of the Federal Government (Bonn 1979).
Wight, M., *Systems of States* (Leicester 1977).
——, *Power Politics* (Leicester 1978).
Wilcox, C., *A Charter for World Trade* (New York 1949).
Wilczynski, J., *The Economics and Politics of East–West Trade* (London 1969).
Willetts, P., *The Non-Aligned Movement* (London and New York 1978).
Williams, P., *Crisis Management* (London 1976).
Williams, W. A., *The Tragedy of American Diplomacy* (New York $^{2}$1962).
Willms, B., 'Dialektische Ansätze der Interpretation von intersystemaren Beziehungen', in G. Zellentin, ed., *Annäherung, Abgrenzung und friedlicher Wandel in Europa* (Boppard 1976), pp. 45–78.
Wohlstetter, A., 'Is There a Strategic Arms Race?', *Foreign Policy*, 15 and 16, (1974), 3–20 and 48–81.
——, 'Racing Forward? Or Ambling Back?', *Survey*, 22 (1976), 163–217.
Wolfe, T. W., *Soviet Power and Europe, 1945–1970* (Baltimore and London 1970).
Wolfers, A., 'The Atomic Bomb in Soviet-American Relations', in Bernard Brodie, ed., *The Absolute Weapon* (New York 1946), pp. 111–73.
Woronoff, J., *Organizing African Unity* (Metuchen, NJ 1970).
Woyke, W., ed., *Handwörterbuch Internationale Politik* (Opladen 1977).
Yahuda, M. B., *China's Role in World Politics* (London 1978).
Yergin, D., *Shattered Peace* (London 1977).
Young, O. R., *The Intermediaries. Third Parties in International Crisis* (Princeton, NJ 1967).
——, 'On the Performance of the International Polity', *British Journal of International Studies*, (1978), 191–208.
Zartman, I. W., 'Europe and Africa: Decolonization or Dependency?', *Foreign Affairs*, 54 (1976), 319–43.
Zellentin, G., *Intersystemare Beziehungen in Europa* (Leiden 1970).
——, ed., *Annäherung, Abgrenzung und friedlicher Wandel in Europa* (Boppard 1976).
*Zusammenschlüsse und Pakte der Welt*, Siegler & Co. (Bonn et al. $^{12}$1979).